D0094888

The Future of Communist Society

PALMER LIBRARY
CONNECTICUT COLLEGE
NEW LONDON, CONNECTICUT

THE FUTURE OF
COMMUNIST SOCIETY

EDITED BY

Walter Laqueur and Leopold Labedz

FREDERICK A. PRAEGER, *Publisher*

New York

335.4
L319.

BOOKS THAT MATTER

Published in the United States of America in 1962
by Frederick A. Praeger, Inc., Publisher
64 University Place, New York 3, N. Y.

First published in Great Britain in 1961
as a special issue of *Survey*

All rights reserved

© Frederick A. Praeger, Inc. 1962

Library of Congress Catalog Card Number: 62-9509

THE FUTURE OF COMMUNIST SOCIETY is published in two editions:

A Praeger Paperback (PPS-68)
A clothbound edition

This book is Number 101 in the series of
Praeger Publications in Russian History and World Communism

Manufactured in the United States of America

CONTENTS

207593

ERRATA

P. 157, l. 18   The date is incorrectly given. It should read: (1956).

P. 164, l. 17
(*from bottom*)   This should read as follows: "The last chinks in the power of the centre had been closed with the *elimination* of Chang Kuo-t'ao and Wang Ming in the later 1930s."

P. 169, l. 3
(*from bottom*)   A few lines were inadvertently omitted. The passage should read as follows: "How permanent these changes launched in 1961 will be no one can say. Yet despite routinisation in Russia and modification of organisational policy in China, the basic systems have remained intact. And thus the differences we have pointed out above continue to exist. Both Soviet Russia and Communist China are very much the products of their political and social histories, their respective revolutionary movements, and their respective societies."

The Future of Communist Society

INTRODUCTION

THE programme of the Communist Party of the Soviet Union, published on 30 July 1961, is the third document of its kind. Russian Social-Democracy adopted its first programme in 1903 ; it had been written in large part by Plekhanov, who submitted it to the second Congress of the party. In many respects it resembled the Erfurt programme of the German Social-Democrats (1891), the Heinfeld programme of the Austrian party (1899), and the Guesde-Lafargue programme of the French Socialists, published back in the eighteen-eighties. On some issues it was more radical; it pointed to the necessity of the dictatorship of the proletariat, but it did not consider this an immediate prospect. The 1903 document consisted of two parts, a maximum programme, and a minimum programme dealing with the immediate political and social tasks of Russian social-democracy. It was the ' bourgeois revolution ' that was on the agenda; the question how and how quickly it would be followed by a socialist revolution had not yet been doctrinally settled. Some of the participants were not altogether happy about this; one Akimov-Makhnovets proposed twenty-two amendments and modifications, and the Mensheviks did not really want the programme to be taken literally; Plekhanov certainly did not like to be reminded in later years of the fact that he had recommended on this occasion limitations on universal suffrage and on political freedom in general, on the ground that salus revolutionis suprema lex.

By 1919 both parts of the programme were clearly out of date, and the Eighth Congress of the Russian Communist Party in March 1919, in the middle of the civil war, adopted a new programme prepared by Bukharin, Lenin, and a few others. This dealt with such current problems as the expropriation of the expropriators, and the establishment of the rudiments of a planned economy. In its preamble it called for war against the ' bourgeois distortions ' of socialism which were said to have gained the upper hand in various socialist parties, trends described as opportunist and chauvinistic. The programme showed great optimism with regard to the future of the revolution : ' We have the greatest confidence in the victory of the world proletarian revolution ' ; the course of the revolution in Germany, Austria-Hungary, and other countries had shown that a new era had begun. The discussion centred on some minor points ; Bukharin wanted to limit the discussion of imperialism to current problems, while Lenin insisted on including once again the theoretical part of the 1903 programme, which contained an analysis of pre-imperialist capitalism, although in the interval his own analysis of the development of finance capitalism had in part rendered the old theses obsolete.

Between the second and the third programme forty-two years have passed, years which witnessed radical changes inside the Soviet Union and in the world in general. So far-reaching were these changes that the need for a new programme was admitted in Moscow in 1939, but it took another twenty years and more for the new manifesto to materialise. But the scope of this book is not confined to an analysis of the programme ; it is equally concerned with the discussions on the future communist society that preceded the publication of the programme (reviewed in detail by L. Labedz), and it deals at even greater length with current trends in the Soviet Union that seem to foreshadow the shape of things to come, whether these trends have found their reflection in the new programme or not.

Marx and Engels did not regard it as their most urgent task to prepare a detailed blueprint of the future communist society, as Iring Fetscher and Thilo Ramm stress elsewhere in this number. Marx, in particular, refused to commit himself in his later years in this respect ; he assumed that the social revolution would triumph only after long struggles, and that during these struggles both the people waging them and the world around them would undergo great change, so that any attempt to predict or prescribe the structure of the future society in detail would be useless. Any such attempt, moreover, would probably have given rise to unnecessary conflicts similar to the quarrels between the various ' utopian socialist ' schools of thought.

Marx envisaged the future society as providing the fullest scope for the individual human being, free from all the restrictions and distortions that affected his development under capitalism and other previous class societies. Interspersed in his work and the work of Engels are various hints and observations of a general character that have become famous : The ' leap from the realm of necessity into the realm of freedom ', the prediction that the government of men would be replaced in the socialist future by the administration of things ; and, of course, most famous of all, their pronouncement that in the second, higher phase of communism, the principle ' from each according to his ability, to each according to his needs ' was to prevail. The formula of the ' withering away of the state ' also derives from Marx, while Engels went on record with his proposal for putting the machinery of state into a museum for antiquities, together with the spinning wheel and the bronze axe.

These and other obiter dicta opened sweeping perspectives and provided ringing slogans, but they are not of much help in working out the details of the ' future communist society '. For this we have to look elsewhere, namely in the work of the innumerable writers from Plato to Thomas More, and from Campanella to William Morris and H. G. Wells, who have all described in great, sometimes abstruse and ludicrous detail, the working of various ideal societies of the future. Nor are such visions absent in Russian intellectual history ; the influence of the utopian socialists can readily be recognised in Belinsky, Herzen, and the Petrazhevtsy, and Anna Pavlovna's cooperative seamstresses in *What is to be done* can be traced back without difficulty to the same sources. It only remains to add that America too has contributed its share of such blueprints from Bellamy's *Looking Backward* to the Goodmans' *Communitas*.

'Scientific socialists' were not excessively eager to stress this part of their heritage ; Marx had no high opinion of the 'utopian socialists' (with the possible exception of Robert Owen). To Kugelmann, in 1866, he wrote that Owen, Fourier and the others had given only 'fantastic expression' to the conception of the new world. Despite these attempts to dissociate himself, Marx, and subsequently Marxism, tacitly accepted not a few ideas of the 'utopian socialists', which were assimilated as self-evident assumptions. Such influences can be followed to the present day ; they have multiplied in recent years with the renewal of discussion on the future communist society. It would be interesting to investigate in detail to what extent the idea of the *micro-rayon* as the basic social unit of the future is related to Fourier's phalansteries and Owen's 'parallelograms'. What Academician Strum-ilin, one of the most prominent participants in the discussions on the future society, had to say about the advantages of having meals in a communal dining hall rather than one's own dining room can be found almost verbally in Fourier's *Fausse Industrie*, and all the arguments for the free distribution of bread (another recent topic of discussion) are contained in Prince Kropotkin's *The Conquest of Bread*. Similar ante-cedents can easily be traced for current discussions about the future of the family, of education, and other topics. The vision of a more just, more rational, in short, an ideal order of society has preoccupied prophets, political philosophers, novelists and other beings for many centuries ; most of them were not even socialists.

So has the idea of the welfare state, even before St. Thomas Aquinas declared that 'nullus enim inconvenienter vivere debet'. The new CPSU programme holds out the promise of social services many of which already exist in Western countries—some for several decades. Other services will be in the nature of a novelty and may act as a spur for those Western countries whose social services are lagging behind. Ultimately it will all depend on the quality of services offered ; even now Soviet citizens pay no more than nominal rent, and the abolition of rent payments would not in itself constitute a revolutionary step— unless, of course, the present very inadequate standard of housing is replaced by something far better.

THE promises may appear relatively modest in Western eyes, but they would mark a tremendous advance by Soviet standards. The Soviet economy will undoubtedly make great progress during the next twenty years, and living standards will continue to rise, as they will elsewhere, given a period of relative peace. But all this belongs to the phase of 'creating the preconditions for a communist society' by raising living standards and reducing the working day. Production would still be for the state ; there would be no *qualitative* change embodying features of the new society. Such radical change could be effected only if the principle ' to each according to his need ' is taken seriously, if money were gradually abolished, and other steps towards that end taken. Since, according to communist predictions, the second and higher stage of communism is expected to arrive during the present century, it is worthy of note that the authors of the programme (in contrast to some of the participants in the discussion preceding it) were extremely reluctant to touch these subjects. They seem to have been aware of the difficulties ahead. Marx and Engels (and in their wake Kautsky, in *Das Erfurter Programm*), relegated the problem of distribution to a secondary place, an issue of interest mainly to bourgeois philistines ; production, they thought, was much more important. But once ' abundance ' is reached (or even a modicum of abundance), distribution becomes the main issue. Soviet commentators will continue to argue that the ' needs ' of the individual mean ' needs within reasonable limits '. But who will fix the reasonable needs in each case? Since individual needs and tastes differ, a system of state control will be required more intensive and thorough than anything ever known in human history. Instead of ' withering away ', the state would become omnipresent and omnipotent, and the individual more dependent on the state than ever.

It is the same with the abolition of money. This was one of the cardinal demands of most 19th-century utopian socialists. Thomas More had written long before that money should be abolished because it was the root of all evil : ' Fraud, theft, disorders, rapine, quarrels, strife, sedition, murder, poisoning . . . die out with the death of money, and fears, anxiety, toils, worries and watching perish along with money '. These ideas can be traced further back still, to the Bible and to Plato. But in a modern industrial society, in contrast to the small agricultural communities envisaged by the utopians, money can only be replaced by a most complicated system of vouchers issued under the strictest state control ; there might be no money and no commodity production, but this would not represent the leap into the realm of freedom.

The prospects of the new twenty-year plan are discussed by Dr Jasny on another page, and perhaps the only further comment called for here is an observation about the revolution of rising expectations, which the Soviet planners may have overlooked. Economists watching developments in the underdeveloped countries have commented at length on what they call the demonstration effect : on the fact that tastes and expectations rise faster than production once a higher standard of living and more diversified and higher quality commodities are in sight. The Soviet people, after decades of being starved for consumer goods, are now in a very similar position, facing for the first time the prospect of the ' good life '. Appetite, as the saying goes, grows with the eating, and Russian appetites are notoriously hearty.

The Soviet Union may ultimately achieve a welfare state more complete and perfect than the welfare states existing now in some Western countries; present priorities being what they are, this would take a long time. But a welfare state is not a communist society where the domination of man by man has been ended and where the free development of the individual is the precondition of the free development of the collective. This could be achieved only with the withering away of the state, an issue that runs persistently through Marxist-Leninist thinking. For Marx and Engels it was the fulfilment of the liberal ideal : As soon as it becomes possible to speak of freedom the state ceases to exist, Engels wrote to Bebel. Lenin, too, dealt time and again with the liquidation of the machinery of state, of ' organised and systematic constraint, of all coercion of human beings in general '. He expected this to happen very soon and wrote that to talk of a ' free people's state ' was ' non-Marxist nonsense ' ; a state was a state, ' an instrument of coercion ; so long as any state exists, a Marxist has no right to speak of freedom '.

Marx and Engels formulated their ideas about the withering away of the state (and incidentally of bureaucracy also) at a time when the functions of the state were infinitely fewer than they are today. In some ways, the latter-day utopians such as Bellamy had more realistic notions in this respect ; when the hero in *Looking Backwards* awakens in the year 2000 in Dr Leete's house, one of his first observations concerns the enormous growth of state activites. Yet neither Lenin nor the present day communists have in their doctrine abandoned the idea of the withering away of the state, despite the fact that the Soviet Union is at present more remote from this ideal than ever before. They envisage (as their programme now says) ' communist self-government ', which is to embrace the soviets, trade unions, cooperatives, and other mass organisations. This subject has been under discussion for several years in the Soviet Union, as Professor Hazard and Mr. Osborn stress in their contributions ; some attempts in this direction have been made, such as establishing the *druzhiny* (to assist the police), and setting up comradely courts. But the ' public bodies ' which are to take over some of the functions of the state have no political power and cannot take any important decisions. They are controlled at every stage by the Communist Party, and whatever the visions seen in Moscow with regard to the Soviet state, no one has yet really advocated the withering away of the Communist Party. On the contrary, according to the programme, the role of the party is to increase in communist society. The talk of the disappearance of the state boils down, therefore, to the take-over of some of the state functions by Communist Party organs. This is not exactly identical with the original ideas of real democracy and the end of systematic and organised constraint.

THE new Party statutes are presented as ' the further development of socialist democracy ', but the new rules are clearly designed to maintain the oligarchic control of the Party leadership and not, as the new programme tries to imply, to get the members to play a real part in shaping Party policies.   Exactly the same applies to the measures enumerated in the new programme which are said to give the ' masses ' an increased role in running the country.   No holder of office is to be permitted to keep it for more than three successive terms, but any threat to those at the top is eliminated by an escape clause, permitting leaders with ' generally recognised authority and high political, organisational, and other abilities ' to stay on the job for a longer period.   The proviso that they must get three-quarters of the vote cast is meaningless in the light of past experience, when they took care never to get less than 98 or 99 per cent of the votes.   The practical implications of the new rules are therefore to ensure stability at the top, with a high turnover in the lower ranks of the Party.   Khrushchev's formula for consolidating the dictatorship is thus to preserve his hold on the Party not, like Stalin, through a permanent purge, but through a constant reshuffle of the Party organs, which has now been institutionalised in the new Party statutes; while it dispenses with the necessity for terror, it gives the Party leaders a powerful lever of legitimate patronage, for, since all office is now constitutionally insecure, it will be up to them to decide when the escape clause should be applied to office-holders, who may or may not qualify for security of tenure as being of ' generally recognised authority.'

The new Party constitution thus makes it impossible for factional groups to consolidate at any level, and particularly within the central committee (procedure for the expulsion of its members has been outlined for the first time in the new Party statutes).

In effect the new ' democratisation ' measures turn out to be another variant of Michels' ' iron law of oligarchy ' and the same applies generally to the principle of ' communist self-government ' in other walks of life. The reality of the Party dictatorship will not be changed if, by the time full communism is achieved, the government of the country is renamed the All-Union Committee for Social Obligations, thus proving that the state had ' withered away '.

THE idea of education as the main key to the liberation of the individual, making it possible to do away with centralised bureaucratic government altogether by enabling the majority of people, through some form of polytechnical education, to participate in self-government, has been one of the basic notions of Marxism.   In the *Deutsche Ideologie* Marx wrote about the future society in which individuals would hunt in the morning, fish in the afternoon, take care of the livestock in the evening, and be critics after dinner without ever becoming professional hunters, fishermen, herdsmen or critics.   Lenin looked forward to the day when cooks would be able to manage affairs of state, and Bukharin (in his *ABC of Communism*) took it for granted that in the government offices of the future there would be ' one set of workers today, and another set tomorrow ', as government by permanent officials would disappear.

There is no doubt that it would be highly desirable to have some form of rotation between different kinds of work in a future society, and the efforts to counteract the ever-growing power of state bureaucracy are highly commendable. Unfortunately, professional specialisation has since Marx's day progressed to an extent that could not then be imagined. One can still imagine people being at the same time hunters, fishermen, and cowherds ; it is more difficult to assume that a plastic surgeon will alternate as a nuclear physicist in the afternoon and as a dustman in the evening (though there have been wistful efforts in that direction in Mao's China). The same goes, a fortiori, for the apparatus of a highly centralised state engaged on thorough economic planning and other highly specialised activities.

What then are the prospects of achieving the ultimate goal—or, to be more modest, what are the chances of approaching it? Two ways of looking at this are possible. One would emphasise that it would be ludicrous even to consider the prospect in view of present day Soviet realities, of the poverty and backwardness that still prevail over many areas, and the repressive character of the Soviet state. These arguments betray a certain lack of imagination: Communism, after all, is a gigantic attempt to change the world; great economic progress has been achieved and more will be attained in the future. The desire to build a better and radically different world may not be as intense as it used to be, but the revolutionary flame has not been completely extinguished. It is very likely that the Soviet Union will create in the course of time what it considers the economic preconditions for the transition to communism.

But what if the goal is not merely ' catching up and overtaking ', not only the establishment of a Soviet welfare state, but the replacement of a totalitarian state by a voluntary association of free individuals? There is secondly the view that freedom will, almost automatically, follow economic progress. Present and past ' distortions ' of the communist ideal in Soviet practice are explained against the background of Russian backwardness ; with the disappearance of backwardness the distortions are expected to disappear too. The continued existence of the whole repressive apparatus is likewise explained as the natural outcome of the West-East conflict, which, with the ending of the cold war or the victory of the ' socialist camp ' would in due course cease to exist. It is conceded that a new elite may have developed, the upper ranks of the party and the new caste of industrial and professional managers ; but these, it is contended, do not constitute a class ; they have no monopoly of education and cannot bequeath their positions of command to the next generation. Because this elite cannot perpetuate itself, it will eventually become superfluous.

Such economic determinism, even in its more sophisticated form, disregards not only the innate anti-democratic trends of modern industrial society (which are hardly likely to lessen with full automation) ;

it disregards equally those trends inherent in the Soviet regime that resist and counteract any movement towards a free society. Lastly, it abstracts itself from an international situation that opens entirely novel perspectives. It is precisely the messianic character of communism, its missionary impulse to redeem the world, that propels the Soviet Union into dangerous situations and makes collision at least a possibility. The emergence of several centres of power within the communist movement is another complication that was not foreseen ; even if communist parties were to prevail throughout the world, the struggle for power would go on, probably with increased bitterness. It has yet to be proved that communist superpowers can co-exist in the long run— especially if the ' external danger ' menacing them and holding them together for the time being should diminish or disappear altogether. Some aspects of Sino-Soviet relations are discussed against this background in the contributions of Professor Eckstein, Professor Schurmann, and Dr Zagoria in the present number.

THE increasing complexity of the division of labour in present day society and of running a modern state has made the concept of the withering away of the state illusory ; this is an objective trend of development, and the most one can hope for is that the individual will not become even more dependent on the state. It is unlikely, to put it mildly, that in this respect the Soviet Union will lead the way for the rest of the world. It is not the communists' fault that the technological basis has developed in a way that makes the realisation of the original ideals virtually impossible. But there are ' subjective ' factors, too, inherent in the Soviet regime, that reinforce the trend. The Communist Party, the new elite, wants to perpetuate its rule and makes no bones about it. It may not be a new class, though in the course of time it may become one ; but it is nevertheless in complete control of all positions of command. Communist Party and society will be one; according to official doctrine, the needs of society, not the needs of the individual, will be the decisive criterion and the supreme value. As the old vision of a free community recedes into the shade, the programme suggests that it may be gradually replaced by a new and different vision. Marx and Engels regarded the reduction of the working day as the decisive prerequisite for the full development of the individual in the future society. Such a reduction is now in sight, but preparations are already under way to ' organise ' his free time in a way that will leave him very little time for himself. The new order will be run by society for society. The collective, and behind it the Communist Party, rather than man, has become the measure of things. The vision of the self-realisation of man is superseded by the vision of the efficient collective ; order and discipline, not freedom, are made the guiding principles of the new society.

If one can foresee, in broad outline, what Soviet society will *not* be like in 1981, what will it accomplish? It may develop in some respects into a more efficient and rational production system than the rest of the world. It may or may not beat the West in the race to the moon. But will it be any nearer to the just and free society of the future that was their ultimate aim in years past? Even if there should be a gradual transformation of the totalitarian state into a relatively enlightened authoritarian regime (after Stalin one has become grateful for small blessings), which in present circumstances is perhaps the best one can hope for, will the regime have justified its cost in human suffering and sacrifice? If all the high hopes, the great efforts, and the idealism have only produced a system with somewhat greater rates of economic growth, and considerably more repression than other industrialised nations, it will be interesting to know how its own proponents will explain its raison d'être. We may have to wait for the fourth programme for an answer, unless, which we doubt, 1981 witnesses the end of ideology in Russia.

Ideology and Utopia

THE NEW CPSU PROGRAMME

Leopold Labedz

THE idea of a golden age, either lost or to come, has been with humanity for most of its recorded history, but political systems promising its implementation in the near future have been rare and, not unnaturally, unsuccessful. The New Jerusalem, the Kingdom of the Saints, and other utopias-in-the-making were historical epiphenomena, whose rulers were unable to establish any enduring political structure. As Karl Mannheim put it, ' the very idea of the dawn of a millennial kingdom on earth always contained a revolutionising tendency ', and this was not conducive to political or social stability. It could be achieved only where the fulfilment of the millennial promise was indefinitely postponed. The church realised that its position in a non-theocratic society could not be stabilised on the basis of a permanent (ecclesiastical) ' revolution from above ' and made every effort to paralyse such tendencies. Later, when secularisation set in and other-worldly objectives were replaced by a dream of happiness here and now, in this vale of tears, the transcendental visions of the kingdom of God on earth gave way to more mundane utopias. Eventually, the chiliastic attitude, which, according to Mannheim, was first ' structually integrated ' with the social revolution in the movement led by Thomas Münzer, found a similar confluence in revolutionary Marxism.

This time, however, utopia paraded as science and ideology as positive knowledge. ' Scientific socialism ' provided a vision of the future which claimed to be free from utopian elements, and the control of the state by a ' party of the new type ' made it possible to combine an enduring rule with a permanent ' revolutionising tendency '. Ever since the party committed to it took power, it has claimed to be moving towards its millennial objective : the 17th Party Congress (February 1934) proclaimed that ' the foundations of socialist economy have been built ' ; the 18th Congress (March 1939), that ' socialism, the first stage of communism, has been achieved in essentials ' ; the 21st Congress (February 1959), that ' the country has entered the period of an extensive development of the communist society ' [1] ; while the 22nd Congress (October 1961) is designed to

---

[1] *KPSS v rezoliutsiakh i resheniyakh syezdov, konferentsii i plenumov Tsk*, Moscow, 1954, Vol. 3, pp. 201 and 336, Vol. 4, 1960, p. 381.

give ' the party and the people the great programme of building the communist society '. [2]

The stage is thus finally set for the realisation of Utopia. Not only is the blueprint ready ; even the approximate date for its completion is given. Khrushchev declared to the Indian journalist, Khwaja Ahmad Abbas, that ' We have every reason to hope that we shall reach our goal between 1975 and 1980, provided there is no war '. This particular interview has not appeared in the Soviet press, which has however published an enormous number of articles on the subject, and the new party programme confirmed this time-table. This made it necessary to give a more specific content to the imprecise outlines previously sketched of the shape of communist society.

But putting the achievement of full communism on the immediate agenda is not without its dangers for the Soviet leadership. There is an obvious incongruity between the renewed insistence on the ideological goals and the prosaic and down-to-earth character of the aspirations of the ' new Soviet man ', aspirations which have something in common with similar appetites in other industrialised and more middle-class societies.

However, this incongruity is neither new nor accidental. The discrepancy between party goals and the private aspirations of Soviet citizens has persisted with different degrees of intensity ever since the revolution, but it is one which the leadership was able to master, and the ' revolutionising tendency' embodied in the party-state continued to surprise all those who from 1921 regularly prophesied a Soviet Thermidor, the end of revolutionary dynamics, ' normalisation '.

Developments after Stalin, and in particular the 20th Congress, reinforced such expectations. Khrushchev's rise to power, the strong ' ideological ' emphasis, and the programmatic outline of the 22nd Congress, must once again cast doubt on such prophecies.[3]

THE latest official projections into the future, like the previous ones, cannot be designated as *la conjecture raisonnée*, to use the concept which Favier introduced in the 18th century, the great age of Utopias. They do not distinguish between the probable and the desirable, and despite all the stress on having established ' a science of socialist construction ' during the decades of Soviet historical experience, the communist *terminus ad quem* is still described in the old, well-worn formulas. No

2 *Pravda*, 21 June 1961.
3 It should be made clear at the outset that Mannheim's definitions of ideology and Utopia are not applicable to Soviet developments. According to Mannheim ' ideologies are mental fictions whose function is to veil the true nature of a given society. They originate in the minds of those who seek to stabilise a social order. Utopias are wish-dreams that inspire the collective action of opposition groups which aim at entirely transforming such a society '. In the Soviet Union, too, ideology is a mental fiction, but its function is not only to stabilise but also to transform Soviet society continuously ; and Utopia does not inspire opposition groups but the rulers. However, Mannheim distinguishes between absolute Utopias, which are not realisable, and relative Utopias, which can be realised. This distinction is more relevant.

attempt is made to check them against real experience ; they simply serve as the ideological veil which covers the realities of party rule and conceals the fact that some of the projections are not at all desirable, while some which are desirable are not probable. Efforts to bring the slogans down to earth were more marked in the debates preceding the publication of the programme than in the programme itself, and it is therefore interesting to compare the two and to disentangle the realistic and utopian elements in both.

The new programme refers to its predecessors as setting forth the historical tasks of the party at that time, tasks dictated by history itself, honourably fulfilled, and replaced only with the transition to the next stage :

> The first programme, adopted at the Second Congress, was carried out in October 1917 by the establishment of the dictatorship of the proletariat. The second programme adopted at the Eighth Congress in 1919 promulgated the task of building a socialist society. . . . Today the Communist Party of the Soviet Union is adopting its third programme, a programme for the building of communist society.

It is perhaps pertinent to recall that the references to the first two programmes are explicitly misleading. In 1903 Lenin considered the establishment of a proletarian dictatorship in backward Russia a heresy, and it took him 14 years to change his mind. The second party programme did not ' promulgate the task of building a socialist society ', as this was considered at the time impossible without revolution in the West ; it became orthodoxy only later with the adoption of ' the theory of socialism in one country '.

Conscious of the need to produce some new theoretical formulation of party aims, the 18th Congress in 1939 appointed a 27-man commission to draft a new programme for the next congress ; but neither that commission, nor its successor appointed at the 19th Congress thirteen years later, produced an acceptable draft. Nor was the third attempt, commissioned by the 20th Congress in February 1956, more successful. It was only after the 21st Congress, which proclaimed the entrance into the higher stage of communism, that the necessity of producing the new theoretical, ideological and programmatic blueprint became imperative.

Although the vision of the glorious future is ' immanently immutable ', being predetermined by history, three questions had now to be tackled in a more specific form : (1) What will communism be like in certain material spheres of life? (2) How is it to be achieved? (3) When will the various stages of ' full communism ' be reached?

TWO traditional topics—the role of property and of money in the communist economy—were discussed once more before the final adoption of the present formulations in the programme.

The debate on property was concerned mainly with the evolution of the collective farms, but other kinds of property (such as *dachas*) were also discussed. The question is of great practical importance, as it is intimately connected with the system of incentives on the one hand, and with the (growing) problem of the market on the other, and not just with the doctrinal problem of the preference for one form of property over another.

The Soviet *kolkhoz* represents formally three different kinds of property : the land belongs to the state, the tools and the output to the collective, and there is the private plot, where the peasant works for his individual profit. For years Soviet discussion centred on the problem of eliminating the third form and the gradual transformation of the co-operative *kolkhoz* property by strengthening the ' indivisible fund ' and tying it up with the state system of credit. ' Full communism ' is by definition compatible with only one form of property, *obshchenarodnaia sobstvennost* (public property).

The 1919 programme envisaged ' the support of agricultural communes as completely voluntary associations of agricultural labourers for the purpose of conducting a communal system of economy on a large scale '. There is no need to recall in detail what happened to this scheme.

Forty years later the Chinese communes movement presented the Soviet ideologists with a new knot to unravel. The Soviet attitude to these examples of Mao's ' creative development of Marxism ' was critical, although for political reasons it was also subdued and indirect. Occasional references to them were couched in esoteric doctrinal language. The most forthright answer, offering positive counter-attractions, came from the pen of Professor Strumilin. He first revealed a plan for the Soviet system of communes in an interview with the East German news agency (17 June 1960), and then developed it in detail in an article entitled ' Working life and communism '.[4] He stressed the standard argument that full communism requires a high-productivity economy ; he developed a plan for Soviet communes, which would not however mature before 1980, which would not be ' miserable community centres with communal kitchens and the perpetual moaning of tormented women and mothers ', but urban and rural centres for a population of about 30,000, with ' 15 communal palaces ', factories, power stations, communal restaurants, libraries, a higher educational establishment (for 1,000 students), some 15 boarding schools, hospital, theatre, club, and sports stadium. Urban and rural communes would have the same features, as under communism the difference between town and countryside would disappear, and would be ' interconnected by a single central plan of action '. Strumilin deprecated the premature use of the word ' commune ' (another clear dig at the Chinese with their low-productivity economy), but although he estimated that each ' communal palace ' alone would cost about 50 million rubles (at current prices), he suggested an immediate

4 *Novy Mir*, No. 7, 1960, pp. 203–220. S. G. Strumilin, who at 84 is a most prolific author, has devoted many of his recent writings to the problem of ' communist construction ': cf. *Na putyakh postroeniya kommunizma*, Moscow, 1959; and articles in *Oktyabr*, No. 3, 1960, *Nowa Kultura* (Warsaw), 6 November 1960, *Krasnaya Zvezda*, 28 February 1961, *Novoe Vremya*, 10 February 1961, and *Soviet Weekly* (London), 13 April 1961.

start to the scheme with the building of the first experimental commune towns on the Angara and Yenisei rivers in Siberia. He calculated that the whole communisation process should be completed between 1980 and 1985.

It does not take an economist to realise that in comparison with the costs of this scheme,[5] the Soviet space programme itself is comparatively cheap. It is not surprising that the idea was not taken up, although not only orbital flights but also flights of imagination were allowed and even encouraged in the Soviet Union during the last two years.

The idea of communes was not included in the new programme, although, as already mentioned, the 1919 programme recommended them specifically both for agriculture and for the distribution of goods to consumers ; in fact the idea was quietly dropped in 1960 from the discussion on the future communist society.

ONE platform for this discussion was provided by the magazine *Oktyabr*, whose editor, the late Fedor Panferov, inaugurated it with an article, ' What is Communism? ' (1960, No. 1), which was followed by a series of contributions by authors from various walks of life, trying to put into words either the concrete forms of the radiant future or ' the growing elements of communism already in existence '. Some of the articles on the latter theme, usually by Heroes of Labour, read like a Soviet version of *Poor Richard's Almanack*, with their sanctimonious insistence on the virtuousness of the Soviet man (' communist consciousness '), or perhaps like the didactic tales of heroism composed for the benefit of the members of the late Austrian Imperial Army, satirised by Jaroslav Hásek in *The Good Soldier Schweik*. Every issue of *Oktyabr* throughout 1960 had a special section devoted to the discussion.

Some of the contributions, however, revealed a good deal about the attitudes of the population and the ideas which eventually found their way into the new programme.

The position to be taken on the *kolkhoz* problem was clearly presaged in articles by Ivan Vinnichenko,[6] who in 1959 proposed, in the magazine *Nash Sovremennik* (No. 4) the transfer of the RTS (Repair Tractor Stations) to the collective farms, in line with the similar transfer of the MTS (Machine Tractor Stations), and advocated something like a co-operative structure for state-farms (*sovkhozes*). By 1960 Vinnichenko had changed his ground, arguing that even with the further amalgamation of the *kolkhozes* (of which he was a foremost advocate), very few of them ' would be able to acquire the repair stations and to secure high quality of repairs '. This followed a similar change of line by Khrushchev himself, who at the December 1959 session of the Central Committee said

---

[5] Assuming the Soviet population by the time ' full communism ' is attained to be about 300 millions, the ' communal palaces ' alone would cost the colossal sum of 7,500,000,000,000 rubles. But of course the problem is not only financial.

[6] *Oktyabr*, No. 6, 1960 and No. 5, 1961. Vinnichenko seems to reflect fairly closely Khrushchev's own evolution of opinions on agricultural problems. Cf. a collection of his articles in *Duma o Kommunizme*, Moscow, 1960.

that the idea of the transfer of the RTS to the *kolkhozes* ' deserves attention ', but rejected it at the January 1961 session.

The attitude adopted in the new programme to the ' private plot ' was presaged in an article in *Kommunist* (June 1961) condemning ' undue haste ' in liquidating the private plots, which ' can only lead to harm '. In the section on ' The Kolkhozes and State Farms on the Road to Communism ', the programme reaffirms this position, stating that only ' when collective production at the *kolkhozes* is able to replace in full the output of the supplementary individual plot of the *kolkhoz* members, when the collective farmers see for themselves that their supplementary individual farming is unprofitable, only then will they give it up of their own accord '. It also stresses that ' all these developments must proceed on a voluntary basis ', and relies on economic improvements in the countryside to ' gradually impart to kolkhoz-co-operative property the nature of public property '.[7]

To achieve these improvements the incomes of collective farmers are ' to double in the next ten years and increase more than fourfold in twenty years '. This growth of the incomes of peasants, intended to be more rapid than that of factory workers, is predicated on the higher rates of growth of farm labour productivity, which should result in a 150 per cent increase of farm output by 1970 and a 250 per cent increase by 1980, both of them dubious assumptions, if not downright impossibilities.

But farm property is not the only form of property existing at present which stands as an obstacle on the path to the achievement of ' full communism '. In an article, ' Communism and Property ',[8] Ts. Stepanyan quoted the following letter which he received after one of his lectures on the future of communist society :

> The immediate task in the countryside is to get rid of privately owned property (cows, gardens, etc.). But what about the personal property of city dwellers? After all, many city residents also have estates (*dachas*, gardens, etc.). Furthermore, individual suburban gardening (the so-called collective gardens) has become widespread in recent years. What does this gardening amount to? A worker receives a piece of land, plants a garden and builds a little house. After all, this is property too. What about it?

He also quoted a letter sent to the journal *Voprosy Filosofii* :

> The principles of socialism do not prevent the working people from spending their labour earnings on the acquisition of such costly articles as automobiles, *dachas*, individual homes, gardens, pleasure boats, and other things that are still luxury items. . . . Probably it is the possibility that the owners of personal transportation and personal housing may receive unearned income that is the basic reason

---

7 For an earlier discussion on the evolution of *kolkhoz* property, see S. Pershin's article in *Voprosy Stroitelstva Kommunizma v SSSR*, Moscow, 1959, pp. 210–217.
8 *Oktyabr*, No. 9, 1960. Stepanyan, it should be observed, came closest in his writings to the actual ' blueprint for communism ' outlined in the programme. Cf. in particular his articles in *Politicheskoe Samoobrazovanie*, 1961, 2, and *Oktyabr*, 1960, 7.

for the application of measures to impede the development of personal transportation and personal home-ownership. I gather that such measures are being carried out from the increased difficulties in obtaining a plot of land for building a *dacha* or garage, or for a personal garden, from the diminishing number of automobiles being put on the market, and from the decline in the supply of spare parts, especially tyres, for personally-owned automobiles. Where do these measures to restrict the growth of personal property lead in practice? In my opinion, they redound to the benefit of those non-working elements that already have personal property capable of yielding income . . . they are the soil on which speculation and bribery flourish. . . . Lastly, these restrictions, in my opinion, violate the Soviet Constitution, since they divide the citizens of our country into two categories—those who have a plot or are in line for one, and those who do not have and are not being granted a plot even though they want one—and lead to unjustified discrimination.

Stepanyan answered these letters by arguing that ' while the elimination of private (*chastnaya*) property is linked with the victory of socialism, the transformation of personal (*lichnaya*) property takes place in the course of the building of communism. . . . The establishment of communism is the objective basis for the intensification of tendencies towards complete equality on the basis of the creation of an abundance of material and spiritual wealth. . . . The construction of the higher stage of communism requires not simply a further development of personal property but also its communist transformation on the basis of the development of the two forms of social property and of their merger into one communist property '.

Although Stepanyan rejects ' radical measures requiring a complete elimination of personal property in general ', he favours measures ' to limit gradually the growth of the surviving elements of personal property, including private *dachas* '.

He admits that ' of course, the most ardent defenders of the " sacredness " of personal property are those who have their own houses, large *dachas* with enormous plots, gardens, etc.', but contends that ' not all comrades have a clear theoretical concept of the question of the fate of personal property in the conditions of the transition to communism, and not all of them take into account the difficulties in correctly solving this problem . . .'. For this ' it is necessary to combine the principle of material incentive, without which one cannot enlist millions of people in the building of communism, with their real progress towards full equality. Otherwise the way may be opened to petty-bourgeois levelling . . .'.

He advises his fellow-members of the privileged strata that ' it is necessary to bring into a co-operative system the existing garden plots and *dachas* personally owned by workers, employees, scientists, and writers '. He assures them, however, that ' as public production develops and the material and technical base of communism is established, public forms of satisfaction . . . will grow and be perfected '.

Is it possible to compare the life of present day *dacha* owners with what model public rest zones will offer? Today many *dacha* owners have to bother about housekeeping chores. . . . And how much valuable time is spent purchasing food and preparing meals! Not only the women but the men as well are chained to the kitchen and to the garden, becoming slaves to housekeeping duties. The situation is radically different in the model public boarding houses of rest, organised in full accord with the interests of the individual-collectivist who is free of housekeeping chores and has sufficient time to develop his mental and physical capacities and to satisfy his reasonable and ever expanding material and spiritual needs.

And when public affluence replaces private squalor, the full stage of communism will be reached (i.e. when nobody will have ' to spend much valuable time ' in queuing at the shops), and the whole country will be covered by cheap restaurant chains and mass holiday camps ; then and only then ' it is to be assumed that . . . people will begin voluntarily to give up their *dachas* . . .'.

Automobiles are not yet choking Soviet roads, but the spectre of the private car is already frightening the Soviet ideologists, who are doing their best to persuade the population that the ' cult of the individual ' should not be replaced by the cult of the individual car. In his 1959 speech in Vladivostok, after his return from the United States. Khrushchev said :

We will turn out a lot of cars, but not now. We will develop taxi pools on an ever broader scale ; people will get a car from them for necessary trips.

The ideological functionaries of the *Agitprop*, who are well-provided with private and official cars, took up the theme, deploring the private ownership of cars. Stepanyan wrote that under full communism ' public garages fully supplied with up-to-date passenger cars for personal use will also be developed '.

In a project for a ' town of the future ',[9] a group of students and teachers of the Moscow Institute of Architecture developed the idea of a ' town of the communist epoch '.

The project is based on the assumption of ' unity of private and public life ' under communism, and of the satisfaction of private needs by public services. In keeping with this, the entry of private cars into the residential area is prohibited ; this idea is directly opposite to the tendency in industrialised countries, where, because of road-jams, the authorities find it necessary to restrict parking and communication in the business zones of the towns. Such a reversal-solution means, as the Polish *Trybuna Ludu* (20 August 1960) observed, ' a serious inconvenience for private car owners '.

However, despite all these discouraging signs, the demand for private cars is growing in the Soviet Union, as indeed it is in other countries of the communist bloc. The Czech *Technicke Noviny* even wrote that

9 *Tekhnika Molodezhy*, No. 8, 1960.

private cars are ' a vital necessity for the modern man ' ; in this one
respect Czechoslovakia is more ' heretical ' than other countries of the
Soviet bloc : it has one car for 68 inhabitants, compared with one car for
255 inhabitants in the USSR (these figures include taxis and official cars).

It would be wrong, however, to infer, by applying strict logic, that this
is as it should be : after all, Czechoslovakia only recently proclaimed the
attainment of socialism, whereas the Soviet Union is on the way to full
communism. The new programme announces that ' production of motor-
cars for the population will be considerably extended '.

It is also necessary to note that the programme is conspicuously silent
on the perennial question of the priority of heavy industry, which not long
ago was still regarded as ' the law of socialist economic development '.
Neither is it explicit on the position of the consumer industries, despite
all its promises to Soviet consumers, the fulfilment of which it defines as
a necessary prerequisite of the construction of communist society.

The implication that the programme reflects a growing tendency
towards a consumer-oriented society has to be balanced against its omission of the explicit statement made by Khrushchev on 20 May 1961 :

> Now we consider our heavy industry as built. So we are not going
> to give it priority. Light industry and heavy industry will develop at
> the same pace.

Obviously, the Soviet leaders do not want to have their hands tied by
any programmatic commitments on the subject. The tendency is rather
to leave the question open (' It is necessary for the national economy to
develop on a strictly proportionate basis ') and to make decisions as the
situation requires, i.e., in the light of balance between consumer pressure
and the power-cum-eschatological commitments. It is the same tendency
which is visible in the decision revealed in the programme that the collective farms are not to be swallowed up by the state farms in the near
future, although it is envisaged that in the long-run there should be
' merging of *kolkhoz* property and the property of the whole people into
one communist property '. As in the other question, the leadership is
left free to decide when the moment is ripe. In the meantime, as trade
unions for the workers in the past, so now *kolkhozes* are proclaimed ' a
school of communism for the peasantry '.[10]

Thus, the programme shows a dual tendency to regard communism as
a short-run (or middle-run) affair, to ' proclaim solemnly ' that ' the
present generation shall live under communism ', and at the same time to
adjudge all the doctrinally difficult questions as a long-term matter.

This is most obvious in the treatment of the problem of money under
communism. No matter how obvious it may be that a highly-developed
economy is bound to be a monetary economy, the Soviet ideologists go on
proclaiming that under communism ' money, trade, and consequently
purchase and sale will disappear '. Stepanyan solemnly quotes Marx and
Engels to the effect that there will be ' personal appropriation of the

---

[10] Cf. also *Kommunist*, No. 8, 1961, pp. 111–20.

products of labour that serve directly for the reproduction of life ', whatever that may mean in the world of growing demand for cars and *dachas*.

However, in treating more immediate problems, the Soviet ideologists are not so starry-eyed. The discussion on the relation of ' commodity circulation ' to the perspectives of communist construction has ended with the defeat of the dogmatic doctrinal tendency. The debate came to a climax in an attack in *Kommunist* (No. 15, 1960) by the two well-known economists, L. Gatovski and M. Sakov, on two representatives of the dogmatic school, I. S. Malyshev and V. A. Sobol. A month later *Kommunist* published another attack on Malyshev by G. Kozlov.

The debate really centred on Stalin's assertion in his *Economic Problems of Socialism* that ' commodity circulation is incompatible with the perspective of the transition from socialism to communism '. The thesis has of course a quite immaculate genealogy in Marxist writings, but is difficult to square with the facts of economic life, and became politically obnoxious after Stalin's death because of the need to improve conditions in agriculture by providing some new un-Marxist incentives for peasants to increase production.

Accordingly, Khrushchev declared at the December 1958 session of the Central Committee :

> Some may say : we are moving into communism and at the same time we are further developing commodity relations ; does not the one contradict the other? No, it does not contradict it.

Malyshev indirectly challenged this view in an article in *Voprosy Ekonomiki* (No. 11, 1960) :

> It is still not clear why we should first develop commodity relations further, and then limit them. . . . It is better and more economic in practice simply not to develop such relations.

The critics, who always have at their disposal the final dialectical argument that in order to ' wither away ' commodity-circulation must first grow stronger, attacked Malyshev as a dogmatist (he branded his opponents as revisionists). The editorial board of *Kommunist* gave to Malyshev and Sobol an opportunity to reply (after seven months, in No. 8, 1961), but firmly associated itself with their critics. This made it clear beyond reasonable doubt that the Party position on the problem is quite settled, and indeed it found an identical expression in the new programme, which promises ' a further strengthening of the monetary and credit system ', and recommends that ' the price system should be continuously improved in conformity with the tasks of communist construction '. It repeats the now ritual formula that :

> It is necessary in communist construction to make full use of commodity-money relations in keeping with their new substance in the socialist period. In this such instruments of economic development as cost-accounting, money, price, production cost, profit, trade, credit, and finance play a big part. When the transition to a single communist form of people's property and the communist system of

distribution is completed, commodity-money relations will become economically outdated and will wither away.

How this will come about is of course left obscure.

IF there was one single term which defined communism to its Founding Fathers it was the concept of ' classless society '.

Yet although there are references to it in the new programme, there is singularly little about what it would mean in concrete detail, and how the differences in status, power, and income in Soviet society will disappear. This is a subject on which the Khrushchevian ideologists cannot afford to be too definite, and they are therefore reluctant to enter into a specific discussion, which might even remotely be called analytical, about the particular problems of ' classlessness ' entailed in the doctrinal perspective of the transition to ' full communism '. Significantly, therefore, no special section is devoted to the subject in the new programme ; only a few scattered pronouncements bear on the question.

It has however been discussed in Soviet publications for years, and an ocean of ink has been spilt on such topics as the obliteration of class distinctions between the Soviet working class and peasantry, between physical and mental labour, leading to the disappearance of the ' social stratum ' of intelligentsia,[11] and of existing differences between town and countryside, and so on. To all these questions the answers are now quite standardised, and they have been included in the definition of communist society given in the programme.[12] But what about the answers to questions which ask not what is to be achieved, but how is it to be achieved? The ' sprouts of communism ' indicated by the theoreticians are not very convincing. As one of the participants in the *Oktyabr* discussion (No. 4, 1960, p. 163) put it : ' We imagine it all, but somehow not quite confidently '.

Some fruits of the imagination may perhaps be quoted, to illustrate the way in which the scholastic dialecticians argue the question of the disappearance of specialisation. That scepticism has crept into the picture is obvious from various pronouncements made during the discussion. Even in Andreeva's model lecture the argument is somewhat blurred :

> With the approach to communism the members of society will take an ever greater part in creative activity ; they will occupy themselves with music, literature, and painting. Consequently, the borderlines between people occupied in the sphere of material production and the professionals, art-workers, and cultural workers will be obliterated.

11 Cf. the present writer's articles, ' The New Soviet Intelligentsia, Origins and Recruitment ', *Survey*, July-September 1959, and ' The Structure of the Soviet Intelligentsia ' in Richard Pipes (ed.), *The Russian Intelligentsia*, Columbia University Press, 1961.
12 For the most authoritative unofficial discussion of the subject see P. N. Fedoseev (ed.) *O Zakonomernostyakh vozniknoveniya i razvitiya sotsialisticheskovo obshchestva*, Moscow, 1960. For a standard popular exposition: G. M. Andreeva, *Na Puti k Bezklassovomu Obshchestvu*, Moscow, 1961.

It is difficult to say if groups of such professionals will remain. Undoubtedly, in communist society too, some people will command exceptional abilities in one or another sphere of art. Obviously, for them, the sphere of art will remain the primary sphere of activity. . . [But] the question who and to what degree is occupied with this or another form of working activity no longer has a social aspect (op. cit. p. 30).

Why this question will no longer have a social aspect is not stated. But even such a mild reflection of scepticism seems unacceptable to Strumilin, who answers the question unambiguously and in a radically fundamentalist manner :

It is true that some contemporary authorities find the idea of the abolition of the division of labour a pure Utopia, and even contemplate an intensification of the division of labour in the practice of Soviet enterprises. But this is wrong (*Oktyabr*, 1960, 3, p. 145).

To fortify his case, Strumilin uses three standard arguments and one unusual one.

The standard arguments are references to : (1) a quotation from Lenin, who said that communism will bring about ' the abolition of the division of labour among people, the education and training of people who are many-sided, trained and developed all round, and who know how to do everything ' [13] ; (2) the ' voluntary ' movement of communist brigades, which it is alleged will replace the principle of the division of labour by the principle of co-operation ; (3) the automation of industry under communism, which is also said to have the same result.

The unusual argument must be quoted in full to get the flavour of Strumilin's ideas about ' the more and more intangible transition from one function to another ' [14] :

If we are not surprised that a piano-tuner even now, when he has finished his mechanical function, completes it like a real musician by performing Beethoven's Moonlight Sonata, a similar joining of functions will be even more natural in the conditions of a shortened working-day under communism.

But such ' realistic ' arguments were not used in all the contributions to the debate on the division of labour. The most thorough discussion took place at a special conference on ' The intensified construction of communism and the many-sided development of personality ' organised at the Moscow University in June 1960. The report reveals far more sober attitudes.[15]

A number of speakers pointed out that automation would not signify the full obliteration of the substantial differences between mental and physical labour. L. N. Kogan criticised the mistaken notion that under communism physical labour disappears altogether and only mental labour

---

13 Lenin, *Collected Works* (in Russian), 4th ed., vol. 31, p. 32.
14 S. Strumilin, *Nowa Kultura*, 6 November 1960.
15 *Vestnik Moskovskovo Universiteta*, Series VIII, Economics & Philosophy, No. 5, 1960, pp. 89-93.

remains . . . members of the communist society would not be ' know-alls '
and dilettantes, without full command of one speciality.

This is, of course, a far cry from Lenin and Strumilin. The new
programme does not enter into any substantial disquisition on the subject, nor does it mention the disappearance of the intelligentsia under
communism, a remark often made during the discussion (Stepanyan
affirmed that ' all the toilers will become members of the intelligentsia ').
It merely limited itself to the short assurance that ' public education
(linked to life and productive labour) will make for the moulding of harmoniously developed members of communist society and for the solution
of a cardinal social problem, namely, the elimination of substantial
distinctions between mental and physical labour '.[16]

The programme is more explicit on another aspect of the problem of
social distinctions, relevant to the question of ' classlessness ', namely the
distribution of income between ' the two classes and one stratum ' in
Soviet society. It indicates the intention to promote a more egalitarian
distribution among them, but does so with qualifications and omissions
which leave the Soviet leadership room for manoeuvre in this sphere too
by keeping some aspects of the problem unexplicit and obscure.

Much of the talk about labour as a social necessity belongs to the
realm of ideological fairy tales. What is real, however, is the increase of
welfare in Soviet society.[17] Some of the recommendations of the programme on questions of welfare (*voprosy byta*) were closely anticipated
in the discussion, but as elsewhere they are less explicit and more non-
committal than some of the ideas expressed unofficially.

Thus, for instance, the question of the working-day was extensively
discussed and Khrushchev himself stated in May 1959, that under communism it may be ' three or four hours a day or even less '. Some of his
theoreticians accordingly constructed a time-table of the shortening of
the working-day *pari passu* with the approach of communism, from six
to three hours.[18] But the programme itself only states that ' in the
coming ten years the country will go over to a six-hour working-day '
(five-hour in underground and harmful jobs). This, like the time-table for
overtaking the United States in industrial and agricultural production
per capita, is an actual postponement of the implementation of earlier
promises, and of course it makes no mention of overtime, or, for that
matter, of the ' voluntary ' labour which is emphasised as such an important feature of the impending communist society. Here is one loophole,
opened in advance, to explain away possible future disappointments.

---

[16] On the background discussion see also : K. Kurilev, in *Kommunist*, No. 5, 1959 :
V. Elnikev, in *Voprosy Filosofii*, No. 8, 1959 ; L. Kogan, ibid., No. 2, 1960 ;
D. Kaidalov : *Kommunizm, trud i chelovek*, Moscow, 1960 : E. Ya. Elremova,
in *Vestnik Moskovskovo Universiteta*, Series VIII, No. 3, 1960.

[17] Cf. *Problems of Communism*, Nos. 1 and 3, 1960, and the Soviet answer to this
discussion on social welfare in the USSR, by P. Mstislavskii, *Novoe Vremya*, No.
4, 1960.

[18] Cf. Strumilin and Stepanyan in *Oktyabr*, No. 3, 1960, p. 142 and No. 7, pp. 152
and 157.

Another, of course, is the statement that the ' complications in the international situation and the resultant necessity of increasing the expenditure on defence may hold up the fulfilment of the plans for raising the living standard of the people '.

As to the proposals for liberating Soviet women from household chores by providing networks of catering services and children's institutions, there was some opposition in the discussion on this to the tendency to reduce the family in the future communist society just to ' married and unmarried ' couples. A Leningrad schoolteacher, N. Dolinina, wrote an article in *Izvestiya*, ' What is worrying Anna Vasilievna? ', in which she defended ' non-working ' mothers, and pointed to their difficulties in running the home and bringing up children. She advocated a part-time working-day for mothers.

The dilemma of ' the two roles of woman ' is, of course, universal in all the countries where the woman's occupation requires her to be away from home and children ; in the Soviet Union the problem is particularly acute because 45 per cent of the working population are women. Dolinina's article was followed by a spate of replies from the readers, published by *Izvestiya* under the characteristic title, ' The interests of production must not be affected '. Most of the replies selected for publication, as could be expected, pointed to the harm which Dolinina's proposal would do to the fulfilment of the seven-year plan. Some advocated an ' equitable ' solution : half of the household duties should be taken over by men. In order to achieve this, Comrade Zhiltsova advocated the ' re-education ' of men.

The topic was taken up in the ' Panferov Debate ' in *Oktyabr*. Vera Bilshaya rejected the proposal in an article, ' Love, family, and female labour ' (No. 3), arguing that ' the only way out is the maximal decrease of women's house-duties through a considerable extension of children's institutions, public canteens, and laundries '. This is, indeed, the position taken in the new programme : sentiments like those reported by UPI from Moscow of a Soviet housewife who said : ' I want my children home with me, all we want to eat is my cooking ', were not reflected in the Soviet press.

But it was possible to express some disagreement with the more doctrinaire schemes on the ' family under communism ' [19] and to bring some elements of the problem down to earth, here and now. Thus P. Dyachuk criticised Vera Bilshaya for not saying anything about how to deal with the household difficulties ' in the present concrete conditions '. He advocated the establishment, following the example of

[19] For a doctrinal analysis of this question see, A. G. Khartchev, in *Kommunist*, No. 7, 1960, and *Voprosy Filosofii*, No. 1, 1961. For a ' discussion ' with foreign critics see I. Solovyev, ' Semya i Kommunizm ', *Oktyabr*, No. 12, 1960. It contains the following passage : ' Not long ago a book by George Orwell with the intriguing title *1984* was published in the USA. In this book the author slanders communism. In the victorious communist world, in 1984, the author writes, all the relations between man and woman will be strictly controlled. The family does not exist. Love is under control and children are produced through artificial insemination.'

Czechoslovakia, of ' councils of grandmothers ' (*sovety babushek*) to take care of the children in the absence of their parents.

But the greatest spate of protests followed the publication of Strumilin's article in *Novy Mir* (No. 7, 1960), which dealt with family and community in the Soviet society of the future and put forward the scheme for Soviet communes. The editors of *Novy Mir* found fit to publish a summary of the letters (No. 2, 1961) with a commentary by Professor V. N. Kolbanovski, playing the role of arbiter between the malcontent readers and the respected Academician. Kolbanovski admitted that some of Strumilin's ' statements were not formulated precisely enough, which, incidentally, gave ground for justly critical remarks by readers '. Strumilin had asserted that children can be educated ' much more successfully by society ' than by the family, and proposed that in fifteen–twenty years all education should be given entirely outside the home. Kolbanovski dismisses the argument that all children need the same amount of the ' vitamins of love ' and those without parents even more. He also asserts that ' the pedagogic illiteracy of parents, feared by S. G. Strumilin, can be eliminated. . . . It is not all that necessary to educate children only in social institutions. . . . It would be a wicked caricature of communism to represent the future family without children, who are the natural aim and the supreme meaning of human love '. This stern reproach echoed readers who ' consider Strumilin's proposals quite unacceptable, for in effect he proposes a complete separation of children from the family and expresses muddled ideas about communes '.

In this latter respect too Kolbanovski called Strumilin to order: ' It is not excluded that the construction of big blocks of flats will be combined with the building of small two- or one-storey houses for individual or common use by separate families or groups of families. This can be admitted without the risk of being accused of individualism '.

Some readers, however, thought Strumilin not consistent enough. One B. Linchevski reproached him because ' on the subject of the formation of the communist family he did not say everything to the end, he did not cross all the t's and dot all the i's '. Perhaps ironically, Linchevski wrote that ' in the future society the conditions of transport will give people the possibility to travel a lot, and this makes for a wider acquaintance [so that] the " old " matrimonial unions will be replaced by new ties and new unions more often '. For such ' anti-Marxist and anti-social reasoning ' Linchevski got a deserved sermon on communist morality from the arbitrating Professor Kolbanovski, duly dissociating the venerable octogenarian who had caused all the dispute from such a frivolous attitude to the family.

GLIMPSES of real life are by no means exceptional in the Soviet press. Judging by the frequency and intensity of the campaigns against loafers and *stilyagi*, against *beloruchki* and private enterprise, other ' sprouts ' than those of communism are flourishing in the USSR. The idealism of youth can still be exploited by the state, but it seems that with increasing affluence other types of motivation will have to be used to keep it in harness ; it takes the obtuseness or the hypocrisy of the true or pseudo-believer to pretend that the manifestations of ' un-communist ' behaviour in the USSR are just ' vestiges of capitalism in the conscious-ness of man ' which will disappear with the approach of communism. The Soviet press itself carries so many testimonials that these phenomena are intimately connected with the social and economic processes of state industrialisation, that there can be hardly any doubt that it is the new *embourgeoisement* and not the survival of the old one which haunts the Soviet exponents of the doctrine.

The campaign against economic ' crimes ' reveals the full extent of the persistence of private enterprise under the surface of the country march-ing to communism. There can be no more telling comment on doctrinal pretensions about the disappearance of the ' vestiges of capitalism ' and the growth of the ' sprouts of communism ' in Soviet man than the intro-duction of capital punishment for ' economic crimes ' (*Izvestiya*, 7 May 1961). In this respect too the Soviet press provides any number of illu-strations contradicting its own ideological claims. For forty years it has been expounding the theory of the economic causation of crime, linking it with the system of class-exploitation and predicting its disappearance with the advent of the ' classless society '. And precisely when this society is officially proclaimed as impending, capital punishment is rein-troduced for economic offences—surely proof enough that the Manichean vision of the ' crime-less ' society counterposed to the iniquities of ' capitalist ' societies, congenitally prone to crime-inception, is false. In reply to Western commentators who had concluded that the new penalties were needed because of an increased volume of crime, the Soviet jurist, Shakhazarov, stated in *Izvestiya*—without giving any statistics about the incidence of crime, which are not published in the Soviet Union—that ' with our country's advance towards communism, the number of people who break the law is diminishing steadily ' ; he attributed the harsher measures to ' purer ' popular morality in a society which, ' as it comes closer to a communist mode of life . . . becomes more intolerant of every-thing that hampers and damages the public well-being '.

The new programme makes the old prophecy : ' There should be no room for law-breakers and criminals in a society building communism. But as long as there are criminal offences it is necessary to punish severely those who commit them '. With due deference to ideological continuity, it then expresses the same pious hope about ' the ultimate replacement of judicial punishment by measures of public influence and education ', as did the 1919 programme which also promised ' finally to replace the system of punishment by measures of an educational character '. As to remedies for the ' vestiges of capitalism ', they were proposed by the head of the central committee's High Party School (the so-called Academy of Social Sciences), Professor Yuri P. Frantsev. His prescription is the same medicine as before, but in larger doses :

Some comrades explained the vitality of the survivals of capitalism in the consciousness of the people by the lagging of psychology, by the gap between consciousness and existence. Others criticised this view, arguing that phenomena of consciousness cannot be explained by (other) phenomena of consciousness. They said that the survivals of capitalism are a social phenomenon. One writer, losing sight of the threads of the dialectic, *began to seek the causes in the social order of our society* (italics added.—L. L.). This of course has nothing in common with the dialectical-materialist approach to the problem . . The existence of the survivals of capitalism in the consciousness of the Soviet people is of course a social phenomenon. But it has no roots in our social order . . . The elimination of the shortcomings in our educational work . . . will secure a decisive success in the task of reconstructing the consciousness of the people all over the country (*Voprosy Filosofii*, 1961, No. 5).

And that is why the new programme states that ' in the struggle for the victory of communism, ideological work becomes an increasingly powerful factor '.

IN analysing Ideology and Utopia in the new Party programme, in disentangling the logic of ideology and the persistence of ' Utopian survivals in the Soviet consciousness ', it is easy to forget that in one sense the content of the programme does not matter at all. Programmatic planks clearly do not play the same part in the chiliastic as in the empirical tradition. To project the later on to the earlier categories is to misunderstand the function of Party programmes in communist countries. But it would be as erroneous to dismiss them altogether as ' irrelevant to reality ' because their promises are not of the same character as the more earth-bound platforms of democratic politicians facing the electorate (of this and not future generations), as it would be to take the specific undertakings of the programme at their face value. Both attitudes disregard the important function of the programme as the symbolic focus of ideology designed to mobilise the population to carry out the tasks assigned to it by the leaders. In this sense, whatever its ideological fantasies and unrealistic elements, the programme is as relevant as the current role of ideology in the Soviet system makes it. Its use of the Utopian formulas of the 19th century is simply anachronistic in the light of subsequent historical experience and general sociological knowledge about the workings of society. This does not mean, of course, that some of its planks, on the development of economy and science, of technical education or social services, are necessarily unrealistic. It only means that no realistic analysis of social change in any society, capitalist or socialist, feudal or communist, can be made on the basis of the naïve 19th-century perspective of human perfectibility through social reorganisation, a perspective descending directly from earlier visions of a Golden Age which found shelter in the pseudo-scientific secular faith of Marxism.

PLAN AND SUPERPLAN

Naum Jasny

AFTER forty years of planning, the Soviets have announced their first general plan of twenty years' duration.[1] No less a task than the completion of laying the foundation of communism is assigned to it.

A single economic plan (single in the sense of covering the whole economy) presupposes the complete tie-in of all its parts. This would not guarantee that the plan is good. Some parts, although well tied-in with the others, may be too high, too low, or otherwise defective. But a plan-like document, in which the individual parts are programmed separately and not tied-in with the others, is not a single plan, even though some parts may be perfectly sensible.

In addition to planning for a time of which nobody can know anything definite, to putting in obviously absurd targets for vital items, and so on and so on, the provisions of the new plan display a flagrant disproportion between such crucial items as the targets for national income and those for labour productivity. This disproportion is so enormous, it so strikes the eye, that the suspicion arises that the real planners may not have seen the document at all. Incidentally, the agency which is supposed to have been working out the twenty-year plan, the Gosekonomsovet, does not appear to be mentioned in it.

The twenty-year plan is part of the programme of the Soviet Communist Party, the draft of which was released on 30 July 1961. The text actually does not use the phrase ' twenty-year plan ' or, for that matter, the standard expression for the long-range plan, the general plan. It speaks simply of two decades, of 10 and 20 years. Features of the new ' plan ', which strike the eye and may possibly be interpreted as showing that, although very, very slowly, the Soviets are learning, are (a) that only few figures are given, and (b) that even those few are given in round numbers.[2] But these are relatively minor matters, included for the convenience of the planners in juggling with those figures that are given, and words of course flow easily. The basic requirement of a good plan is that it must be realistic. This was recognised at the party central committee meeting in December 1956, and was clearly in evidence in the annual plans of the subsequent years and in the targets of the general plan (a 15-year plan) for 11 industrial commodities announced in November 1957. This policy has now been

[1] The Soviets count the Plan GOELRO (State Committee on Electrification of Russia) of 1920 as the first general plan. But it did not embrace the whole economy even as drafted. The only part of it approved was the construction of thirty electric power plants. The rest was propaganda.
[2] The figures are frequently qualified with such phrases as ' not less than ' or ' more than '.

abandoned. The targets of the new 'plan' are on the strongly optimistic side in almost all cases, and some important targets are clearly absurdly high.

On the technical side, it should be added that the new plan does not contain even a trace of a breakdown into 5-year periods, as seems to have been expected by writers in the Soviet press. The usual breakdown in the plan is by decades, but such important targets as those for grain and steel capacity have only one figure, that for 1980. At least in one case (real incomes of low-paid hired labour) there is a target only for the first decade.

While only a few figures are given, they enable us to form a rough idea about the expected development, although one would want to have in addition numerical data at least for the output of industrial consumer goods and for investment. For the first of these items one has to speculate from the data on the expected growth in personal incomes; for the second conclusions have to be drawn from the high rates of growth expected for the whole economy and from some verbal statements (the 20-year plan states that investment will have to be huge). Nobody expects from such a document as the new plan specific information about expenditure on the armed forces, but it goes out of its way to emphasise that 'defence' is fully taken care of.

Calculations as to the size and disposition of labour are one of the most important components of a plan. Not only are these items missing from the new 'plan', but such immense errors have been made in respect to this question that it is impossible to accept the economic provisions of the programme as a plan.

PRODUCTION

The few figures which can be extracted from the published document are set out in the table below :

| | Attained 1950–60 | | Percentage growth as given in the 20-year Plan | | |
	official	corrected	1960–1970	Planned 1970–1980^a	1960–1980
National income	159	97–113	almost 150	not less than 100	400
Industrial output	204	140	almost 150	not less than 140	not less than 500
of which:					
electric power	220	—	208–242	200	825–921
steel	139	—	—	—	284b
Farm output	60^b	—	about 150	40	250
of which:					
grain	62	—	—	—	more than 100
meat	82^c	—	about 200	nearly 33·3	nearly 300
milk	80	—	more than 100	—	nearly 200
Labour productivity:					
industry	104	—	more than 100	—	300–350
agriculture	—	—	not less than 150	100–140	400–500

	Attained 1950–60 official corrected	Percentage growth as given in the 20-year Plan		
		1960–1970	Planned 1970–1980*a*	1960–1980
Real income per employed person: Workers and em-				
ployees	62*c* —	almost 100	—	approx. 200–250
of which:				
low-paid	— —	approx. 200	—	—
kolkhoz peasants	85*c* —	more than 100	100	more than 300

a Implied.
b Capacity.
c 1950–59.

As far as can be seen from the data in this table, there is a violent contradiction between the targets for national income and those for labour productivity. The first implies a marked slowdown in the rate of growth in the second decade (1970–80) as compared with the first (1960–70), while this development is scarcely reflected in the targets for labour productivity. If the targets for national income are regarded as basic, as they should be, the question arises as to the reason for the slowdown. Since the Soviet planners are of course unable to visualise what will happen in the 1970s, the reason for the big discrepancy may be that the Soviets were mainly interested in having high rates of growth in the first decade and therefore set the target for this decade much higher than that for the second decade.

Because, clearly, the target for the growth of the national income in the 1960s, providing as it does a 2·5-fold rise and implying an annual growth of about 10 per cent, is very much on the optimistic side. The official estimates indicate a growth in national income in 1950–60 of almost 11 per cent per year, but there is no doubt at all that this figure is excessive. Most Western analysts agree on a figure of about 7–8 per cent.

Some analysts believe that the new plan is a projection of the development in the preceding years, but this is true only for output of electric power, as will be shown. The target for national income, the index which summarises the whole economy, clearly reflects expectations of a substantial speeding up in the first plan decade as compared with the preceding decade. A rate of growth approximately equal to that in the past is provided only for the second decade. In 1959 and 1960, the last two years, even the *official* indices showed a growth of 8 per cent per year, i.e. considerably less than scheduled for the 1960s. The first half of 1961, i.e. the initial portion of the 20-year plan period, was not better than 1959 or 1960.

The 20-year plan foresees a growth of 150 per cent in industrial output in 1960–70, or 10 per cent per year, i.e. the same as for the national income, and, incidentally, for the growth of agriculture.

The official estimate for the growth of industrial output in 1950–60 (about 11 per cent per year) is probably exaggerated, but much less than that for national income. (It is a mystery to this writer how this discrepancy comes to exist.)   A growth of 9 per cent per year is assumed by this writer for this period.   Thus here, too, the new plan goes beyond the previous attainments.   The target of the new plan for industrial output also exceeds the targets of the 7-year plan for 1959–65, adopted little more than two years ago, which set a growth in industrial output of 8·6 per cent per year.   The Soviet authorities may feel justified in raising this percentage because, according to their calculations, the rate of growth scheduled by the 7-year plan was exceeded in the first two years of its operation.   According to these official calculations, industrial output grew by about 10·5 per cent in both 1959 and 1960. But, like most other recent indices, the indices for industrial production in 1959 and 1960 are likely to be at least moderately exaggerated. The real growth in industrial output in these two years is unlikely to have been as high as 10 per cent, the rate implied in the 20-year plan for 1960–70.   And even if it were, can a 20-year plan be based on a 2-year development?

The growth of agricultural output of 150 per cent, or of 10 per cent per annum, foreseen for 1960–70, reflects nothing but Mr Khrushchev's exuberance.   There can be no doubt on this score.   He takes the failure of his past predictions about the growth of farm production with amazing equanimity ; his urge to get estimates down from the sky does not abate.   Farm output grew at no more than 5–6 per cent per year from Stalin's death to 1960, with the growth in 1959 and 1960 definitely bogged down (even with the effect of unfavourable weather eliminated, this might still be true).   The new target for the growth of agricultural output of 150 per cent in 1960–70 is also substantially above the target of the 7-year plan for 1959–65 of 70 per cent in seven years, which was in any case wholly unrealistic.

It has already been mentioned that the new plan shows a great decline in the rate of growth of national income from 150 per cent in 10 years, or about 10 per cent per year in 1960–70, to 100 per cent in 10 years or about 7 per cent per year in the 1970s.   Whether even this rate can be realised, nobody of course can say.   The growth in farm output is to go down substantially in the second decade (40 per cent instead of the 150 per cent for the first decade).   Industrial output, however, is to continue its growth at almost the high rate of the first decade (about 9·5 per cent for the second decade as against about 10 per cent for the first).   If the target of the 20-year plan for national income were to be fulfilled, this would mean that the national income of the USSR would in 1970 be slightly greater than the 1960 national income of the United States, and would be not much less than 2·5 times the latter after twenty years.   The United States has of course

10 and 20 years respectively in which to counter these pleasant prospects.

Official Soviet indices (exaggerated) show that the output of heavy industry was increasing at a rate of almost 13 per cent in 1950–60, while the output of consumer goods was growing at a rate of not quite 10 per cent. The difference in the rate of growth between producer and consumer goods was actually not as large as indicated by these figures, but it should be noted that the share of consumer goods in total industrial production fell from 60·5 per cent in 1928 to 31·2 per cent in 1950,[3] and to less than 28 per cent in 1960.

At a reception in Moscow on 20 May 1961, Khrushchev is supposed to have said : ' Now we consider our heavy industry as built. So we are not going to give it priority. Light industry and heavy industry will develop at the same pace.'[4] There was every reason to assume that this important statement had been taken from the 20-year plan, then (according to Khrushchev) in preparation, that indeed it was one of the foundations of the whole plan and especially of its industrial component. Yet no such statement is to be found in the 20-year plan. Neither is there any statement on the priority of heavy industry, which has been present in every plan for over 30 years. The 7-year plan for 1959–65, approved little more than two years ago, still gave predominance to the growth of heavy industry. Instead of this, the importance of heavy industry is stressed in the programme without reference (even by implication) to the growth in output of consumer goods. Heavy industry ' insures the development of the economy ' and therefore ' deserves unflagging attention '. Of consumer goods it is said : ' The CPSU will concentrate its efforts on insuring a rapid increase in the output of consumer goods.'

It has been suggested in the Western press that the omission of Khrushchev's statement about an equal rate of growth in output of consumer and producer goods was due to a conflict at the top level, in which Khrushchev was defeated. It is, however, not very likely that one of the foundations of the plan was really changed at what should have been a very advanced stage of its preparation. The targets of the new plan, giving the same rate of growth for consumer and producer goods, may have been retained[5] (there may have been some manipulation to make it easier to reach statistical equality) and only the words altered to omit the precise text of Khrushchev's statement ; the specific rates of growth for the two groups of industrial goods, and possibly the targets for one or two individual consumer goods, were presumably present from the start. This assumption is reinforced by the very high target for output of farm products in the first decade,

---

3 *Soviet Statistical Handbook for 1959*, p. 149.
4 *New York Times*, 31 July 1961.
5 But there may have been difficulties in setting this level of output of consumer goods for the second plan decade, when the rate of growth in output of farm products is scheduled to decline sharply.

as well as the figures for real incomes, although the few round figures that are given in the new plan might well have been totally revised in the two months which elapsed between Khrushchev's declaration and the publication of the programme. Nevertheless it is still significant that, with the share of consumer goods in total industrial production as low as 28 per cent, the programme does not go so far as to ensure expressly that this percentage will be maintained in the future. There is not the smallest reason to treat Mr Khrushchev as an entrenched advocate of consumer goods output and of adequate personal incomes in general. When he got the better of Malenkov, his victory signified *inter alia* the abandonment of Malenkov's efforts to speed up the expansion of the output of consumer goods and a return to Stalin's priority of heavy industry. Still, consumer goods are treated in the 20-year plan better than they were by Khrushchev in 1954–55, and in the 7-year plan for 1959–65. Indeed, no previous plan in the USSR has given anywhere near as much space to the well-being of the population as does the new plan. There is reason to believe that the change is due to the pressure of the population, which can make itself felt in spite of the dictatorship.

The new plan has only two individual industrial targets, namely, electric power and steel. Both are producer goods. The target for electric power provides about a trebling in each decade. This is equivalent to a rise of not quite 12 per cent per year, and represents an almost exact projection of the development in the decade 1950–60. In fact, this scheduled rate of growth seems somewhat too small relative to the target for total industrial growth, especially in view of the considerable reduction in the costs of constructing electric power plants. As for steel, the new plan speaks only of the technical production possibilities, i.e. of capacity to produce, which is not necessarily to be fully used. A capacity of 250 million tons of steel—the 1980 target—seems huge when compared with the present output of the United States. It is almost double the capacity of the United States plants; but it does not seem particularly large in the context of the other targets, specifically that for total industrial production. The implied annual rate of growth, almost 7 per cent, even appears small compared with the rate of increase attained by steel production in the preceding decade. Of course it is hoped to economise on steel by making machinery lighter, and more attention will certainly be paid to the substitution of plastics for steel.

Three specific targets for farm products are given. Like the target for total farm output, these must be judged as being more or less on the fantastic side, considering the limited possibilities for the expansion of farm production at anything like the rates implied.

When referring to overtaking the United States in total output, the planners concentrate on the prospects 20 years hence, but with reference to agriculture they say : ' In the first decade the Soviet Union will out-strip the United States in output of the key agricultural products per head of population.' It is not difficult to overtake somebody who is not running. There is no reason for the United States to expand its farm output which already exceeds the demand.

The scheduled increase of more than 100 per cent in the grain output in 20 years implies a rise of approximately 4 per cent per year—a great rate for a crop like grain and for a country like the USSR. Most of the grain areas are located in regions with inadequate moisture supply, and where, therefore, commercial fertilisers have only a limited usefulness, which in turn limits the possibilities for raising per-acre yields. A threefold increase in meat output in 10 years would mean a per capita output of real meat of not much less than 100 kilo-grams in 1970. The further increase in the second decade is then scheduled to be relatively moderate (equal to about 15 per cent on a per capita basis). At anything like present prices, this meat output might well outrun demand. But Mr Khrushchev does not really need to worry about this right now, when people are standing in long queues for meat. The nearly trebled milk output scheduled for 1980 implies a per capita output of over 700 kilograms. Butter consumption is apparently believed to be capable of rising almost indefinitely.

Labour Productivity and Labour Force

The crucial point in the development of the Soviet economy in the coming two decades or so, in any serious plan, is the speed with which labour productivity will grow. The provisions of the 20-year plan are extremely optimistic on this score, especially of course in words but also in figures.

Labour productivity in industry is to rise by fully 7 per cent per year on the average in each of the 20 years. For some reason, its growth is scheduled to be larger for the second than for the first decade. The official statistics show, it is true, exactly the same rise in 1950–60, but the index of labour productivity in industry is exaggerated about as much as the index of industrial output. The target of the new plan for labour productivity in industry is definitely, and moreover substan-tially, higher than the past performance.[6] The new targets for labour productivity in agriculture far surpass even those in industry, and are wholly unrealistic. In the first decade labour productivity in agriculture is to grow by about 10 per cent each year. This would certainly be a great achievement, but the target for the second decade makes it a pygmy. It provides that labour productivity in agriculture, after having risen to 2·5 times its present performance, will go on growing at a not

[6] N. Kaplan and R. Moorsteen, ' An Index of Soviet Industrial Output ', *The American Economic Review*, June 1960, p. 316, calculated for industry other than machinery (including armaments) an average growth of 5 per cent in 1950–58. The addition of machinery would raise this percentage to say 6.

much slower rate for a further 10 years. By 1980 it would have reached a 5–6-fold level as compared with 1960. The official estimates indicate a rise in labour productivity in agriculture in 1953–59 of not quite 7 per cent per year. This was, however, an overestimate and, moreover, the 6 years covered by the index are the most favourable ever, and the start was from a very low level.

The improbability of the labour productivity targets is enhanced by the comparisons with the United States made in the programme, where it appears that the USA is pretty backward compared with the level easily attainable on paper in the USSR

It seems reasonable to assume that the rates of growth in labour productivity should decline as time passes. It has been increasing at a good rate in recent years, and it is obvious that the greater the growth of labour productivity in the past, the less remains for the future. Such gains as this are not repeatable.

There is however one thing which may prevent such a decline, possibly even permit an increase (but of course not over twenty years ; this writer refuses to put down on paper his speculations on what will happen after 20 years). This is the great amount of irrationality and inefficiency in the Soviet economy. The partial removal of these features, now certainly in progress, may for a time prevent the decline in the rate of growth in labour productivity which is otherwise probably inevitable.

The immense amount of irrationality, inefficiency, and downright waste in the Soviet economy is apparently not generally realised.[7] Part of it is inherent in the Soviet system and cannot be eliminated. (This is not to say that this part is necessarily greater than that inherent in the capitalist system.) But a large part is unnecessary, and the Soviets are doing something to remove a good bit of it. Here only two items, electric power and fuel, will be briefly discussed. There is an immense waste of labour in Soviet agriculture, but the complications here are so vast that merely an attempt to touch on the topic would burst the permitted bounds of this article.

Of the electric power plants put into operation in 1950–59, 21·4 per cent were hydro-electric. One competent Soviet author has said : ' As is known, hydro-electric plants cost four times as much as thermal plants per kilowatt to construct.'[8] Moreover, the reported construction costs of hydro-electric plants are minimised in various ways in the USSR. It seems reasonable to assume that the relatively small proportion of hydro-electric plants among the 1950–59 constructions nearly doubled the total construction costs of all power plants.

---

[7] The beginning of an analysis of this very important phenomenon may be found in my ' Note on Rationality and Efficiency of the Soviet Economy ', *Soviet Studies*, April and July 1961.

[8] *Economic Effectiveness of Fixed Investment and New Techniques*, ed. T. S. Khachaturov, Moscow, 1959, p. 466.

On 10 August 1958, Mr Khrushchev announced that the preferred treatment of hydro-electric power was to be discontinued ; henceforth preference was to be given to thermal electric-power plants. The idea was incorporated in the 7-year plan for 1959–65, and in spite of Mr Khrushchev's assurances that the change in policy would only be relatively short-lived, it may be regarded as accepted for good. If the share of hydro-electric power plants will be only 10 per cent of the total new capacity in the next 20 years, this alone may involve a saving on construction costs of about a quarter of what they would otherwise be. In addition, the majority of whatever hydro-electric plants will be constructed in the next 20 years, will be located behind the Urals, where the topographical conditions are much more favourable than in European Russia and construction costs are said to be only about half as large per kilowatt. Finally, if large thermal power stations are built, construction costs per unit of power will be substantially reduced.

After a delay much longer than the twenty years now envisaged, the Soviet rulers awoke to the idea (they did not need to develop it themselves ; they could have borrowed it from the United States) that petroleum, and natural gas in particular, are very much cheaper to produce and, for that matter, to transport than coal, especially since this is particularly expensive in European Russia. The investment, including exploration costs, required for petroleum and gas is somewhat greater than for coal, but this hardly matters because the additional investment can be repaid from savings in less than two years, and for gas in less than one year. By the end of the 1970s the share of coal in total fuel is unlikely to be much higher than 25 per cent (it was 66·1 per cent in 1950), with the shares of petroleum and gas correspondingly higher. It has been calculated on the basis of the provisions of the ' general plan ' announced in November 1957 (this scheduled a decline in the share of coal to about 30 per cent) that 36 milliard rubles would have been saved on this score by 1972,[9] a sum equivalent to roughly 3 per cent of the total 1959 national income. The savings (in rubles, not in per cent of national income) would of course be even greater by 1980, what with the total amount of fuel steadily rising and the share of coal in total fuel steadily declining.

All such savings are likely to affect favourably the growth of labour productivity in industry and construction. What can be expected is no more than holding on for some time to the relatively high rates of growth of labour productivity in the past few years, not its growth beyond this level and not for as long as 20 years.

So far as agriculture is concerned, the Soviet leaders presumably expect great savings of labour from the conversion of collective into

9 *Economic Effectiveness*, op. cit., p. 82.

state farms, accompanied by the elimination of the private plots and livestock of the collective peasants. These sources indeed may permit a temporary growth in labour productivity in agriculture greater than in the past several years, but nothing even remotely resembling a 2·5-fold rise in 10 years and 5–6-fold rise in 20 years is likely.

To turn now to the vital problem of the relation between the rate of growth of labour productivity and that of national income.

Assuming that the access of persons of working age will be about the same in percentage terms in both the 1960s and the 1970s, there should be a marked parallelism between the rate of growth of labour productivity and that of national income. This is, however, not the case. In the programme a somewhat greater rise in labour productivity in industry is set for the 1970s than for the 1960s. The target for the rise in labour productivity in agriculture is slightly less for the 1970s than the 1960s. Yet the rate of growth of national income is to decline from 150 per cent in the first plan decade to only 100 per cent in the second.

This glaring inconsistency can also be seen from the following data : In the first plan decade labour productivity in industry is to rise by ' more than 100 per cent ', that in agriculture by ' not less than 150 per cent '. If the access of new labour during the decade is taken into account, the growth in national income of ' nearly 150 per cent ' seems to have at least an outward appearance of a tie-in with that in labour productivity in industry and agriculture combined. But in the second plan decade we have a rise in labour productvity of 100–125 per cent in industry and of 100 to 140 per cent in agriculture. Taking into account the continued access of new labour to the extent of roughly 20 per cent, these rates of growth in labour productivity correspond to an increase in national income of not very much less than 150 per cent. Yet the new plan has only a 100 per cent rise. The reason for this immense discrepancy can only be guessed at. It may possibly be due to failure to consider the changes in the labour force.

An indispensable part of a 20-year plan should be concerned with accessions to and utilisation of labour. Not a word can be found on these vital items in the document. The point is not only not discussed, it was obviously not given any thought. If it had been, the new plan would be a different document. The planners possibly thought that with the immensely optimistic prospects for the rise in labour productivity there was no need to worry about a possible shortage of labour. It seems to have escaped their notice that the combination of the provisions for output with those for labour productivity in the plan implies a tremendous amount of unused labour. After having boasted about the absence of unemployment for some 30 years, they suddenly programme unemployment on a fantastic scale. The relevant provisions of the new plan are shown in the table below :

LABOUR FORCE AS IMPLIED IN THE PROGRAMME

First decade (as % of 1960)

	Industry	Agriculture	Total
Output	250	about 250	—
Labour productivity a ...	more than 200	not less than 250	—
Labour force b:			
Millions in 1960	21	33	54
Percentage increase	25	less than in 1960	—
Millions in 1970	26	32	58
Second decade (as % of 1970)			
Output	not less than 240	133⅓	—
Labour productivity b ...	almost 200–225c	200–240	—
Labour force:			
Millions in 1970	26	32	58
Percentage increase + ...	+ about 15	− 30–40	—
decrease −			
Millions in 1980	30	19–22	49–52

a The calculations of the changes in the labour force are only rough owing to the nature of the data.
b Implied in the targets for output and labour productivity.
c A formula 'almost 100–125' does not make much sense but this is implied in the targets of a 'more than 100 per cent' rise for 1960–70 and an 'approximately 300–350 per cent' rise in 1960–80, and one naturally does not wish to meddle with official data more than absolutely necessary.

With the great rise in labour productivity in industry, the situation turns out very favourably for the industrial labour force. The targets for output and productivity in industry imply a rise in the industrial labour force in 20 years of only one-third to one-half. This compares with an increase of around 50 per cent in the 10 years from 1950 to 1960.

The corresponding data for agriculture imply a really fantastic development, if they were anything more than words on paper. For the 1960s the data of the 20-year plan imply an almost unchanged labour force in agriculture (for output we have a rise of 'about 150 per cent' and for labour productivity one of 'at least 150 per cent'), while in the next decade the labour force in agriculture, and consequently the whole farm population in about the same proportion, is to be cut by not less than 30–40 per cent. (This is expected to occur at a time when the real incomes of the peasants are rising fastest.) Ten to thirteen million workers (actually more because the figures for labour cited in the tabulation are not in physical terms but in units, and one unit is larger than one physical person) would be released from agriculture. What will happen about housing them? Is housing to be provided outside the village for this mass of people? And, most important, what will this mass of people be doing in the way of work and earning a living?

In two decades industrial and farm employment would go down from about 58 per cent of the total to little more than one-third. As the table shows, in the first decade industrial and agricultural labour together will increase by less than 10 per cent. The total access of labour may amount to say 20 per cent, and the economy, other than farming and industry, would have to expand its labour force by more than 30 per cent to make use of all available labour. Possibly it will be able to do so. We will not start guessing.

But the second decade shows an impossible situation. Industrial and farm labour together is scheduled to go down by 6–9 million. Employment other than industry and agriculture would have to double to take them in. The ' planners ' certainly did not realise it, but their beautiful plan implies unemployment on a vast scale.

DISTRIBUTION

Of the roughly 10,000 words devoted to economics in the programme, a large part deals with the well-being of the population. ' The CPSU puts before itself the task of world-historical importance—to insure in the Soviet Union the highest living standards as compared with any country of capitalism '. It might easily escape the reader that the prospects are not quite so rosy, when one turns from words to examine the few figures given in the programme.

It must be remembered that the industrialisation drive was based on the severe exploitation and deprivation of the population, and that the share of personal incomes in national income was reduced by the time of Stalin's death to an incredibly low level and then held at approximately that level until today.

With all the great benefits, free lunches, etc., provided for the population in the programme, the extremely low share of personal income in national income is apparently going to remain almost stationary (an exact calculation is impossible because of inadequate data). The huge funds allocated for investment and the armed forces will grow (this seems to be implied in the data of the plan) only insignificantly less than personal incomes. Moreover, part of these incomes will reach the population in a form which will not be counted at full value (see below).

National income is scheduled to rise 5-fold in 20 years. (It is not stated, but is definitely implied in the combination of the rise in national income and the rise in personal incomes, that the funds in the hands of the State for investment and armed forces, huge even now, are to rise almost as much as national income, i.e. almost five-fold, during the same period.) This implies a per capita rise of 245 per cent during this period. Total per capita incomes of the population, which include all free public services, are to rise ' more than 3·5-fold '. The balance in favour of the population with reference to the distribution of the national income thus shifts only negligibly. The share of personal incomes, including free services, remains virtually at the low level at which it stood in 1960.

Real wages (targets for real wages include public gratuitous services throughout) are scheduled to rise by 200–250 per cent. The real incomes of the kolkhoz peasants (only few will be left by 1980 at the present rate of conversion of kolkhozy into sovkhozy), are to increase by more than 300 per cent.

Even a trebling of real wages in 20 years, the minimum 'ensured' to hired labour in the plan, not to speak of the more than quadrupling provided for the kolkhoz peasants, would by no means be bad. But the fulfilment of the targets for real incomes obviously depends on attainment of the much too optimistic goals for output, especially for farm output. This dependence is even emphasised in the programme in reference to peasant incomes.

The policy of reducing the stratification of real wages is continued ; it is indeed stated that by 1970 there will be no low-paid hired workers. The 7-year plan provided for the following increases in real wages :

All hired labour, 40 per cent.

Minimum wage, about 80 per cent.

The provisions of the new plan until 1970 are as follows :

All hired workers, almost 100 per cent.

Minimum wage, about 200 per cent.

The relationship in pay between minimum and average is more favourable in the new than in the 7-year plan. It must be remembered, however, that the 7-year plan is realistic and the new plan is not. The rate of increase in the minimum real wage is scheduled to reach by 1970 the level foreseen for increase in pay of all labour in 1980, but there is nothing about the course of the minimum wage in the 1970s. There are, however, provisions in the new plan which, if carried out, must further substantially improve the relative position of low-pay hired labour.

One feature of the new plan, potentially of importance, is the great increase in free services. Before discussing this point, it must be recalled that the rise in real wages is calculated *inclusive* of the ' social funds '. This phrase, however, is omitted from the statements on real incomes of the peasants. ' Social funds ' are the funds for providing gratuitous state services to the population. These are bestowed on the whole population, rather than on hired labour only. The reason for the use of different concepts in planning growth in real wages and the real incomes of the kolkhoz peasants is not made clear. Perhaps the peasants are not expected to get all gratuitous services.

The programme promises a vast expansion of these services. ' In the movement towards communism, personal needs will be ever more satisfield at the expense of social funds of consumption ; the rates of their growth will exceed the rates of growth of the individual payment according to labour.' Some of the existing services are to be enlarged and a number of new ones added. Among the latter are the maintenance of children in children's homes and boarding schools (if the parents desire this), support of the disabled, free housing and some free communal services, lunches at the place of employment, etc.

Lack of space prevents a detailed examination. These services as a whole are to account by the end of the 20 years for ' about half the total real incomes of the population '. This phrase in the programme is given greater precision in an unsigned and consequently official commentary on the programme of great length in *Pravda*, 2 August 1961. According to this, social funds are to rise in 1960–80 ' about eight-fold ' on a per capita basis—a huge increase, if reached. A combination of these figures relating to gratuitous services yields the implication that the paid-out real wages are to be in 1980 about double those in 1960. The increase in cash payments is to be less, possibly much less, for those in the higher wage-brackets. It may be fairly assumed that the population would, in regard to at least many of these services, prefer cash, and that the relatively small increase in cash payments actually implies smaller rises of total wages than those stated in the programme. Since so much depends on the rise in the labour productivity of the better-paid labourer, the attempt to carry out the provisions for free services may become a handicap to growth in labour productivity, on the high targets for which the whole programme depends.

The fact that half of the real pay is to consist of gratuitous services, bestowed upon the population without regard to the amount of their labour, implies of course a great reduction in both stratification of real wages, and the differentiation in incomes between hired labour and kolkhoz peasants, especially since the wording of the programme seems to aim at reduced stratification in individual payments as well. If the minimum real wage paid out individually equals 50 per cent of the average wage payment, the total minimum real wage will have to be equal to about 75 per cent of the average total real wage. A full share in the gratuitous services on top of their incomes from the kolkhozy and their own farming enterprises would also mean higher incomes for the kolkhoz peasants. There is no indication how this difficulty is to be resolved, but it is impossible for peasants' incomes to differ substantially from the incomes of low-paid hired labour.

Expansion of gratuitous services is to go on after the expiration of the twenty years, and when all pay consists of gratuitous services, then, according to Mr Khrushchev, there will be communism, the realisation of the principle ' to each according to his needs '. As compared with the ideas held for the last few hundred years, there is however this difference, that previously it was thought that the individual would himself decide what he needs. Now it turns out that the rulers will decree what the free Soviet population needs. A minor difference, to be sure.

CONCLUSIONS

Soviet planning is rich in bad plans. But to find an equivalent of the new ' 20-year plan ' one has to turn back to Stalin's initial drive with its bacchanalian planning, the period called by this writer the All-Out

Drive,[10] when in February 1932 an output of electric power of 100 billion Kwh was planned for 1937 (actual attainment, 36 billion Kwh), and this was by no means the only, or even the worst, target set in this period, which extended from Stalin's pernicious article in *Pravda* of 6 November 1929 to early in 1933. The deterioration in planning techniques in the new plan is especially marked as compared with the seven-year plan for 1959–65.

The question arises, how did all this get into the programme? It is impossible for real planners to have produced it. An explanation which seems least damaging is this : the Gosekonomsovet, with or without the participation of Gosplan, produced, on directions from above, a draft of the plan. Because these directions came from on high, the targets were made very optimistic, but probably the provisions were, if only crudely, tied in one with the other. The immense increases in productivity of farm labour may have been absent, and so, consequently, the precipitous decline in farm labour in the second planning decade, and so on. This crude draft was then, possibly very belatedly, taken to the central committee Presidium, where the planning ' experts ' drastically revised the draft. Mr Khrushchev no doubt contributed his ideas on how agriculture had to develop. Tie-ins? Who at that level cares for them or understands the need for them? The real planners may not even have been given a chance to see this ' plan ' when the printers got to work, but they knew the moment they read the programme in the papers that the ' plan ' was absurd. Will they report their findings to Mr Khrushchev? And will their advice be heeded?

In November 1957 Mr Khrushchev announced the so-called general plan, in actual fact targets for the output of eleven industrial commodities, to be reached in about fifteen years. Even at that time the targets seemed not the product of serious prolonged work, co-ordinated with the probable development of the rest of the economy, but a hasty *ad hoc* affair, and they were dropped by March 1959 at the latest. The 20-year plan now announced seems no more serious. The targets for the eleven commodities constituted part of a pageant, the celebration of the 40th anniversary of the Revolution, and this function they fulfilled more or less successfully.

It looks very much as though the targets of the 20-year plan were designed to play the same part in the pageant called the XXII Congress of the CPSU. If the economic provisions were not incorporated in the programme, they might die at an even earlier age than the eleven targets of the 1957 general plan. Their incorporation in a more lasting document will make it more difficult to bury them, even if they become a corpse.

[10] See *Soviet Industrialization, 1928–52*, Chapters 4 and 5.

MAN AND THE IDEAL ECONOMY

Peter Wiles

THE concept of Full Communism, as a problem of communist theory and practice, is primarily of interest to communists; but it is equally important for non-communist countries to have a view of where they are going: an image of the far future to oppose to Full Communism, or even conceivably a peaceful road to the same state of affairs. For while the far future as a whole cannot be foreseen in an open society—in a closed one, naturally, it can—at least certain tendencies and probabilities can be spotted, and encouraged or discouraged according to taste.

This article is an impertinent attempt to supply the economic side only of a non-communist Statement of National Purpose. It is obviously deficient on the sociological and political sides, and no attempt is made to remedy this. It is also of its nature deficient on the side of foreign aid and backward countries, but then so are most doctrines of Full Communism. The mere fact that most of the world is extremely poor does not mean that affluent societies have no problems of their own.

Can there, then, be other forms of Extreme Affluence than Full Communism? We answer by asking three more questions :

(i) Is indefinite economic growth likely? For clearly only so can any form of Extreme Affluence be achieved.

(ii) Can any type of organisation achieve it, or only some types?

(iii) What are the *natural* economic and social consequences of Extreme Affluence in a democratic, capitalist society? Could they be described as Full Communism?

It is my thesis that 'Capitalism' will in fact autonomously grow over into something rather more desirable than Full Communism, without any intervening nonsense of 'Socialism', 'Proletarian Revolution', etc., if only it is left alone in peace.

As to question (i), the merely technological side, we must take it here for granted that growth has no limits.[1] But there is also the institutional side. If indefinite economic growth is possible at all, is it possible through the market, and with our present economic organisation and political democracy?

---

[1] It is not obvious that this is so, and it cannot be rigorously proved. Cf. my article in *Ost-Europa*, 1961.

That it should be possible without a command economy but through the market, if only by means of a Titoist economic structure, is reasonably obvious. Indeed it so happens that the most rapidly growing economy in the world is at present a capitalist one : Japan, the runner-up being precisely Yugoslavia.

It may be objected that this is a very short-run view : that a market is only possible if decisions are decentralised, and that this depends on the size of decision-making unit that technique imposes. But the trend of technical progress is no longer so obviously towards yet more centralisation. Marx could always effectively jeer at Proudhon, how would he run a railway? The modern liberal has a retort : how would Marx run a million motor-cars? Indeed, if the future is with the personal helicopter we may go still farther, for motor-roads require a large central planning body in their building if not in their use, but the air is there already. Similarly the old medium-wave broadcasting was suited to a few monopolistic transmitters, since its range was long and the possibilities of interference great. But we now have VHF and FM, which make possible a multiplicity of competing stations. Or take the supply of power. When the industrial revolution began it was practically synonymous with the concentration of artisans into a single building where their machines all ran off a single source of power : first water, then steam. Electricity takes us in two directions from the position thus achieved : its own supply is by technical necessity vastly more centralised than that of water or steam, but its use can be almost as decentralised as that of man- or bullock-power. Full many an obsolescent craftsman, or do-it-yourself enthusiast in his basement, depends on the electric grid. Undoubtedly society will never be so technically decentralised again as before the industrial revolution, but in which direction is it moving at the moment?

Moreover, even when the size of the decision-making unit does increase the market still has functions to perform, in that large enterprises each produce many products, and must choose between them. The simplicities of textbook economics, which deal with one product per diagram, entirely obscure this basic point. Furthermore large enterprises produce things for themselves, since they tend to be vertically integrated ; they thus need *internal* criteria of choice. Central planning *could* provide these two kinds of criterion, after various technical developments have taken place. At present it cannot, and even when it can it might not perhaps show such serious advantages over a market as to make us wish to sacrifice our social structure.

Technology, therefore, shows some bias against the market mechanism, but not a big one. It certainly does not go far enough to show that indefinite economic growth technically entails collectivism.

It *is* however necessary for any economy aiming at Extreme Affluence within measurable time to grow fast. This means at least to maintain full employment and to force the overall volume of invest-ment. Now while this is entirely compatible with a free market in everything else, political freedom is quite certainly a brake here.

In that great right-wing anarchy, the United States, there is serious and successful opposition to even such a trivial strengthening of central power as is needed for perpetual full employment. And a really large increase in investment is more difficult still. That it should be financed by voluntary savings is out of the question. To accommodate it to Western institutions with least damage to them we need heavy taxation, the accumulation of a large ' above the line ' surplus in the budget, and its disposal by a public investment board to public or private capital-users. The really difficult item is the higher taxes, i.e., the increase in the abstinence of the population ; we may reasonably suspect that freely elected parliaments will never for long impose the taxation needed. What the people will not voluntarily save they will not in the end permit their representatives to save for them.

Then again Western democracy means letting economic agents do more or less what they like, and therefore tolerating many comfortable abuses, restrictive practices and traditional ways of carrying on that have little or nothing to do with the volume of abstinence. How serious are these really? First accept the pessimistic assumption that few of them could be abolished without a dictatorship ; then I believe that paradoxically most of our economically inefficient institutions can be tolerated.

For we must distinguish most carefully between institutions that reduce the *level* of productivity (' handicaps '), and those that retard its *rate of growth* (' brakes '). However, by a merciful dispensation of providence the ones with deepest social roots are mostly handicaps. Upon the rightness of this generalisation nearly everything turns, so we must take at least one example before leaving the subject of brakes versus handicaps.

This is the case of restrictive practices, including trade unions, cartels, and the withholding of new knowledge by patents. These on inspection turn out also to be only handicaps. Invention goes on, technique after new technique is developed ; what happens to a country or industry that refuses to adopt them? It simply stagnates, becoming more and more backward, until finally the dam bursts. No restrictive practice lasts forever, and then one of two things must happen. First it may go straight for the most advanced technique available. At this point it benefits from all the usual ' advantages of immaturity ', and grows faster than those who have kept up all the time, reaching, more-over, the same point in absolute development as they over the same long period. Over the average of all industries such a country will of course suffer a lag, but it is unlikely to increase or diminish. Or, secondly, the restrictive practices merely impose a permanent lag in techniques, the adoption of every successive innovation being delayed in each industry. This obviously has not even a temporary effect on the rate of growth. Only if, thirdly, the technical lag increases all the time do restrictive practices become a brake as well as a handicap, i.e. they must become more and more restrictive for growth to be slowed down.

The principal brake, then, is a low volume of investment. For technical lags can be caught up in giant strides, or if kept constant are irrelevant to the speed of growth. But if the national capital is not increased in a given year this simply leaves us with the task of greater saving and investment next year. That apart, a free economy and society seem to suffer mainly from handicaps. The superiority of communist growth is, if this analysis is correct, partly due to a single continuing factor : more abstinence ; and partly to many historically circumstanced, once for all factors : the exceptionally rapid removal of all the old handicaps of an underdeveloped economy, without permitting the new ones to arise that characterise an advanced one.

IT is, then, clear that different forms of Extreme Affluence are technically possible, since the volume of investment is the main permanent determinant, and many free societies in fact invest enough to grow quite quickly. To Full Communism will be opposed here two of these possible forms : Affluent Individualism and Affluent Socialism. The former offers of course the more perfect contrast. It is based simply on the notion of increasing wealth, without moral ' improvement ', whether inevitable or induced. Money, the market, and private ownership of the means of production are entirely retained, and the social services disappear as people become more and more able to support themselves. The ideal is, as under Full Communism, a rich, fully developed individual ; only this time there is no bias towards Puritanism and uniformity. And there is one other big difference : the Affluent Individualist works for himself and his family, not for society ; his virtues are not self-sacrifice and enthusiasm but responsibility and self-support. He has no more ' socialist consciousness ' than twentieth century John Smith, or that regrettable survival of outmoded capitalist mentality, twentieth century Ivan Ivanov. This, precisely, is why the market mechanism has to remain.

Affluent Socialism differs from Full Communism in that while the government is not totalitarian, minimal demands are yet made upon the individual for moral ' improvement '. The social services are, however, built up and eventually engulf the market sector : in stark contrast to Affluent Individualism, in which the social services are confined at first to the provision of a minimum for all, and eventually wither away. Thus the question of ' socialist consciousness ', i.e. of the will to work without private reward, does arise. But Affluent Socialism, being less in a hurry than Full Communism, simply permits the falling will to work to slow up the rate of growth.

It may well be asked, why have Affluent Socialism at all? Surely the choice lies between the two extremes, the one quick-growing but totalitarian, the other both preserving political and creating economic freedom.[2] The writer himself can see no advantage in Affluent Socialism, but feels it must be included ; first in order to show that there are very many practicable models of Affluence ; and secondly because many people find individualism as morally repulsive as totalitarianism. Such people should be consoled with the prospect of a genuine third way, though one cannot help asking why they need it.

Why, after all, is collectivism more moral than individualism? Charity is moral, the succour of the needy ; and if there are many needy, charity must be collectivised or it will not be big enough. But when there are no needy all this falls to the ground. Collectivism without charity has no visible charms. It is good to work for society if society is helping the poor. But it is rather silly to set up all these centralised pooling arrangements otherwise. It remains, of course, altruistic, but what superiority over individualism has the altruism of one millionaire working for another?

This is an awkward question, more suitable to the theologian or politician than to the economist, even should he be an off-beat economist with leanings towards heresy, eschatology, and institutionalism. Such a person may be pardoned, however, for asking whether sometimes ethical judgments are not unconsciously predicated upon contingent circumstances. Female chastity seemed good before contraceptives : now one begins to wonder. So also economic altruism—we do not here speak of altruism in other respects—may possibly be found to rest on the assumption that ' the poor ye have always with you '. Or again, to attribute to central planning some moral superiority over the market—or vice versa—is surely too absurd and eccentric for serious consideration. There are of course people, at both ends of the political spectrum, who continue to feel ethically here. For such, and they are many, the writer has only blank incomprehension ; to him these two different ways of allocating resources are morally quite neutral. When —as is surely inevitable—they one day become equally efficient, the choice between them will be political : the more decentralised is the more compatible with personal freedom.

WHAT would be the fate of money under Affluent Individualism? To do absolutely without money is probably incompatible with any system unless rationing is used instead ; and ration cards are a

---

2 It will be observed that I do not fall into the trap of equating a free market with economic freedom. Economic freedom is a nebulous and troublesome concept. It either means freedom from material anxiety, i.e. great wealth and leisure, or freedom to ' do what I like with my own '. On the former definition it is assured by any form of Extreme Affluence. On the latter it arises from a *combination* of affluence and a free market; only the rich can have it, since only they have any ' my own ' to do ' what I like with '.

mere substitute for money, so that it is a mere play on words to substitute them and call it a moneyless economy. The reason for this is that some things will always remain scarce, such as natural amenities and new goods. The latter are the more important category : owing to innovation there will always be in any economy many things that are ' marginally technically possible '. They are still difficult to produce (for those that are impossible to produce there is no effective demand, since they do not exist), and therefore use up significantly more resources than the old lines, now easy to produce. Again, demand for new goods is elastic, so to charge nothing for them would be certainly to overload the economy, and therefore to render resources scarce, and thus to render old lines of production scarce as well.

Thus the ' marginally technically possible ' presents an insoluble problem to all systems alike. Leaving it on one side, we find that under this particular system moneylessness has special aspects.

First, as people get richer they become more and more careless about little things. Consider the contemporary American, whether corporate or individual. He expects and gets a large number of *small free things* : free paper napkins, free water in the train, free lavatories, free air in his tyres, a free wipe of his windshield, free matches, free road maps, etc. etc. ; above all free information. And these things are not part of the public sector, like free entry into museums (which he also enjoys, more than a Russian). Nor are they really advertisers' giveaways. For although they mostly began as such they are now regarded by one and all as a right. Secondly, Americans create a lot of *usable waste* : cars that still go, picnic leavings, cast-off clothing. These things have no money value, yet with sufficient ingenuity and determination a man can live off them : the United States is a paradise for bums, beatniks, *et hoc genus omne*. Then, thirdly, an American does not count the cost : he uses either the telephone or the mail on no sort of calculation, but as mood and convenience urge. He appears more hospitable, in that he makes his guests free of more facilities in his house—this in addition to the unconnected fact of *being* more hospitable, i.e. giving up more of his time to guests, being more genuinely pleased to have them. Nor is he interested in petty economic crime : he hardly picks pockets in areas where an *unskilled* honest man can get a decent living with no risk. Major economic crime, and especially the corruption of government and the police, still interest him ; and crimes of violence of course persist—but the pursuit of a modest competence by physical theft has almost died out.

Yet all the instances we have mentioned are very small beer, and it is hard to see how any important production could be carried on under laissez-faire except for money ; for what other motivation could voluntary economic activity have?

It might be objected that this holds until the time when labour is provided free of charge ; i.e. when productivity is so high and consequently the working week so short that men's natural abhorrence of continuous leisure drives them to work. At this admittedly almost unthinkable level of productivity a moneyless version of Affluent Individualism becomes possible. People voluntarily produce, without any central planning, as much in total and in particular as people want to consume, although their consumption is not disciplined in any way. All the organisation there is, is that shops give orders to factories, and the work of people in their workplaces is hierarchically organised as at present. That is, people do not on the whole sabotage the system ; they not only work without pay but observe labour discipline and commercial commonsense without economic sanctions.

A plausible picture but for four points. The first is that people must for some reason rather do the unpleasant jobs than no jobs at all. But this surely cannot be brought about under laissez-faire. For the jobs they really want to do will still be relatively scarce. These are the jobs that people already at our present standard of living do for nothing, or at least put in overtime at for nothing : i.e. local government, entertainment, the administration of sports, university teaching. Disappointed in their applications here, but still over-burdened with leisure, people must in fact volunteer to become dustmen,[3] or the system breaks down. No doubt technical progress will have much lightened the task of the dustman, but even so it is difficult to imagine labour freely allocating itself among all the required activities. Pleasant jobs would have to be rationed by a central authority, and labour directed to unpleasant ones.

Secondly, there is the problem of the transition to moneylessness. If any single firm ceases to demand money for its products it must cease to pay its factors ; they will go elsewhere and it will go out of business.[4] Affluent Individualism provides no means whereby moneylessness can take root and spread—in contrast to Affluent Socialism and Full Communism, which can both convert more and more things into social services. The act of abolition would have to be an act of state, affecting everybody at once.

Thirdly, what of capital (i.e. abstinence from present consumption) and land? It is easy to see that when labour need not be paid saving need not either. Indeed, a permanent superfluity of saving is a very near possibility, and Western economics have long been familiar with the zero rate of interest. But land, meaning all the gifts of nature, is a quite different matter. It is grossly improbable that these, or many of

---

[3] When in his vision Marx said he would be a huntsman in the morning and a literary critic in the afternoon, he never mentioned collecting the garbage!

[4] In full communism there is much to be said for beginning with things in inelastic demand, and it is true also in Affluent Individualism that the prices of such things could be reduced to zero without a re-allocation of demand. But they would still lose the factors of production at present employed on them.

them (especially minerals), will lose their scarcity until long after labour has. They will therefore continue to command a price.

So while there is psychologically nothing impossible in people saving or even working for nothing they will only do so if enterprises can be induced to supply goods free in the shops. For naturally if money is required for goods people must have money, and will charge it for such labour and abstinence services as they provide. But if land continues to command a price enterprises will continue to need money, and therefore to charge it for their products. There is thus a vicious circle : so long as something somewhere is ' scarce ', money will be needed for it, and it is impossible under laissez-faire to keep money out of nearly all other transactions as well.

Moreover, even supposing that *all* the fundamental factors of production become so plentiful as to be free, there remains the problem of motivating investment. For it is easy enough to see why people would save—they would have no need to consume all their output ; and why they would work—they would like it and need it. But why should any manager invest, and expand ' his ' enterprise? Deprived of all pecuniary motive, we are thrown back on the will to power, or the mere will to expand business. Power, however, in turn becomes a doubtful motive. For in what sense, in so affluent a society, can the means of production be said any longer to belong to anyone? When our incomes are simply whatever we choose to take out of shops, plainly ownership of capital is not required to yield an income. Titles to capital will then tend to lapse, and the whole concept of property will ' wither away '—including personal property, which will be so easily replaceable as to be not worth protecting. This is in itself a highly desirable and easily comprehensible situation, but it leaves the maintenance and further accumulation of capital goods very oddly placed. The writer cannot see how they could be provided for under laissez-faire without money.

Indeed, even the close approach to moneylessness would lead to stagnation. As the rate of profit finally fell towards zero in any line, research and investment would be choked off and diverted elsewhere, until they finally ceased everywhere. Not only the actual transition, but also the final steps towards it, would have to be an act of state. It is, then, perhaps as well that the close approach too can only be made on very special assumptions : a cessation in product innovation, the willingness of people to work for nothing at jobs they do not like, and a plentiful supply of *all* raw materials.

WHY would anybody *want* to switch from Affluent Individualism to Full Communism? Taking some sensible mixture of Affluent Individualism and Affluent Socialism we can say :

    (a) distribution according to need is far advanced in Western capitalism, which shows no fewer social services, and very much better ones, than any communist country. Moreover the social service approach to distribution according to need is not the only, nor in the writer's opinion the best. The alternative is some form of co-ownership or ' people's capitalism ', in which the capital itself—i.e. the private ownership of the means of production—is ' distributed according to need '. The individual can then fall back on his own capital and decide his own needs. He thus escapes from the probably totalitarian consequences of submission to a central authority that decides what he needs.

(b) money will indeed not wither away, but this is in no sense a disadvantage. The prejudice against money is absurd and has no intellectual basis. It is absolutely vital as an alternative to compulsion, in any remotely likely society. In purely economic terms, the abolition of money leads to waste and irrationality. It does nothing to raise production—rather the contrary—and therefore nothing to raise the standard of living.

(c) many of the items in Full Communism are soulless and humourless, delighting in uniformity for its own sake. In particular the difference between town and country is a delight to all, and the very stuff of life to many. There are, by nature and nurture, urban and rural types, and urban and rural phases in the life of an average man. Extreme Affluence would enable these demands to be met far more fully than at present: as indeed all other demands for differentiation. There is no case for deliberately assimilating the internal structure of the farming enterprise to that of a factory: many people *like* small personal enterprises, the present structure of capitalist farming caters to a genuine human need. It is tyrannical to try to alter both the farm and the farmer. Moreover the undoubted cost of small-scale family farming in efficiency is offset by the economic cost of compulsory collectivisation, the unpopularity of which makes it equally inefficient. The correct way out is the natural, voluntary, American way : the heavily capitalised medium-scale family farm. In a word, Affluent Individualism would preserve the *institutional* laissez-faire that Full Communism would destroy. This is an unmixed blessing.

(d) the further collectivisation of consumption is a monstrous objective, having no economic necessity and being exactly contrary to many tendencies within any Affluent Society. Indeed, we may boldly generalise about the present trend of technical progress as follows : it at no point actually favours small-scale operation, since small units can always be reduplicated and large-scale management of such combinations is an established technical possibility.[5] But it may quite well operate less

---

[5] i.e. the L-shaped long average cost curve is in a sense an a priori law. See my *Price, Cost and Output*, 2nd ed , Oxford, 1961, Chap. 12.

sharply against small-scale units at some times than at others, and especially so if there is urgent demand for inventions suitable to small units, so that research is directed that way. Now it so happens that all over the world two small economic units have immense social advantages and traditional prestige : the family and the family farm. Their obstinate survival has created those deeply un-Marxian objects, the individual washing-machine and the rotavator. The loss in efficiency compared with the laundry and the large tractor is perceptible but not tragic. And in any case the loss is only a ' handicap ' not a ' brake ' ; technical progress is as likely in these small things as in big ones. In a word, if people like to live that way they can certainly afford it. If they lose a decade or so in their march towards the economic Utopia they at least do not lose sight altogether of other human values, unknown to Full Communism.

(e) It is not only Puritanism and uniformity from which those suffer who live under communism. The very generalised feeling of constraint and effort makes the whole of economic activity unpleasant. The tension inherent in physical planning—the physical struggle to beat some target—is the main item here : it takes enjoyment out of work at all levels, and encourages corruption, the cutting of corners, etc. etc. A man should be happy while he works; and this matters because work is such a large part of his life.

So even if we look into the farthest future, more liberal systems of economy, while necessarily less dynamic, can be made dynamic enough given the will, and are on all other grounds vastly superior. Bert Brecht used to say of Capitalism and Communism : if you had enough drug to cure only one person of a fatal disease, and two people lay dying of it, an elderly roué and a pregnant prostitute—to whom would you give the drug? It is out of place to be dogmatic, and more than foolish to be complacent—the writer for one has no great confidence that the capitalist will to grow will ever be sufficient. But still, surely Brecht had the roles mixed up.

VALUE, PRICE, AND PROFIT

Alfred Zauberman

AS expected, the economic—and psychological—pièce de résistance of the CPSU draft programme is a list of facilities which are promised to every citizen ' free of charge ', that is, paid for by the citizenry out of the communal rather than the private pocket. There is no reason why in principle the Soviet Government should not as now promised distribute half the population's real income on a communal basis by 1980. (If anything is striking about the list of ' free of charge ' goods and services, it is that it makes one realise that it will take the USSR two decades to catch up in many respects with the Western welfare state.) The really crucial point is the negative statement implied in this pledge : that even at the threshold of full communism, half of the real income will have to be distributed on a wage basis of one kind or another. Hence the inevitability of operating a system of incentives (Mr Khrushchev may still try to be a Utopian in the ethical code he proclaims; but in the economics of his scheme he does not rely on the idealistic attitude to work which this code demands from people). Hence also the preservation under full communism of value relations, money, and prices. The interconnected question of private property is deliberately framed in ambiguous terms, but the guarantee of private ownership of consumer goods shows that the orthodox Marxian puritans have been routed on this point too. All this disposes effectively of the egalitarian dream and makes nonsense of the principle ' to each according to his needs ', in spite of the solemn lip-service paid to it time and again in the programme. The programme also makes nonsense of this principle where it quantifies the state of plenty under full communism. My very rough calculation (based on Soviet prices) would suggest that if and when the Soviet worker enters the promised land of superabundance, his total real income will equal, or perhaps be just above today's British levels. Would anybody seriously suggest that at these levels the average British man and woman can satisfy all his or her heart's desires? It is left to the bureaucrat to decide whether and to what extent a citizen's need deserves to be satisfied, and this has influenced the organisational and institutional solutions adopted. The idea of communes has been discarded; even in agriculture, the state—or the Party, which will come to mean one and the same thing—will have the monopoly of productive enterprise ; it will centrally plan and control production, consumption, and investment. In a word, as against the flights of fantasy of those who built up the traditional vision of communism, Mr Khrushchev's charter is quite pragmatic ; it provides for no more than a moderate change in the existing mechanism of the system, and in many respects may therefore not prove unrealistic.

IT is a measure of the formidable difficulties encountered that in spite of the Soviet Union's claim that it is already approaching communism, no attempt has yet been made in Soviet official thinking to formulate a definitive view of the economic organisation of a fully communistic society. Indeed, until very recently, all that had been written in this domain by economists were some more or less poetic flights of imagination—variations on the few lines to be found on the subject in the classics. Representative of them is a portrait of Arcadia produced by Strumilin in his well-known *Novy Mir* essay (1960, No. 7). Commenting on it, a Soviet writer remarked that ' the subject of transition to a communistic distribution, and in general to life under communism, is very often expounded [in Soviet literature] almost in the same terms as were previously used by the great Utopian socialists '. The 1960 Strumilin version of communism shared its framework with that of Thomas More (1516) or of Campanella (1623). But, the critic went on, ' the degree of development of the sciences, of techniques and productive forces, and of the people's cultural levels in our era can hardly be compared with those in the time of the early Utopians. Yet old Utopian ideas still exercise a strong influence on our scientific [*nauchnye*] propositions with regard to the passage to communism and to the organisation of work and life in a communistic society '.[1] However, a critique of the state of Soviet thinking on these matters is far easier than a constructive contribution. Engels noted that the more fully the Utopians worked out the minutiae of their system, the more they were forced into fantasy.[2] Reticence on these questions was regarded by Marxists as a distinctive trait and a virtue of scientific as against Utopian socialism. The predicament starts where this virtue stops : where it has to yield to a political necessity to insert down-to-earth details into the vision.

The first attempts to introduce some precision into Soviet thought on full communism have now been made, with the emergence of the new mathematical school in economics. The practical aim of the school is to provide a formal scaffolding for certain planning methods and techniques, but for the present theme their work is noteworthy as an attempt—interesting and unique in Soviet literature—to put some accepted concepts on the economics of communism to the test of logic. To begin with, the mathematicians' hypothesis of a communist economy differs from the conventional one in its point of departure. Traditionally the theme is approached from the consumption end, from an axiomatic state of abundance, whereas the mathematical school—or

1 E. Manevich, *Voprosy Ekonomiki*, 1961, No. 5, pp. 83, 84.
2 *Anti-Dühring*, Eng. ed., Moscow, 1954, p. 356.

to be more precise, one of its leading lights, Novozhilov [3]—does so from the opposite end, from the conditions of production. The crucial question for him is whether under communism, there will still be a need to measure disparities in factors applied in production. His answer is yes, and this broadly on three principal grounds. First, because of the varying effectiveness of the wealth with which nature endows us. For would it not be absurd to assume that with the advent of full communism the yield of, say, all coal seams to be mined would be miraculously equalised, regardless of geological, geographic, or climatic differences? His second argument concerns technological progress : together with the assumed beneficial psychological effects of the very change to total collectivism, technical innovation has always been seen as the basis of an era of unlimited abundance. It may be agreed that we are moving at present on the wave—or that we are perhaps only on the threshold—of a major technological revolution : and it may also be readily conceded that technological progress is likely to extend the sphere of free goods. In the portrait of the future drawn in the presidential address at the congress of Soviet scientists (May 1961), energy was one day to become as free as water is today. This need not be rejected as unrealistic, but it leaves the issue in doubt, since—to come back to Novozhilov's reasoning—far from eliminating differences in the efficiency of ' reproducible instruments of labour ', i.e. of man-made capital, it is precisely technological progress that generates such disparities. This is indeed incontrovertible. Suppose that nuclear power has been made technically accessible for practical application under a regime of full communism : would thermal and water sources of power be discarded? Whatever the structure of society, the assumption of efficiencies equalised throughout the economy would be tantamount to an assumption of stationary technological levels. Is this the environment envisaged for eventual communism?

The third and interconnected argument concerns the time-factor. Time is the resource in incurably short supply, independently of the way in which communities are organised. This implies the necessity of ' converting ' the future into the present, of ' discounting ' it in one way or another under full communism (and even more under socialism —the point which the Soviet mathematical economists are actually out to establish).

TAKING them as a whole, the arguments boil down to the proposition that the world of communism will be a world of continuing scarcities. Consequently—and it is the purpose of these arguments to demonstrate it—the rational organisation of a communist (and a fortiori of a socialist) economy, presupposes the weighing up of opportunities

---

[3] V. V. Novozhilov, *Izmerenie zatrat i ikh rezultatov v sotsialisticheskom khoziaistve*, in *Primenenie matematiki v ekonomicheskikh issledovaniakh*, ed. V. S. Nemchinov, Moscow, 1959.

against each other ; in other words, it implies the use of opportunity cost as a yardstick in choice-making. In still other words, it calls for some techniques of an optimal calculus.

Long before *Capital* appeared, Engels suggested that the balancing of ' useful effects ' and labour outlays was all that would be left of the concept of value in a communist society.[4] Decades later he returned to this theme in his polemics against Dühring, and insisted that ' the useful effects of the various articles of consumption as compared with one another, and with the quantities of labour required for their production will, in the last instance, determine the plan. People will be able to manage everything very simply without the intervention of the much vaunted " value ".' [5]

It is anything but easy to decipher the true meaning of this obscure passage, though it is perhaps here that classical Marxist writing goes furthest in trying to lend some precision to the idea of a value-free society. How are the ' useful effects ' to be measured and ordered? How should they be compared as between goods? How should they be set against the socially necessary labour time required for their production? One would try in vain to find an answer.

I shall take up the point of the survival of value in a somewhat different context. For the present my concern is with the implications of scarcity of resources in the ultimately perfect society as the basic environmental background for the planners' decision-making. For, once scarcities of factors are brought into the picture of full communism, this picture appears discordant with the conventional vision of abundance. Scarcities of factors used in production must necessarily entail scarcities— relative at least—of the consumables which they are employed to produce. Novozhilov emphasises in particular that the ' scarcity ' of the time factor affects distribution as well as consumption.[6] And it is clear what he means by this. Assuming a continuous advance in production techniques, the saturation of potential demand at any point of time becomes an untenable proposition. Suppose, for example, that some new synthetic fibre has been invented and used for the production of material for women's dresses ; it will take some time before the demand is fully met, and in the meantime some new invention may create new tastes and demands, and consequently result in new scarcities of consumer goods and so on, ad infinitum. Unsaturated demand means, in turn, putting the consumers into a queue of one sort or another, and this in turn raises the question how to make the queue behave in an orderly fashion.

Now let us leave the queue for a moment and turn to some institutional problems. We have taken for granted throughout that full communism involves economy-wide planning. What is the authority for

---

4 F. Engels, *Umrisse zu einer Kritik der Nationaloekonomie*, Marx-Engels Gesamtausgabe, I, 2, pp. 379 ff.
5 *Anti-Dühring*. p. 430.
6 Op. cit., p. 164.

doing so? Hints to this effect were made in the Marxist classics, by Engels in particular. One has already been quoted ; here is another from his critique of Dühring's vision of communes : ' anarchy in social production is replaced by plan-conforming conscious organisation '. With the end of capitalism, he goes on to say, ' socialised production upon a predetermined plan becomes possible '.[7] Precious little can be found in Engels about the mode of operation of the plan system, and here too the Soviet planimetricians (to adopt Professor Nemchinov's term), are trying to fill the gap, by offering solutions which they believe to be both realistic and effective. How far these are compatible with the classical image of final communism, will appear in the course of this essay.

We can now take a closer look at the architecture of the Novozhilov model. In the world of scarcities, he contends, two kinds of centralism are possible in planning. In one the planner thinks in physical terms ; makes his allocational decisions in these terms ; and frames in them the orders he passes down the line for implementation. The alternative, the indirect variety of centralism, relies on value terms. The planner will think in terms of uses rather than users of resources. The planning ' centre works out general standards (*normativ*) for the solution of allocational tasks and the subordinate organs (*mesta*) apply these in each individual case '.[8] The crux of the matter here is the indirect limiting of the use of resources. Under socialism this can be achieved by means of prices, and this is the word used ; and ' under communism by means of norms of efficiency ', the euphemism for prices coined in deference to Engels for whom, as we have seen, there could be no place for price in a value-free society ; goods would cease to be ' commodities ' in a socialist society. It was hard enough for Soviet doctrine to grant commodity production a reprieve for the era of socialism ; it would fly too openly in the face of the inherited doctrine to perpetuate the reprieve and to give value and price theoretical sanction under full communism. Only ' by combining the two forms of [direct and indirect] centralism can the widest expansion of the planning principle and the widest democracy be achieved ', and this structure will be characterised ' by an exceptionally high level of centralism '.

What kind of economic democracy does this imply? The answer is that the democratic principle will be given scope in the wide range of economic choice-making left to the lower echelons. Whose choices will these in fact be? When the planner decides and passes on his fiats, directly in physical units, the answer is clear. What is meant by indirect, democratic centralism is that the planner should guide the lower echelons, by means of prices, towards his own choices. In other words, the lower echelons are provided with parameters of choice ready for use, and the stronger the compelling force of these parameters the better they serve their purpose. The ideal is thus the elimination as

[7] *Anti-Dühring*, pp. 392, 395.

[8] Novozhilov, p. 172.

far as possible of an *independent* choice. (The question may arise, at what point does a " dependent " choice cease to be a choice at all?) In a word, the kind of economic democracy envisaged for full communism would involve changing the channels and instruments of guidance—broadly in agreement with the present trends in Soviet planning —rather than an abandonment of the command system.

ALL this links up with the institutional framework of the future communist society. Present-day Soviet literature on this question as a rule follows tradition in virtually identifying it with a system of communes. Strumilin, for instance, has been concerned with showing why—in contrast to the discouraging historical pre-socialist experience— a commune will be viable under full communism, rather than with justifying the need for the commune, which he in fact takes for granted.[9] But at least one writer has grasped the incompatibility between a closely knit and centrifugal collective and a centralist command economy, and has rejected it as anachronistic, arguing that it is possible to have ' communism without communes '.[10]

We may now take up some of the loose threads. We have seen how the planimetrician has been led from the classics to the logical conclusion that ' to each according to his needs ' does not in itself prejudge the answer to the question, who is going to determine what individual needs are. It now appears that it will not be the individual himself, and not the lower echelons of the economic administration nor the commune, the need for which is now denied, at least by some writers. Novozhilov makes the position quite unambiguous in a footnote intended to clarify certain sequences in planning procedures : ' with a very high level of productivity, when distribution according to needs becomes feasible, their volume [i.e., the volume of needs] could be calculated for many products by reference to scientifically established standards of consumption '.[11] It is arguable that in a society better off than the Soviet Union today, the conflict between individual scales of preference and those of the planner may be expected to relax ; the more affluent it becomes, the less intense the clash is likely to be. But the crucial point is that—whatever the degree of intensity of the conflict of preferences—what in the classics is an allocation ' according to needs ', turns out to be allocation according to what the administrators believe *should* be the needs under prevailing conditions (deduced from ' norms ' or arrived at in some other way). Has not allocation in centrally planned and controlled systems, always been, in this sense, ' according to needs '?

In the classics the alternative version of the postulate ' from each according to his abilities, to each according to his needs ' reads as ' equal obligation to labour, equal right in the product '. Engels describes this

9 S. Strumilin, *Soviet Weekly* (London), 13 April 1961.
10 E. Manevich, loc. cit.
11 Op. cit., p. 165n.

rule, in a reference to Owen, as one feature of 'the most clear-cut communism possible'.[12] The two versions would mean the same thing only if both were very severely qualified. For the accent on egalitarianism in the second version, while removing some ambiguities from the first, adds new ones : one man's wants will be deemed his needs if, and only if, they equal those of any of his co-citizens. It is easy to imagine the planner's headaches if, on the assumption of scarcities, he is instructed to follow both precepts at the same time.

It is not surprising that some Soviet economists tackle the concept of allocation according to needs in a more pragmatic way. They shift the emphasis of the processes of communisation of consumption towards 'social funds'. (Strumilin, not always consistent in these matters, belongs to this school; he would like to see the growth of real wages, at the 'approaches to communism', kept within the limits of, say, about 2 per cent per annum, any surplus over and above this rate being turned over to communised 'social funds'[13]; surely his critics are right in pointing out the depressive effect this would have on the productivity of labour.[14]) This school insists that in fact the communistic principle already governs a substantial part of consumption, especially in the sector of communal, cultural, health, and other social services. It should be noted on this, first, that the expansion of this sector fails to provide a differentia specifica for socio-economic systems : the Soviet Union is outstripped in the 'free' supply of at least certain goods and services of this kind by some welfare-state capitalist societies; and, secondly, that the consumer can claim for himself unlimited satisfaction of his needs only within a very narrow segment of the sector.

The revised concept of 'needs' as a principle of distribution which emerges from the confrontation of the classics with life, has its corollary in society's right to draw on the individual's capacity for effort. The classics borrowed from the Utopians, and transmitted as their own legacy, the idea of a society in which work becomes a pleasure pursued for its own sake. It is unnecessary to dwell on the question whether the belief has been confirmed by the experience of socialist societies as life there has become easier. (Recent Soviet legislation against idlers seems rather a pointer in the opposite direction.) Leaving trends in ethical consciousness aside, the logic of the vision is still dubious.

If the planner has to aim at his goals amidst scarcities, he has to determine the recognised 'needs' of the citizens in such a way as to coax them towards his goals. Allowing for any meta-economic inducement he can mobilise—moral impulse on the one extreme, and outright compulsion on the other—the input of the individual's effort becomes inevitably the effective distributive criterion. For the plan to be consistent and balanced, the scale of reward for effort has to be harmonised with its goals, and here the problem of adequate incentive arises. It is

[12] *Anti-Dühring*, p. 366.
[13] S. G. Strumilin, *Na putyakh postroeniya kommunizma*, Moscow, 1959, p. 89.
[14] Manevich, op. cit., p. 83.

indeed hard to devise any nation-wide economic plan, of the kind envisaged, without an effective mechanism to ensure that the flow of the citizens' efforts—patterned as required by the plan—*will* be forthcoming. From the planner's point of view, this effort is yet another of the resources which, if his construction is to be consistent with an optimum, have to be accorded a scarcity price. The shortening of the working day, in keeping with rising productivity—as conveniently postulated in the vision of full communism—would tend to perpetuate this scarcity, and though, in Soviet thinking, much is now being made of what is termed the trend towards ' polytechnisation ' of labour in a communist society, technical innovation is likely to result in continual scarcities of specific skills. Novozhilov evades the issue by exempting labour from his scale of ' efficiency normatives ' for communism as well as socialism, but he does so at the expense of the consistency of his model (another eminent Soviet planimetrician, Kantorovich, has been more consistent on this point, but it has landed him in ideological trouble).

ONE subject which is being given major attention in current Soviet writing on the economics of communism is that of personal property. Economists, lawyers, and philosophers have contributed to the voluminous literature, and it is not difficult to see why. Marx's fullest treatment of man's moral progress as related to the institution of private property can be found in one of his earlier writings, *Nationaloekonomie und Philosophie* (1844).[15] So long as society is ' infected ' with vestigial forms of property, he argued, not even the abolition of the state could complete the process of communisation. Only their complete elimination would bring about the end of ' human self-alienation ' and produce the ' social, that is the human man '. Until this happens, only ' crude communism '—whether ' dictatorial or democratic '—is conceivable. And conversely, once this goal is reached, the ultimate form of communism becomes a reality.

The language of this passage may not be lucid, but Marx's attitude to ownership could not be clearer or less uncompromising : it leaves little room for any exegesis of the kind which would provide loopholes for those in the Soviet Union who aspire to a less extremist solution of his fundamental ' riddle of history '. But the vested interests of the growing number of actual and potential owners of cars and dachas are at stake. It is on this point then that the mood of the Khrushchev era—the mood of ' *enrichessez vous* '—clashes most patently with accepted ideals. The puritans—in the words of one of them, Stepanyan [16]—are aligned against the many who try to ' immortalise ' the features of the ' first stage of communism ', who ' advocate the unrestricted development of personal property ' and ' think like Galuska in Korneichuk's comedy, *In the Ukraine Steppes* : " Why have communism

15 See in particular the chapter on ' Privateigentum und Kommunismus '.
16 Ts. Stepanyan, *Oktyabr*, September 1960.

when we live well even under socialism? " '. The debate is of rather limited theoretical interest, except perhaps for those philosophers who would like to be able to determine precisely the point at which the trend makes its inevitable dialectical turn. Clearly, the growing tolerance towards personal property is determined largely by the system of rewards and incentives which has proved to be more necessary the more affluent the society becomes.

Our last point concerns the vexed question of contradictions inherent in production relations in the post-capitalist society, a subject of endless dispute between Soviet scholars. At the 1958 session of the Academy of Sciences on the construction of communism, Academician Kronrod debunked the accepted thesis on the nature of production relations under socialism which, as we know, defines them as ' cooperation ' and ' mutual aid '.[17] These terms, he argued, are moral and ethical (Professor Pashkov expanded this to mean ' purely propagandist '), and irrelevant from the economic angle ; from that angle what is crucial is distribution according to effort, since it implies a contradiction between an egalitarian system of ownership of the means of production and a non-egalitarian distribution of the product obtained by their use. Hence contradictions are bound to remain so long as Soviet society retains the present principle of rewarding labour, and in so far as the principle holds good under communism, communism will not be free of these contradictions either. (We shall not try to relate the kind of economic communism which emerges from these remarks to the political organisation envisaged for that society, though the hankering after the stateless state has of course always been indissolubly connected with the communist economic ideal. Saint-Simon foretold the ' complete absorption of politics by economics ' ; this was another feature of the Marxian picture of the ultimate stage of full communism borrowed from the Utopians.)

Stalin, the realist, reprieved the State indefinitely. To Khrushchev, the process is an evolutionary one towards an undefined form of communistic self-government conditioned by various factors, in the first place by an abundance of material goods. His goal is located not on some distant horizon, but in the foreseeable future. Indeed, with the due amount of pragmatic redefinition and revision of the various elements of the classical heritage, it becomes a not-impossible objective. Conceived as a society in which scarcities remain and highly centralised planning operates, where the planner's scale of preferences dominates and the national product is divided on lines determined by himself, and where contradictions persist, the image of the ultimate phase of communism becomes at last the projection of a possible reality. The point is, however, that as it takes formal shape it becomes less and less distinguishable from the present phase. If anything is ' withering away ', it is the conceptual communism from its model.

[17] *Voprosy Ekonomiki*, 1958, No. 9, p. 104.

THE WITHERING AWAY OF THE STATE

I. Philosophy and Practice

George L. Kline

IT is tempting to speculate upon the shape of the 1961 Draft Pro-gramme of the Communist Party of the Soviet Union had it appeared a generation earlier, say, just after Lenin's death in 1924. In certain minor respects it might have been much like the new programme, e.g. in mentioning no Russian name except Lenin's—which occurs about a dozen times. But in at least one important respect a Party programme published in the 1920s would have looked very different indeed, for it would have placed much greater emphasis upon the eventual ' withering away ' of institutions, attitudes, and ideas considered inappropriate to ' full communism '. The 1920s were marked by an enthusiastic advocacy and confident prediction of the withering away of such institutions as law, the state, private property, the family, trade unions, material incentives, money, the wage system, bureaucracy, religion and the church, morality, even formal education—not just by academic theorists, but by such hardened politicians and ideologues as Trotsky, Bukharin, Zinoviev, Lunacharski, Bogdanov, and Alexandra Kollontai—to say nothing of Lenin himself.

In this paper I shall try to clarify the theoretical presuppositions of the notion of withering away, indicating which Soviet institutions have been removed from the original list of candidates for withering away, and offering some tentative explanations for these doctrinal reversals.

*　　*　　*

The metaphor of ' withering away ' (literally ' dying out '—German *Absterben*, Russian *otmiranie*) presupposes the metaphor of society as a plant with roots and leaves. When the root of the social plant is cut or extracted, the leaves wither. The ' root ', of course, is the *Unterbau*, the economic ' base '; the foliage constitutes the *Überbau*—the socio-political and ideological ' superstructure '. Classical Marxist doctrine holds, in effect, that capitalist society is a kind of weed or *flora monstrosa* ; its baneful roots—economic exploitation of man by man, based on private ownership of the means of production, etc.—nourish the perverse leaves of ' bourgeois ' law, religion, morality. When the socialist revolution cuts the root, the leaves will droop and wither, eventually dying out com-pletely. No Marxist would speak of the ' withering away ' of ' exploita-tion of man by man ' or of the ' private ownership of the means of production '. These are the roots, and roots do not wither ; they are cut and die immediately—although in the Soviet Union their death-agony happened to be prolonged for several years by the exigencies of the New Economic Policy.

Two points should be noted at once : (1) The ' withering ' metaphor presupposes a causal link between base and superstructure, as well as an order of priority such that changes in the former automatically produce corresponding changes in the latter. This is not the place to argue the exegetical question as to how Marx and/or Engels really conceived base-superstructure interaction, or to what extent they admitted reciprocal action. Whether or not *Wechselwirkung*—in whatever degree—be admitted, the Marxian analysis remains essentially causal.

Nor is this the place to discuss the theoretical issues in any detail. I shall merely say that the Marxist doctrine of superstructure seems to me to rest on two false assumptions. The first is that anything non-material —institution, attitude, idea, or value—is a ' function ' or ' product ' of something material (i.e. ' social existence generates social conscious-ness '). The second is that economics is somehow material, or material-istic (hence the doctrine of economic determinism is called ' historical *materialism* '). This dogma rests, I suspect, on a confusion of the distinct ethical and metaphysical senses of ' materialism '. In the (popular) ethical sense, a ' materialist ' is someone who is money-minded or money-mad ; he may or may not be a metaphysical materialist. In fact, some Marxists have argued that ' *theoretical* idealism (non-materialism) ' entails, and is entailed by, ' *practical*—i.e. ethical—materialism '. In any case, there would seem to be nothing peculiarly ' material ' or ' material-istic ' about the forces and relations of economic production. Economic activities and institutions are a product of human ingenuity, inventiveness, and industriousness. As between the available Marxist-Leninist categories of ' matter ' and ' not-matter ' (i.e. mind or consciousness), the ' economic base ' would surely have to be assigned to the latter.

Thus an analysis built upon the categories of ' base ' and ' super-structure ' must, in consistency, admit that the one is no more ' material ' than the other. But such an admission wholly undercuts the causal analysis of base-superstructure interaction, grounded as it is on the assumption that the base—a predominantly material entity—produces changes in the superstructure—a predominantly non-material entity. It would seem that the most sensible theoretical move, in this predicament, would be to abandon the entire base-superstructure model. But that, from a Marxist point of view, would be inadmissible heresy.

(2) The above remark is focused upon the *economic* aspect of economic determinism, or the ' materialist ' aspect of historical material-ism. If we now look to the *determinism*, we discover a further implication which bears crucially on the *Absterbenstheorie*. I shall not go into the question of determinism *versus* voluntarism in Marxist-Leninism theory. Whether one claims, with the Lenin of *What is to be Done ?*, that iron-willed activists make and remake history in their own Promethean image.

or, alternatively, with the Marx of *Capital*, that broad general forces and tendencies, independent of individual human wills, are the motive forces of historical change, it is still the case that—short of abandoning the theory of superstructures—one regards the economic base as the lever of all social change. Whether free men or necessary ' historical forces ' move the lever, its motion causes automatic changes in the superstructure. In terms of the earlier metaphor, neither the voluntarist who cuts the root of capitalism with a blow of the axe, nor the determinist who watches the root being destroyed by impersonal historical forces, will need to stir himself to remove the *foliage*. In both cases the leaves—lacking nourishment—will ' wither away ' of themselves.

It has been remarked that Marx put forward the theory of the withering away of the state as a tactical device to forestall the ideological inroads, in the First International, of Bakunin's anarchist doctrine of immediate and total elimination of the state. The Marxists agreed with the anarchists—it is held—that the final goal should be a stateless society, but differed in maintaining that the approach to this goal must be gradual and deliberate. Historically, this is doubtless true. But it is misleading if taken to imply that a Marxist could—for tactical or ideologically competitive reasons—put forward a doctrine that might otherwise have been suppressed. The doctrine of withering away follows naturally from the base-superstructure model ; *both* are essential to classical Marxism. Only a drastic ' revision ' of the doctrine—such as that suggested by Engels in certain letters written after Marx's death—which assigns major causal influence to elements of the superstructure, could force one to modify the root-leaf metaphor. But this, it seems to me, would constitute an abandonment of what is distinctively ' Marxian ' in the doctrine of historical materialism.

This is not to say that the doctrine of withering away is a consistent or coherent one simply because it is entailed by the theory of super-structures. On the contrary, it shares the general theoretical weaknesses of historical materialism. For example, the fundamental tension between deterministic and voluntaristic elements in Marxism-Leninism is echoed in the relation between ' withering away ' and ' liquidation '. ' Withering away ' should mean the same thing as ' self-liquidation ' or ' liquidation by history '. The line between what will wither away of itself and what must be actively ' liquidated ' by dedicated individuals and groups is vague and shifting. This vagueness reflects the ambiguous vacillation between deterministic and voluntaristic versions of Marxism-Leninism on the part of Soviet political leaders and ideologists.

To the dichotomies of base and superstructure, root and leaf, we must add another dichotomy, that of form and content, if we are to pursue the career of the concept of ' withering away ' in Marxist-Leninist theory. The continuing identity of a social institution depends upon its form. If this form can be given new social and ideological content, the institution in question can be transformed, ' socialised ', and preserved. If not, it must inevitably wither. The notion of putting ' new content ' into ' old forms ' may help to explain the doctrinal shifts among Russian Marxists over the past half-century with respect to the detailed schedule of withering away.

(1) In the first decade of this century Gorky, Lunacharski, and other Bolshevik ' God-builders ' asserted that ' bourgeois ' religious institutions and attitudes could and should be given a new ' socialist ' content. The old content—supernatural, authoritarian, anti-scientific—would be replaced by a new one—humanistic, libertarian, ' scientific '. This ' religion of socialism ' or ' religion of feeling ' would provide a sense of supra-individual unity, inspiration, and even consolation. Gorky and Lunacharski insisted, with Nietzsche, that in twentieth-century Europe ' religious feeling was growing powerfully, but rejecting theism '. Plekhanov and Lenin took the opposite view, denying that religion could assume a new ' socialist ' content and insisting that it must inevitably wither away under socialism. With the end of exploitation of man by man, Lenin asserted, every variety of religion will disappear. On his view, religious attitudes and institutions are generated by insecurity and fear of unanticipated socio-economic change, due in the last analysis to the fluctuations of the capitalist market. Hence religious beliefs are ' rapidly . . . being thrown into the rubbish-barrel by the very course of economic development '.

That the withering away of religion has taken forty-four years in the Soviet Union, and remains far from complete—believers are still numbered in tens of millions—is now explained as a result of new insecurity and fear generated by the threat of thermonuclear war. Since such a war would allegedly be launched only by ' capitalist ' governments, the persistence of religion in the Soviet Union is officially explained as a result—now indirect rather than direct—of the evils of the capitalist market ! In any case, religion is still expected to wither away completely with the approach to full communism, although the new draft programme cautiously avoids assigning any date to its final disappearance.

(2) In contrast, the institution of the family, and monogamous marriage, which early Marxist theorists considered just as much an ' opiate ' as religion, and as surely destined to wither away, has been wholly reclaimed for socialism. Lenin did not take an unequivocal position on the future of the family, but Marx, Engels, Trotsky, Lunacharski, Bukharin, Krylenko, and—of course—Alexandra Kollontai were quite certain that the ' bourgeois ' content of the family and monogamous marriage—including inheritance rights, dependence, possessiveness, and exclusiveness—could not be liquidated without breaking the form of the family,[1] and substituting ' free love ', ' erotic friendship ', polygamy, and/or ' sequential monogamy ', along with free ' social '

---

[1] Kollontai in 1920 modified the ' rubbish ' image which Lenin had applied to religion, describing the family as ' no more than a bit of debris from the past ' (A. N. Kollontai, *Communism and the Family*, New York, 1920, p. 3). The draft programme takes an antithetical view, asserting that it is capitalism which tends to break up the family (' Proekt Programmy KPSS ', Pt. I, sec. iv, *Pravda*, 30 July 1961, p. 3)

upbringing and education of children (whether ' legitimate ' or not), inexpensive and eventually free housing, food, domestic goods and services—to relieve women once and for all of the drudgery of housework and child-care. Kollontai spelled out the glowing details in the early 1920s ; these are repeated in the new draft programme without any reference to Kollontai, or to Trotsky, Bukharin, and other ' old Bolsheviks ' who shared her views.

The crucial difference is that there is now no slightest suggestion that the Soviet family will *ever* wither away. On the contrary, the draft programme, like all Soviet statements since 1936, stresses the proposition that a new kind of family, the ' firm, stable, socialist family ', has made its appearance on the stage of history, and is here to stay—until and including the final phase of full communism. In other words, the family as a social institution has been fully ' socialised ' ; its ' bourgeois ' form has proven capable of taking on a ' socialist '—and eventually ' communist '—content.

(3) The case of law and the state is intermediate between the two preceding ; here the doctrinal shifts have been less pronounced. Lenin leaned farthest towards anarchism in *The State and Revolution* (1917), declaring that the ' dictatorship of the proletariat ', which is ' not a state in the strict sense ', but a ' semi-state ', would begin to wither away as soon as it was established. However, after he gained power Lenin made no effort to encourage such withering, and he gave at least tacit approval to Trotsky's assertion that the dictatorship of the proletariat must be firmly consolidated, developing a powerful juridical system and apparatus of coercion, before the process of withering could even begin. Trotsky's image is that of a kerosene lamp which flares up strongly just before going out : so proletarian ' statism ' will be enormously intensified before it begins to die out.[2] This view was taken over by Stalin and Vyshinski in the 1930s, though of course without reference to Trotsky. Many Mensheviks opposed the Lenin-Trotsky policy of strengthening the ' dictatorship of the proletariat ', insisting that without the immediate abolition of its military and bureaucratic features, and the ' democratisation ' of the whole state apparatus, there could be no talk of socialism. A similar view is taken by some contemporary ' revisionists ', especially in Yugoslavia, who consider the ' dictatorship of the proletariat ' incompatible with political democracy, and assert that the state must wither away under *socialism* rather than communism. This view is as emphatically rejected by contemporary Soviet writers as was the Menshevik view by Trotsky, et al.[3] During the 1920s leading Soviet

---

2 L. D. Trotsky, *Terrorizm i kommunizm* (Moscow, 1920), pp. 158–159. The Russian term *gosudarstvennost*, used in the 1870s by Bakunin, occurs several times in the 1961 draft programme. The transition to full communism is described as a development from ' socialist statism ' (' *sotsialisticheskaya gosudarstvennost* ') to ' communist social self-government ' (' *kommunisticheskoe obshchestvennoe samoupravlenie* '). I suspect that the Soviet passion for acronyms will colloquialise these unwieldly expressions into the snappier *sotsgos* and *komobsam*!

3 Cf., e.g., L. M. Karpetyan and V. I. Razin, ' Ob issledovanii razvitiya sotsialisticheskoi gosudarstvennosti ' *Voprosy filosofii*, No. 6, 1961, pp. 154, 155, 159.

' juridical nihilists ' such as Stuchka and Pashukanis argued in detail that law, the state, and morality could not take on a ' socialist ' content, since they were inextricably bound up with private property and a market economy. Needless to say, this position too was repudiated by Vyshinski.

The orthodox view since the 1930s has been that the state will indeed wither away—but not yet. ' It would be incorrect to assume ', Vyshinski declared in 1937, ' that the withering away of law and the state will occur in some mechanical or automatic way, that it will not be preceded by a vast period of time and, probably, not by a single period, but by a whole series of periods, of epochs '.[4] The image is almost geological ; one pictures centuries, if not millennia ! Stalin, of course, made this time-scale authoritative when he declared at the eighteenth Party Congress (in 1939) that the state would have to be preserved at full strength even after the achievement of full communism—defined primarily in terms of ' distribution according to need '—so long as there was capitalist encircle-ment and the threat of aggression from without. One of the few explicit references to ' withering away ' in the new draft programme repeats Stalin's position (without mentioning his name) : the state will finally and fully wither away when there is (a) full communism in the Soviet Union and (b) full communism throughout the world. But before this the ' dictatorship of the proletariat ' will already have disappeared.

At the sixteenth Party Congress (1930) Stalin had made the famous statement : ' We are for the withering away of the state. [A voluntaristic claim, of course. There would be no point in being either ' for ' or ' against ' an objectively determined historical process.] But at the same time we stand for strengthening of the proletarian dictatorship, which constitutes the most powerful, the mightiest of all governing powers that have ever existed. The highest development of governmental powers, this is the Marxian formula. Is this " contradictory " ? Yes, it is. But this contradiction is life, and reflects completely the Marxian dialectic.'[5] Contemporary Soviet commentators—without mentioning Stalin—repeat that ' the withering away of the state occurs through its strengthening ', and attack ' revisionists ' who ' do not wish to understand that the strengthening of the socialist state and its withering away are not mutually exclusive processes '.[6]

(4) More problematic is the question of the withering away of various forms of institutionalised coercion. Most early Russian Marxists had assumed that all coercion would disappear under communism, and Lenin made at least one statement that appears to confirm this, declaring in *State and Revolution,* that under communism ' the elementary rules of social living ' would be obeyed ' without force, without compulsion '. Some contemporary Soviet theorists assert that the coercion exercised by the state and by trade unions will increasingly give way to persuasion. But other Soviet writers take issue with this view, asserting that, although

[4] A. I. Vyshinski. *K polozheniyu na fronte pravovoi teorii* (Moscow, 1937), p. 54.
[5] Quoted in J. Towster, *Political Power in the USSR* (New York, 1948), p. 13.
[6] Karpetyan and Razin, *loc. cit.*, p. 158.

state coercion will indeed disappear, ' this does not mean that *all* coercion will be eliminated '. The individual in communist society will still be required to bow to ' the interests of the majority ' and to follow the instructions of ' specific organs of self-government even if these instructions go counter to his own opinion or desires '.[7] This naturally raises the question of the withering away of ' coercive ' moral norms under communism.

(5) Most early Russian Marxists, especially those who may be called ' Nietzschean ' revisionists with respect to their ethical and social theory —Gorky, Lunacharski, Volski, Bogdanov, and Bazarov—assumed that the morality of duty, epitomised by Kantian ethics, would wither away soon after the elimination of capitalism. The imperious ' you must ' (' *ty dolzhen* '—' *du sollst* '), they declared, would give way to the free ' I want to ' (' *ya khochu* '—' *ich will* '). The only remaining imperatives, Bogdanov insisted, would be hypothetical rather than categorical. Expressed in his own terminology, ' coercive norms ' would be wholly replaced by non-coercive ' expediency norms '. This view was defended during the 1920s by Bukharin and Kollontai, among others.

But since the 1930s a contrary view has become dominant, according to which *legal* obligation will eventually wither away, but *moral* obligation will remain, even under full communism, sanctioned by the inner voice of ' consciousness ' or ' conscience ' and the outer voice of public opinion. The 1961 draft programme repeats this position, referring to ' labour for the good of society ' as a ' sacred obligation of every human being ', which will be enforced by ' consciousness ' and ' public opinion '. The new draft statutes of the CPSU also make this point, detailing the same set of ' moral principles ' as the draft programme—among them ' a high consciousness of social duty '.[8]

Only two changes with respect to moral obligation are envisaged, neither involving any withering away of morality : (a) Moral obligation will increasingly take the place of legal obligation, and (b) ' Internal ' sanctions will increasingly take the place of ' external ' sanctions. Soviet writers usually express this in terms of an increasingly habitual or automatic obedience to the internalised voice of social obligation, or even as a response to a ' vital need '. In Kantian terms one might say that the voice of conscience will infallibly prevail over the selfish tug of individual interest or impulse. The point is put in deliberately ambiguous and ' dialectical ' language in the draft programme : ' The whole system of state and social organisations inculcates in the workers a spirit of voluntary, conscientious fulfilment of their obligations, leading to an organic union of rights and obligations in the unitary norms of communist social-living '. For example, there is the ' unitary norm ' (right-plus-obligation) to ' work for the good of society '. It seems clear at least that

---

7 G P. Alekseyev and Ye. A. Ivanov, ' Teoreticheskie osnovy leninskovo ucheniya o sovetskikh profsoyuzakh ', *VF*, No. 4, 1961, p. 23; Karpetyan and Razin, *loc. cit.* Italics added.

8 ' Proekt Ustava KPSS ', sec. vi, *Pravda*, 5 August 1961, p. 2.

moral obligation will continue to operate under communism, and that it will remain both categorical and imperative.

(6) Crime, too, we are assured, will disappear (' be liquidated ') with the approach to communism. Earlier Soviet theorists had predicted that crime would wither away with the prior attainment of socialism. But since crime, like religion, has tended to persist in the Soviet Union, its disappearance is now postponed to a remote future under conditions of (a) economic security for all, (b) a ' higher cultural level ', and (c) an appropriate communist ' consciousness ' (' *soznatelnost* '). Meantime, violators of Soviet laws will be punished with utmost severity. This harsh tone would seem to be related to the recent introduction of the death penalty for embezzlement and other ' crimes against (state) property '.

(7) The party, like the state, will be further enlarged and strengthened before it can begin to wither away. The approach to communism, as the draft programme puts it, ' involves the further growth of the role and importance of the Communist Party '. The number of salaried full-time party (and state) functionaries will decrease but their place will be taken by volunteers or part-time workers. One Soviet source insists that the party will remain strong and active until (a) all the links in the chain of ' communist social self-government ' (*komobsam* !) are functioning smoothly, and (b) every Soviet citizen has attained ' a high level of communist consciousness '.[9] This, like the above-noted conditions for the eventual withering away of the state, would appear to offer a pretext for the perpetuation of the party during what Vyshinski had called ' a vast period of time and, probably, not . . . a single period, but . . . a whole series of periods, of epochs '.

(8) Like the party, trade unions will assume more and more complex functions with the approach to communism, becoming fused with the state apparatus. They already seem very closely linked to the state apparatus in many ways. Recent Soviet writers admit that many ' social organisations '—presumably including trade unions—arose at a time when ' almost all social life was directed by the state ', and thus tended to take over ' the work methods of the state organs '. A number of these organisations, we learn, are still burdened with ' bureaucratism ' and an over-inflated staff of salaried administrators.[10]

*   *   *

Two final remarks : (1) If the theory of withering away is understood in the determinist sense, namely, as a prediction that certain institutions and attitudes will ' liquidate themselves ' or ' be liquidated by history ', then the fact of the non-withering of religion and the family in Soviet society will have to count as disconfirming evidence, and the theory will stand invalidated.

(2) If, on the other hand, the theory is understood in the voluntarist sense—as Lenin, Stalin, and apparently Khrushchev have understood it—

9 Karpetyan and Razin, loc. cit., p. 155.
10 Karpetyan and Razin, loc. cit., p. 159.

then *no* fact of historical withering or non-withering could either confirm or disconfirm it. On this view the statement that a given institution will wither away is not a prediction, but a programme for action. ' *X* will wither away ' means roughly ' we will strive to liquidate *x* '. ' *X* will not wither away ' means ' we will strive to preserve (and perhaps transform) *x* '. Somewhere between is the deliberately ambiguous and vague: ' *X* will wither away, after a very long time, when such-and-such (improbable) conditions are finally met '. Current references to the withering away of law, the state, and the party are couched in this cloudy idiom.

Since plans of action are neither confirmed nor disconfirmed, but either carried out or not carried out, and since Marxist plans of action, unlike Marxist predictions, can be modified at will, this pragmatic approach leaves ' the path to communism ' wide open. But it gains this openness at the price of abandoning a central Marxist doctrine, tacitly undercutting both the base-superstructure model of social interaction and the root-leaf metaphor which derives from it. In this sense the 1961 draft programme of the Communist Party of the Soviet Union continues the doctrinal ' revision ' of Marxism-Leninism which was initiated by Stalin. And Khrushchev, to the extent that he is responsible for its doctrinal content, must be regarded as an even more uninhibited revisionist than was Stalin himself.

II. The Function of Law

John Hazard

EVERY Soviet jurist since the Russian revolution has anticipated the ultimate end of law. The debate has concerned only the two questions : when? and how? In 1917 the answers varied, but many of those around Lenin expected the change to come soon and progressively, although Lenin was rather cautious in his own predictions.[1] In 1930 Stalin settled the matter for twenty-three years by declaring authoritatively that the withering away could occur only in the far future, and then only suddenly on all fronts without progressive preparation.[2] One morning the world would find that no further compulsion was needed.

Today the answer is mixed, but the majority of those appearing in print seems to be saying that the end will not be soon, although preparations of some sort should be made for the progressive transfer of social control from a system of law to a system of morals.

It often seems Utopian to western trained minds to speak of a stateless and lawless society, but for the Soviet legal philosopher, and for the Soviet man in the street, it is the logic of their doctrine. The logic of a society without law is made clear to Soviet schoolboys from the moment they are taught the origin of the state, for they learn that it is related to the emergence of a class society at the end of the tribal epoch in history when covetous individuals are said to have seized what had previously been the property of the entire tribe.[3] Born as an instrument of class warfare, and utilising law as its strong right arm, the state is shown to have continued its function throughout history as the preserver of authority in each of a succession of powerful classes, fortified by ownership of the supremely productive type of property of the epoch and unseated only by violent revolution led from below by a previously suppressed class that has gained economic power by degrees with the emergence of a new means of production. Inexorably the progression of epochs leads to the victory of the proletariat over the bourgeoisie ; the end of multi-class society and consequently the end of the state and its agent, the law.

Communism's social fabric is to be held together not by law but through the efforts of all citizens joined in a single class of toilers, the members of which are to live together harmoniously on the basis of common acceptance of a system of morals proven desirable by the benefits it has bestowed : namely, satisfaction of creature comforts and intellectual desires, but also strengthened by self-restraint inculcated in the hearts of all except the mentally ill by mass education and the continuing guidance of the communist party.

[1] V. I. Lenin, *The State and Revolution*, Chap. V, sec. 2 (Eng. trans., Moscow, 1935), pp. 86-87.
[2] J. V. Stalin, *Leninism* (Eng. trans., Moscow, 1933), Vol. II, p. 342.
[3] Frederick Engels, *The Origin of the Family, Private Property and the State* (Eng. trans., Chicago, 1902), p. 119.

Nothing has occurred in the forty-four years since the Russian revolution to alter this vision. It is as vigorously pronounced today as in 1917, although perhaps sometimes with a rueful suggestion that the hopes for immediate achievement were premature in the early days. It was made the theme in 1960 of the closing pages of the communist party's post-Stalin manual on political theory in which it is declared, ' There is no need for the state. The need for legal regimentation withers away '.[4]

WHILE the goal of a stateless and lawless society has been held constantly before the eyes of Soviet citizens since 1917, Stalin silenced any further speculation on how it would be achieved, when he told the XVI communist party congress in 1930 that before the state could wither away, it must first become stronger than any state the world had known. His was the thesis that the dialectical method of social development required a juxtaposition of opposites. He took his old colleague, Nikolai Bukharin, to task for arguing that the withering process must proceed progressively, with the withering of instruments of repression, one by one, beginning with the army. By 1937 Stalin had purged his Commissar of Justice, N. V. Krylenko, and his principal legal philosopher and constitutional draftsman, E. B. Pashukanis, because they had sought to implement in law the concept of progressive withering.[5] Through A. Y. Vyshinsky, whom he made his right arm to revise legal thought, he castigated the attempts of the jurists of the early years to categorise law as primarily of bourgeois origin, destined to wither as the market economy of the N.E.P. was taxed and hounded out of existence.[6] He had Vyshinsky proclaim that law had become socialist in both content and form, and could be expected to retain its full vigour right up to the moment when society moved into communism.

Nikita Khrushchev reopened the gates that Stalin had closed to speculation on the role of law during the period of transition to communism when he rose in 1956 at the XX communist party congress to denounce what he termed the absurd theory that as socialism progressed, the class war must sharpen.[7] Since the gates have been flung wide, the Soviet legal fraternity has revelled in its new opportunity to speculate on the future of communism and the role of law during the transition period. The Minister of Justice has called upon his colleagues to bend their energies to devise new institutions to replace the police and the courts, and to draft new laws that will prepare the way for a communist society.[8]

4 *Fundamentals of Marxism-Leninism* (Eng. trans., Moscow, 1960), p. 868.
5 For a fuller account, see *Soviet Legal Philosophy*, translated by Hugh W. Babb with an introduction by John N. Hazard (Cambridge, Mass., 1951).
6 See Andrei Y. Vyshinsky, *The Law of the Soviet State* (New York, 1948), pp. 56-57.
7 For text, see Leo Gruliow, editor, *Current Soviet Policies III* (New York, 1957), p. 177.
8 ' Dalneishee razvitie sovetskoi demokratii ' (The further development of soviet democracy) *Sovetskaia Iustitsiia*, 1959, 3.

Preparation for a transfer from law to morals, from a society controlled by a state through law to a society controlled by public self-government through deep concern for the common good, expressed in a new system of morals, has inspired extensive writing on a system of classification for law. To the common law mind of the Anglo-American school, classification has little interest because the common law has grown as a series of responses to immediate needs rather than as a logical pattern of prohibitions and commands devised as a scheme of inter-related provisions adopted to implement a philosophy. To the continental mind generally, and to the Soviet mind in particular, nothing is more important than classification, because through the system of classification adopted for the law the future is created. Thus, E. B. Pashukanis, when trying to formulate conditions for the progressive withering away of the law in the 1920s, decided that economic relations between citizens and between public producing-distributing enterprises should be separated into two different categories. He thought such division would make the way easier for the withering away of the law governing relationships between citizens while permitting the preservation for a longer time of the law governing relationships between state enterprises. He called for a sharp line to be drawn between the former, which he called ' civil law ', as the relic of the law created for the governing of private relationships in the Romanist systems of law, and the latter, which he called ' economic law ', for which he claimed novel qualities as the emerging rules of a socialist society destined ultimately to retain only regulations for the administration of things, in accord with Engels' dictum that ' the government of persons is replaced by the administration of things, and by the conduct of the processes of production '.[9]

Pashukanis was a man of action, and he took concrete steps to relegate civil law as he understood it to the background. It was removed from the curriculum of the law schools, and from the titles of legal textbooks. Since it was admitted that for a time—short though it would be—young lawyers would have to assist clients in meeting the requirements of the law in regulating their personal relationships with other citizens, Pashukanis condescended to include civil law matters at the end of courses on economic law, and in final chapters of legal textbooks on economic law, but the subject seemed to him to have little importance to any but historians.

Vyshinsky put a stop to Pashukanis' system of classification, declaring that it led to a disrespect for the individual and to concentration on state enterprises alone. What he really seems to have been worried about was revealed in his recognition of the reaction abroad among opponents of the Soviet regime, who were using Pashukanis as proof that socialism spelled regimentation of citizens like robots. This was damaging Soviet efforts to win friends abroad. Further, he is thought by outsiders to have

---

[9] Frederick Engels, *Anti-Dühring*, Part III, Chap. II (Eng. trans., Moscow, 1934), p. 315.

been worried lest a system that belittled civil law create such a lack of social respect for the property of private citizens that Stalin's formula for increasing production, through wide adoption of the differentiated wage incentive system, would fail in its purpose if the law provided no protection for those who acquired wealth through piece-work. These were the days of *Stakhanovism*, i.e., encouragement of productivity through large bonuses for exceeding work norms, and legal thinking that relegated protection of citizens' property to a short-lived branch of the legal system nullified the incentive schemes.

WITH the purge of Pashukanis in 1937 no one talked of classification systems in terms of preparing the way for the withering away of law. All had to accept as permanent the system written into the 1936 constitution, in which provision was made for codes of civil and criminal law, civil and criminal procedure, domestic and labour relations, and land use.[10] With the opening of the gates to speculation in 1956, classification again became an issue. Numerous articles were presented to the editors of the state's law reviews, so numerous as to permit only summary of the bulk of them after publication of those by the men with distinguished names. A congress of law professors was held in Moscow in the autumn of 1957 to which not only specialists from the USSR were invited but from the People's Democracies as well.

The 1957 congress considered the arguments of a new school, who contended like Pashukanis that civil law should be split from the law governing public enterprises, and the latter should be called economic law. The proponents of this view declared their independence of Vyshinsky's ghost, and although they nowhere mentioned Pashukanis and his writings, they mentioned his colleagues and used some of his arguments. A bold Armenian, V. S. Tadevosian, led the attack, writing, ' The scientific workers among the civilists must increase the attention they give to the legal questions raised by economic development, and they must give their help to the improvement of the work of these organs. Incidentally, work in this area has been noticeably slow since 1938, when, without any basis, the proponents of the theory of economic law were declared enemies of the people on the legal front, and economic law was excluded from the system of law.' [11]

In spite of strong support for separation of civil and economic law, the congress decided to retain the union created by Vyshinsky. Subsequent attempts to shake the decision, even taking the form of a letter signed by many of the eminent jurists of the Institute of Law of the Academy of Sciences in Moscow, including its Director, P. S. Romashkin, failed to shake the decision, and the general principles of civil law published in 1960 for public discussion prior to enactment embody the

---

[10] *Constitution of the USSR*, 1936, Art. 14.
[11] V. S. Tadevosian, ' Nekotorye voprosy sistemy sovetskovo prava ' (Some questions on the system of soviet law), *Sovetskoe Gosudarstvo i Pravo*, 1956, 8.

union.[12]   This position has been taken in spite of the fact that the
Tadevosian group has denied any thought of promoting the withering
away of civil law as Pashukanis would have done, and in spite of the fact
that two of the People's Democracies, Czechoslovakia and the German
Democratic Republic, have separated their civil and public enterprise
codes.

Tadevosian has not accepted his defeat. In criticism of the new draft
of general principles he has found it possible to say that the combination
of two different relationships in a single code makes for absurd complication in drafting,[13] but P. I. Orlovskii, a leading civilist and former
Director of the Institute of Law, continues to support the combination,[14]
and it now appears likely that the draft will be adopted without change
in this feature. If the civil law is to wither, leaving in force only the
provisions regarding the administration of public enterprises, it will do so
without the help that might have been provided by a system of classification of the branches of law creating separate categories for civil and
economic law.

Facilitation of withering through classification is not, however, entirely
out of the minds of Soviet jurists. The summation of the 1957 discussion
on classification, as it appeared in 1958 from the pen of Professor I. V.
Pavlov, then Deputy Director of the Institute of Law of the Academy of
Sciences, related the system he proposed to the transition from regulation
by law to regulation by morals.[15] He removed at the outset some
branches of law from the field of argument by saying that some social
relationships were to be explained exclusively by the existence of the
state, these being constitutional legal relationships, administrative law
relationships, criminal law relationships, and those having to do with the
structure and procedure of courts. But, in contrast, other social relationships that had taken form only at given stages of history were expected to
pass out of the legal category as socialism advanced. These were the
relationships of property, land use, labour, and family. For these latter
he saw a transition beginning even in socialism. He put it in these
words : ' In socialist society, in which in these relationships there are
coming together and constantly developing ever different and completely
new fundamentals, these relationships will be endowed with legal form
in some degree, but in some measure they will be beyond the boundaries
of the law and exist only as factual relationships '. Pavlov closed his
study by suggesting that the development of law depended not only upon
objective criteria but also upon a subjective factor, namely the will of the
ruling class. By this he was reasserting that since the Russian revolution

---

[12] Published as a supplement to *Sovetskaia Iustitsiia*, 1960, No. 7.

[13] V. Tadevosian, ' K proektu osnov grazhdanskovo zakonodatelstva Soiuza SSR i
soiuznykh respublik ' (On the draft of the fundamentals of civil legislation of the
USSR and of the union republics), *Sotsialisticheskaia Zakonnost*, 1960, 8, p. 47.

[14] P. E. Orlovskii, ' O proekte osnov grazhdanskovo zakonodatelstva ' (On the draft
of civil legislation), *Sovetskoe Gosudarstvo i Pravo*, 1961, 1, p. 92.

[15] I. V. Pavlov, ' O sisteme sovetskovo sotsialiticheskovo prava ' (On the system of
soviet socialist law), *Sovetskoe Gosudarstvo i Pravo*, 1958, 11, pp. 3-18.

man was not the prisoner of objective situations but could mould his future in some degree, having come to understand the rules of social development. Systematisation of law was to be related, therefore, to what the ruling class wanted to achieve, and there was an opportunity for the exercise of the will in the creation of categories of law. For Pavlov, the exercise of the will could not ignore objective reality, but the systematisers were not prisoners of this reality. They could influence the future by selecting the branches of law to be codified, and do so through systematisation for social progress. Pavlov expected old branches of law to disappear as one after another became unnecessary because, with the growing respect for morals, the given spheres of social activity were becoming orderly.

The specialists in domestic relations were among the first to take up the challenge. A woman judge argued that family relations had advanced so far towards the monogamous family espoused by Engels that law was no longer necessary to enforce unions necessary to the preservation of a healthy home environment.[16] Two authors suggested in a conference devoted to the future of family law that the law of divorce should be dispensed with.[17] Labour relations also seemed to some to be moving in the direction of voluntary work without regard to the compulsion of labour law epitomised in the severe legislation of 1940 freezing workmen in their jobs. Fellow workmen's disapproval of drifting from job to job would be enough to prevent unnecessary labour turnover. Freedom from compulsion was in the air as it had not been since 1917, when the hated chains of Tsarist legal restraints had been broken. Thus the end of the decade of the 1950s approached.

THE years 1959 to 1961 have brought some more sobering second thoughts, if the record may be taken as indicative of what is being said in the intimate circles of the communist party. The leading article in *Kommunist* for March 1961 [18] tells its thousands of readers that ' The complex social process of growing from the socialist governing process to the public self-government of communism requires a correct theoretical explanation. The words of Engels to the effect that in place of the government of persons there will under communism be the administration of things must not be understood literally. Any society, including communist, is senseless without definite forms of social control, without a firmly established order within which the whole complex social organism functions. The " withering away " of the state, about which V. I. Lenin wrote, puts the realisation of the process in the time of " complete communism," and it does not mean simply the liquidation of some state

16 A. Pergament, ' K proektu kodeksa zakonov RSFSR o brake i sem'e ' (On the draft of the code of laws of the RSFSR on marriage and the family), *Sovetskaia Iustitsiia*, 1957, 4.
17 ' Vo Vsesoiuznom institute iuridicheskovo nauka ', *Sovetskoe Gosudarstvo i Pravo*, 1957, 6.
18 ' Lenin—znamia nashei epokhi ' (Lenin, the banner of our epoch), *Kommunist*, 1961, 5, pp. 7-8.

organs, but means first of all a change in the character of their activity, the loss of their political nature, the transformation of the apparatus of state compulsion into an apparatus of public administration, co-ordination, regulation.'

The theme of caution as regards the withering away of the state and especially of law has been reflected since 1959 in a growing number of articles against revisionism in law. In October 1959, an author in the Ministry of Justice's journal declared that the issue is not as to the withering away of the state, to which the USSR is committed ; the issue is what is meant by withering. The author calls for a state law up to the time that communism is achieved, and demands the strengthening of the Soviet state, in the first place by means of its further democratisation through the increasing activity of public organisations in the Soviet manner and not in the Yugoslav manner.[19]

Another attack on revisionist thinking on law says that ' The tasks of constructing and developing the socialist system of economy, of raising the level of socialist culture, and of the defence of the country from the imperialist world, necessarily require attention on all sides to the strengthening of the socialist state and law, to raising their role in economic and cultural construction '.[20] While the author seems to be concerned primarily with the economic might of the USSR, his language is sweeping and might be taken to mean that there should be no more discussion about preparing for the progressive withering away of law in those realms of social activity not related to production, such as domestic relations.

Some indication that the door has not been completely shut on the progressive withering away of law comes from the pen of Dr. N. G. Aleksandrov, distinguished senior legal theorist of the Communist Party. Writing in mid-1959 he was able to say: ' The process of development of socialist law in the direction of its future transmutation into social norms of communist society, which enter into the habits of members of society, is already going on and will accelerate as there are further successes in the building of communism. As communist society unfolds there will be accumulated, and increasingly accumulated, those prerequisites for the future withering away of law under the conditions of communism. Such prerequisites are, in particular, the consolidation of the voluntary observance of the norms of socialist law, elevating the role of society in protection of the socialist legal order '.[21]

While extending some comfort to those who have championed the

[19] B. Lazarev, ' V chem sut revizionistskikh kontseptsii otmiraniia gosudarstva ' (What is the substance of the revisionist conceptions of the withering away of the state), *Sovetskaia Iustitsiia*, 1959, 10.

[20] A. F. Shebanov, ' Protiv revizionizma v voprosakh obshchei teorii prava ' (Against revisionism in questions of the general theory of law), *Pravovedenie*, 1959, 4, pp. 24-25.

[21] N. G. Aleksandrov, ' Razvitie kommunizma i prava ' (The development of communism and law), *Pravovedenie*, 1959, 3, pp. 15-16.

progressive withering away of law, Aleksandrov ends with some enigmatic words which tend to postpone the commencement of the progression, for he concludes : ' But the development of these prerequisites in conditions of the lowest phase of communism, during socialism, means elevating the role of law in the life of the public, and makes possible the further strengthening of socialist legality and the socialist legal order ', [22]

Alexsandrov sounds much like the Stalin of 1930, for he is saying that before withering can begin there must first be a strengthening of law. The only difference lies in the hope he holds out of a progression starting at some future point, when the moral fibre of the new Soviet man is stronger than it is at present. Stalin, in contrast, postponed all withering until the last shred of necessity for compulsion had vanished. The difference is immaterial for the policy makers of 1961 ; that they see no difference is shown by the spate of measures adopted in 1961 to strengthen a criminal code adopted only a few months earlier, when there seems to have been some expectation that the severity of the criminal law could be lessened.[23] Yet there is a difference between Alexsandrov as spokesman for the Soviet leadership of today and Stalin. It lies in what each would envisage as the policy of the year 1980 or, perhaps, 2000.

But the year 2000 seems still far off, and if one is to believe that communism is ever to come, one will have to assume that people can learn to conduct themselves always with constant attention to the good of the community and without regard to personal advantage. In professing to believe that, Soviet philosophers show themselves to be singularly optimistic.

[22] The same severe position is taken in his popular brochure; see N. G. Aleksandrov, *Rol prava v sovetskom sotsialisticheskom obshchestve* (The role of law in soviet socialist society), Moscow, 1957.

[23] See for example the law of 5 May 1961 instituting the death penalty for a series of offences including the theft of state property as a business, *Vedomosti SSSR*, No. 19, item 207, and that of 4 May 1961 instituting a procedure for banishing parasites to remote parts of the Russian Republic either by court action without appeal or by action of neighbours through a social assembly, *Vedomosti RSFSR*, 1961, No. 18, item 273.

III. The Role of Social Institutions

Robert Osborn

L IKE most of the world's industrial nations, the Soviet Union has only gradually and tardily come to grips with the problem of giving its new city dwellers the capacity to meet the evils which beset growing urban concentrations. These evils are physical, governmental, and social, and in all three areas the Soviet problems have parallels elsewhere. The failure or absence of urban planning is a consequence of the very advantageous position occupied by industries, which are able to manage the new population centres around them to suit their own short-run advantage. Political cohesion is blocked by a splintering of local authority which leaves local governments too weak to resist the demands made by industries. Social cohesion must be built from the ground up. The new city dwellers, coming as they do from farming and small towns, find no easy form of association which might permit them to take action and to repair official neglect. In the case of the Soviet Union we are tempted to ascribe urban chaos mainly to Soviet political circumstances and the forced pace of industrialisation. These have played their part, but fundamentally the cause was a system of priorities which has had both intentional and accidental features, and which the West has known in a different form. Everywhere attention to the success of production has taken precedence over attention to the living conditions which the productive mechanism created. And everywhere the new urban populations acquiesced in this neglect as part of the price they paid for exchanging the insecurity of agricultural life for the security offered by an industrial wage.

While the urban dilemma may have similar causes throughout the world, the vision required to find a way out of it—if any vision emerges at all—depends on particular national experiences. The Soviet Union, even with its formidable planning mechanism and its projects now under wide discussion, for 'satellite towns' and 'micro-districts', has still to develop a concept which unites human, governmental, and physical elements. This is not surprising in itself, but only in the light of Soviet claims for the possibilities of planning. The non-communist urbanised nations have certainly had their troubles even in producing a concept which presumes great local diversity. The Soviet 'lag of vision', as opposed to the Western lag, is rooted in the especially bitter circumstances of the rural-urban transition and in the omissions of Marxist thinking. Europe and North America are strongly influenced by a half-conscious reverence for a pre-industrial way of life, real or imagined. Even the experience of dust bowls and collapsing agricultural prices has not erased the feeling that a life existed, within the memory of our grandparents' generation, which we must somehow recapture to the extent that urban circumstances permit. America's suburban development and Europe's fastidious preservation of pre-industrial appearances, grotesque though the results often are, bear witness to the reaction against over-urbanisation. Russia's urban migrants, although they clung for a time to village associations, could hardly share this emotion. They were and perhaps still are too close to precarious dependence on agriculture, complicated by inequitable taxes and tenure systems before the Revolution, by more taxes and unfavourable trade terms in the 1920s, and finally by the rigours of the collectivisation period. The choice between industrial and agricultural occupations presented itself as a question of security versus insecurity in terms more severe and uniform over a period of decades than had been the case in the West. For a fixed wage and the goods it bought, the urban migrant would give a good deal else in exchange : a small family house and garden for part of a barracks room ; village associations for an anonymous factory crew ; the security of a cohesive community for a world where mistrust among strangers bred immorality in new and vicious forms. The road back to the older way of life is closed not only by economic circumstances and population growth, but psychologically as well. The modern Soviet dacha colony is the Russian's way of escape from the town. But economic circumstances have loomed large in the rise of the dacha : the acute housing shortage and the great value of even a tiny garden plot. Just to make sure that nostalgia does not gain the upper hand after all, Soviet theoretical writers have been erasing the dacha from any possible vision of the good life under communism. If the *agrogorod* plan is carried out on a major scale, the villages themselves will vanish and with them the prototype of the family house and garden.

Marxism-Leninism speaks of man's alienation from the productive process, not from the community as such, except perhaps as an incidental by-product. Under communism man is said to be associated with man through the productive process itself. It is true that during the past few years there has been much discussion of the community as the embodiment of values, particularly as the organiser of leisure. But if any true vision is to emerge from this, it will be only after considerable experimenting. Meanwhile the exaltation of industrial production as the greatest and best source of meaning in life is a tenacious dogma whose primacy will not easily be challenged. As an ideal it has clashed repeatedly with other ideals since 1917, and so far has always emerged triumphant. The ideal of a community bending every effort towards fulfilment of its industrial production plans left no room for the ideal of a local soviet, assembled like a giant town meeting, drafting plans for apartments, theatres, streets, and parks. Economic scarcities were only part of the reason for this. A priority of ideals provided strong reinforcement for economic priorities. The absence of a workable ideal to guide even the more ambitious communities meant that

local initiative withered, and that potential local organisational talent
was diverted to other matters. Secure in the support of the party and
the higher government apparatus, the industries managed local government as a secondary concern.

IT is not surprising, therefore, that the economics and psychology of
the ' company town ' are known to the Soviet Union as they are
to other industrial nations. In the newer industrial areas particularly,
it is the industries themselves that command local resources, build
apartments and other facilities as suits their convenience, and divert
these same resources to production whenever the plan is in danger.
Stalinsk, with a 1959 population of 366,000 which doubled over the
preceding twenty years, controls only a small part of its housing. A
metallurgical plant commands about 40 per cent of the total, and the
rest is divided among 155 different enterprises. The main difficulty is
that the various landlords constantly violate their contractual obligations
to both the city and their own workers regarding housing space.[1] The
assignment of housing is a vital channel of influence for the enterprise
or local government which controls it, and the authority of the Stalinsk
city administration can be judged accordingly. Other enterprises such
as hospitals, schools and clubs may be neglected because the enterprises
feel they cannot afford them. The regional administrations of the
Soviet railways in many places command the housing, utilities, and
trade network of entire communities, a practice which has been the
source of numerous complaints.[2] In 1957 roughly one-third of all city
housing not privately owned was still under the jurisdiction of bodies
other than the city soviets. Furthermore, the cities managed less than
half of such facilities as water supply systems, laundries, and public
baths.[3] One provincial executive committee complained that in 1959 its
local soviets received 2,000,000 (old) rubles for building water mains while
the economic council received 54,000,000 rubles for the same purpose.[4]
Angarsk, a raw young Siberian city of 134,000 is going through a
typical Soviet boom-town phase in which one industry controls the
street lights, another the transportation network, another the telephone
system, and so forth. When the city's executive committee complained
to Russian Republic officials that Angarsk was barred from using the
plentiful local natural gas supplies, it was told that the city was not
' municipal ' (*gorodskoi*) but ' administered ' (*vedomstvennyi*). This
was meant as a reproach, since the latter category does not exist in
published local government statutes. When the executive committee
then approached the Irkutsk Province government and economic council

---

[1] *Izvestiya*, 26 January 1961, p. 3.
[2] *Sovety Deputatov Trudyashchikhsya*, No. 2 (August), 1957, p. 76; No. 7 (July),
1959, p. 61; *Izvestiya*, 24 May 1960, p. 2; *Pravda*, 25 March 1961, p. 2.
[3] *Planirovanie Mestnovo Khozyaistva i Kul'turnovo Stroitel'stva Administrativnovo
Raiona* (Moscow, 1957), p. 207.
[4] *Izvestiya*, 24 May 1960, p. 2.

for funds to build a local gas system, officials of these latter bodies pointed out that the Angarsk industries were acting illegally and must be fined by the city before anything could be done.[5] This was done, but in practice fines have little effect : industries pay them and continue to derive an advantage from an illegal state of affairs. Fines levied on industries for water pollution, for example, are paid with such regularity that many enterprises provide for them in their annual financial plans, and some local governments compound the offence by relying on them for income.[6]

Eventually these questions of jurisdiction and responsibility are settled in favour of the local governments. Moscow, Leningrad, and the older urban centres usually control the bulk of their own housing construction and allocation under a centralised city authority, and other cities will gradually reach this important goal. Where local governments are still unable to manage all their own affairs, they try to work out a tolerable arrangement with the most important local enterprises.[7] Recent legislation has given them somewhat more financial independence.[8] Territorial amalgamation is bringing suburban areas and nearby villages under the control of city soviets, permitting better land-use planning.

Meanwhile a good deal of damage has been done. Housing has gone up haphazardly and cannot be torn down for redevelopment because the shortage of space is still acute. Industries have been built with no regard to sanitary conditions and residential zoning, while the appropriation of city lands by enterprises for future industrial use has wrought havoc with city planning.[9] Water pollution, for example on the upper Donets, has become not only a health problem, but also very costly to correct, and the difficulties increase with the passage of time. In short, the Soviet Union did no better than Europe or the United States in avoiding the squalor and disorder of young industrial nations. This was not so much a failure of planning as the silent omission to do what could not be planned anyway in the circumstances. It was understandable that a nation fanatically intent on industrial investment could not at the same time set its industries down in ideally designed communities.

5 Ibid., 12 February 1960, p. 4.
6 Statement by S. V. Kurashov, USSR Minister of Health, reported in *Pravda*, 8 June 1960, p. 4; I. Demin and D. Bilenkin, ' A River Calls For Help ', *Komsomolskaya Pravda*, 27 April 1960, p. 2.
7 Magnitogorsk, for example, made a long-range agreement with the Southern Urals Railroad for improving the water supply, local transportation, and other public services. E. I. Kozlova, *Ispolnitelnye Komitety Gorodskikh Sovetov* (Moscow, 1960), p. 52.
8 The Russian Republic, for example, now permits the more important local governments to invest 30 per cent. of above-plan profits from industries of local subordination in housing. *Biulleten Moskovskovo Gorodskovo Soveta*, No. 13 (July), 1958, p. 27.
9 Statement by V. A. Kucherenko, Chairman of the USSR State Construction Committee, reported in *Pravda*, 8 June 1960, p. 2.

But the jeopardy to future city planning may be the lesser half of the total damage that has resulted. The other half of the story is that little ground was left in which civic initiative can take root. The plight of a city is the spur to creative action, which may be taken even under unfavourable political circumstances if there is enough leeway for local public leaders to build an organisation. Joseph Chamberlain's reforms in Birmingham, and the municipal reform organisations which arose in the United States more than a half-century ago, gathered strength in response to the political and physical chaos created around them by industry. But they could do this because in both countries the central government was either indulgent or powerless to act. The Soviet system will scarcely produce reform movements in this sense. The fact that so many separate hierarchies reach down into local affairs would stifle them even if one-party rule did not forbid them in a political sense. The reproach that the Soviet system maintains a ' vested interest in confusion' applies to the local government scene even though the consequences of this policy are frequently deplored in the Soviet press. Besides this, the rapid turnover of deputies in the local soviets and their standing commissions can be understood only as a deliberate policy of preventing these bodies from developing a will of their own. Where local combinations of one kind or another do succeed in setting improvements in motion, they lay themselves open to the charge of ' localism '. Perhaps this is justified in the cases where administrators show too great a fondness for huge stadiums and expensive government buildings, as often happens.[10] Local governments are also at fault when they proceed blindly in their new projects without consulting the higher authorities and institutions that could give them badly needed advice. The real tragedy, however, is that local governments and public organisations are given nominal responsibility to correct situations of glaring disorder and corruption against which they are in fact powerless. Demoralisation and apathy may be the lot of corrupt cities anywhere in the world. But the public frame of mind is abysmal indeed where reform is said to be desirable while the initiative for reform is blocked.

IT is useful to consider the slogans which have been brought into play regarding the character of the new community. They are not very enlightening if examined solely in the context of Soviet Marxist theory, but they are used with a certain practical effect in mind, and each one serves as the justification for certain specific measures. The fact that well-worn slogans are stretched to fit present needs does not necessarily diminish their effectiveness or their convenience as levers for certain programmes. For example, the ' elimination of the distinction between town and country', which the

---

[10] Examples are cited in *Izvestiya*, 8 February 1961, p. 3; *Pravda*, 22 February 1961, p. 6; 29 March 1961, p. 1.

Communist Manifesto set forth in the literal sense of breaking up existing cities, now serves to bracket three programmes : the *agrogorod* idea, growth ceilings for the larger cities, and the accommodation of future population increments in more and more new cities spread throughout Siberia, Central Asia, and the Soviet Far East.[11] While economic necessities dictate the last-named measure, there is obviously a growing concern with the physical problems of urban congestion, perhaps even a tinge of official uneasiness at the massive population concentrations which would build up if no energetic measures were taken to block this trend. For the ' magnet of the metropolis ' exerts its force in the Soviet Union just as it does elsewhere. Even where new industries are systematically excluded from the western cities and located in Siberia instead, they crowd their way into the existing cities, where they show a preference for the already congested central areas. There is concern, for example, about Novosibirsk, whose population is approaching 900,000. Local governments are criticised for their ' narrowly ministerial attitude ' in allowing this to happen. There are even suggestions in the press that Soviet cities, like growth-concious cities elsewhere, seek to lure more and more industries without considering the human consequences of urban growth.[12]

' Public self-government,' *obshchestvennoe samoupravlenie*, is a far more nebulous idea both in its theoretical context and in its present application. Strictly speaking, it means a technique of performing administrative tasks and does mean greater autonomy for the local authorities. However, since it is advertised as a method of doing the work of local administration, it is simultaneously held up to view as the first and greatest hope for stronger local government. With it is bracketed Lenin's call for ' the *unpaid* fulfilment of state obligations by *every* working person ', which alone, Lenin said, could guarantee the transition to socialism.[13] The idea in this form had faded by the 1930's, but now it has been revived as a condition for attaining the higher stage of communism. The demand of the 1919 Party Programme for obligatory work by all soviet deputies was interpreted in local government statutes of the 1920's to mean their obligation to join one of the soviet sections, the predecessors of today's standing commissions. The sections did not administrate, but served as advisory councils to the executive committee departments, with the department heads serving as chairmen. The department head pretty well dominated his section, and was removed first from the chairmanship, then from the section altogether. Some proposals in the magazine *Vlast Sovetov*

---

11 This slogan was revived and reinterpreted in the massive theoretical statement published shortly after the 21st Party Congress, *Osnovy Marksizma-Leninizma* (Moscow, 1959), pp. 698-701.

12 S. Shumski and N. Shchetinin, ' Urgent Problems of Urban Construction ', *Sovety Deputatov Trudyashchikhsya*, No. 9 (September), 1960, pp. 20-21.

13 Voroshilov quoted this at the 21st Party Congress. The italics are Lenin's. *XXI S'ezd KPSS* (Moscow, 1959), Vol. 2, pp. 307-8.

in 1929 and 1930 urged that the sections at last take over the operation of their departments, but nothing came of this. In 1938 Vyshinsky's well-known legal manual buried the whole idea by suggesting completely innocuous ways for the public to be brought into administration.[14] The present-day standing commissions, first organised in 1940, have functioned more independently than the sections, but have also stressed self-help activities in order to make up for the authority which they seldom gained. They have lost contact with the administrative departments, so much so that proposals have been made to revive the old advisory council concept in the hope of overcoming the unwillingness of department heads to be bothered by delegations of deputies.[15]

Against this background, the goal of drawing volunteers into the process of local administration still appeared distant when the 21st Party Congress proposed to bridge this gap once and for all. Local government departments were to become 'public departments' run entirely by volunteers. The permanent bureaucracy would vanish from an ever-wider sphere of administration, and with it the stigma of 'bureaucratism' from those governmental offices with which the public has the most contact. A campaign to this end was taken up in Sverdlovsk Province, now a highly important industrial area whose urban population represents more than three-fourths of the 4,000,000 total. Its First Party Secretary, A. P. Kirilenko, is the only province Party chief who also sits on the Party Presidium (as a candidate member), and several of the articles describing the Sverdlovsk experiment have appeared over his signature. The change-over to voluntary departments began at the borough level in Sverdlovsk city, where a volunteer staff of 22 took over the October Borough Department of Trade and Public Catering in January 1960. At the time this occurred, the former Department had only one inspector to look after the 57 shops and restaurants entrusted to it, and neither he nor the corresponding standing commission had been able to cope with the job. The new volunteer director was the director of a local technical school specialising in trade and distribution, and one-third of his volunteer staff consisted of his own faculty members.[16] Pensioners formed another third of the staff, and the rest included three production workers, three housewives, and two book-keepers. The staff was divided into sections according to subject-matter, and each section operated according to quarterly plans for such activities as inspections, conferences at the enterprises, public education measures, and co-operation with local public organisations such as street committees. Regular

[14] A. Ya. Vyshinsky, *Sovetskoe Gosudarstvennoe Pravo* (Moscow, 1938), pp. 436-37.
[15] *Izvestiya*, 1 March 1959, p. 3.
[16] This recalls the old *shefstvo* arrangement, in which a factory collective or other organisation assumed guidance over a local soviet or one of its departments. Like some of the better standing commissions, the voluntary departments will be run by experts.

working hours were established with two daily shifts, the later being left to those with regular daytime occupations.[17]

Within a year some 50 voluntary departments were reported to be functioning in Sverdlovsk Province, 20 of them at the borough level in the larger cities, and some of the others at the district level. Most were departments of trade or culture, and there were some sanitary inspectorates and councils of vehicle inspectors. Similar experiments on a more modest scale were undertaken in some Ukrainian cities, likewise at the borough level. Dneprodzerzhinsk claimed to have transferred all its borough departments to the standing commissions. It was a cautious beginning on a humble plane, as the 1959 theoretical statement predicted.[18]

IT does not appear that the gulf between bureaucratic authority and local voluntary effort was bridged in any real sense, at least within the limits of these first experiments. The charters which the borough executive committees issued to the new departments did not empower them to issue obligatory directives of any kind, or to impose or collect fines. They could not employ or dismiss personnel in the enterprises entrusted to their care, and their approval of economic plans was not required. Their main function was to organise, inspect, and educate; for example, the Sverdlovsk department already described was set to work organising new shops on the city's neglected periphery, and collecting public complaints about inadequate facilities or service. What appears to have happened is that the voluntary departments were set up in those parts of the soviet apparatus which had never functioned as they were intended to do, which had little authority, suffered from the low level of their personnel, and had been unable to mobilise the communities around them. Many borough soviets are being abolished anyway, and the departmental staffs of others are being trimmed to a bare minimum as a matter of administrative principle. When Tomsk, a city of 250,000, abolished its boroughs recently, it did so partly to gain the advantage of more centralised administration of housing, utilities, and certain other matters.[19] Officials of the various Ministries of Finance keep close watch over all paid offices in the soviet apparatus, and may demand staff reductions or the abolition of local soviets altogether where there seems insufficient justification for their existence.[20] The boroughs, being the very lowest links, have existed mainly

---

[17] *Izvestiya*, 25 August 1960, p. 1; 23 November 1960, p. 3; Yu Tikhomirov, ' Something New in the Work of the Local Soviet Apparatus ', *Sovety Deputatov Trudyashchikhsya*, No. 8 (August), 1960, pp. 21–23.

[18] *Izvestiya*, 23 October 1960, p. 1; 10 February 1961, p. 3; 1 April 1961, p. 3; *Osnovy Marksizma-Leninizma*, pp. 718–20.

[19] V. Antonov, ' After the Abolition of Boroughs ', *Sovety Deputatov Trudyashchikhsya*, No. 7 (July), 1960, pp. 62–68.

[20] For example, the Crimea Province Department of Finance put pressure on Kerch to abolish its three borough soviets altogether, having already brought about a sharp reduction in their staffs three years earlier. *Izvestiya*, 24 September 1959, p. 4.

for the purpose of mobilising street committees, pensioners' committees, women's groups and others for self-help projects, inspections, and public education campaigns. If they fail in this, they might as well be replaced by groups whose basis is voluntary, and who thus have a bias towards enlisting still more volunteers.

This having been done, the volunteers with their new official-sounding title find themselves burdened with all the disadvantages of not being a regular link in the professional soviet apparatus. The articles describing Sverdlovsk experiments stated that the lack of communication between the city departments and the boroughs which existed before the reforms had hardly improved afterwards. Requests from the boroughs to city officials went unanswered more often than not, with the result that most of the public departments lacked office space, telephones, and funds, and had not even won themselves a place on the city's official administrative list.[21]

It would be wrong to judge the vision of ' public self-government ' by this failure to move towards what may be an impossible goal, namely the substitution of volunteer committees for professional bureaucrats in vital areas of administration. Certain functions not involving the exercise of authority do still hold a certain promise, such as inspection, consultation, and the processing of public complaints. These have been used in many different contexts since the early days of the revolution, partly in order to divert public dissatisfaction to the lower bureaucracy and to keep the latter aware of its responsibility to the public. But the formula for creating a self-sustaining interest has invariably escaped the organisers of the public committees. The present trend is towards investing these groups with greater status, to give them the feeling and appearance of authority without, in most cases, any real powers beyond the right to investigate, consult, and report. Statutes have been issued in great quantities by the local soviets in order to legalise the status of a great variety of groups. The groups in turn have developed an appetite not just for statutory recognition, but for greater authority.[22] There is something ironical and incongruous in the value placed on legal capacities by the very organisations which supposedly embody the new stateless society in the making. Reliance on administrative authority, however clumsy its procedures, is not just a system but a deeply ingrained habit which cannot be rooted out simply by transferring authority from one kind of group to another.

THE distinction between voluntary service and paid administration will remain fundamental for a long time, no matter how closely the volunteers are integrated with the work of a local executive

21 Ibid., 23 November 1960, p. 3.
22 See *Uchastie Obshchestvennosti v Rabote Mestnykh Sovetov; Sbornik Dokumentov* (Moscow, 1960).

committee or department. Nevertheless certain things can be done. The Commission of Soviet Control has been obliged to rely heavily on volunteer inspectors and controllers following the sizable reduction of its paid staff in 1957.[23]   The control of housing allocation offers a particularly interesting task for volunteers, since it is a problem which concerns most people intensely and brings deep-rooted egalitarian feelings into play.   The one danger here is that, in housing matters particularly, volunteers lack the authority to act against injustices dictated by powerful local interests.   Like poll watchers at elections in a machine-run city in the United States, they may soon tire of the monotonous dishonesty they are forced to observe.   On the other hand, the possibilities for reforms stimulated by group initiative do exist. With each volunteer group, the problem must be solved of giving its participants enough autonomy to promote a feeling of status and importance, enough drama in their tasks to impart a sense of forward motion, and enough cooperation from the authorities to keep them from dissolving in frustration.

If the vision of ' public self-government ' means only another campaign for more voluntary activity under the direction of the same old authorities, we can perhaps dismiss it as something the Soviet Union has seen many times before. Even a successful and sustained campaign of this kind would do nothing to clear away the entanglements which today still block local self-government in the usual sense of the word. At best there will be some more progress on the ' second plan ' the local improvements for which no specific provision is made in the economic plans of the USSR and the Republics.[24]   Many of these improvements, whether in the form of self-help projects or checking on local administration, will be carried out by amateurs working under great handicaps, expending a great deal of time and effort, when they might as well have been done professionally.[25]   Perhaps volunteers must do them if they are to be done at all ; this, in any case, is what the ' second plan ' concept seems to mean.   Insofar as the projects concern checking on local administration, they testify to the failure of the local soviets and their standing committees to do this job themselves.   Against this judgment must be balanced the Soviet principle of using every conceivable channel, every type of organisation, to secure active participation in local affairs by every person in one way or another.

[23] A. Stoyantsev, Chairman of the Soviet Control Commission in the Ukraine, writing in *Izvestiya*, 1 April 1959, p. 2, and 18 December 1960, p. 3.

[24] The phrase ' second plan ' is not often used in Soviet descriptions.

[25] The Soviet Union is in a better position than almost any other nation to encourage self-help projects, in view of the large proportion of its citizens which has technical training in some form.   The self-help apartment construction projects which began in Gorki in 1956 rely to some extent on these skills.   By contrast, the long struggle of a street committee (in Yoshkar-Ola) to pave its streets, even with some trained participants, is described in *Sovety Deputatov Trudyashchikhsya*, No. 11 (November), 1960, pp. 61-63.

The strength of mass-participation campaigns must be recognised no matter how poorly their reality compares with the high-flown claims made for them. Given the proper organisation and motivation, volunteer groups can secure both material and psychological ends which governmental action by itself cannot duplicate. The sense of regeneration and forward motion which they create has been discovered by Asian and African nations, and to their advantage.[26] The fact that these movements are centrally directed in a monolithic one-party state is not necessarily a disadvantage.

All this still does not add up to a vision of the future community in operation in any accepted sense of the word. There is little indication so far that the kaleidoscopic field of public participation in planning and running the community will crystallise, establish traditions, and become a force in its own right. This is not what is intended, at least at present. The device of periodic campaigns, with their cycles of decay and resurgence, offers political and psychological advantages to the Soviet regime ; furthermore, it has become a habit and a kind of tradition itself. This being so, there is just as little prospect that local public organisations will gear into any sustained effort to solve the *major* problems of the urban and industrial environment. No local organisation or combination of them has shown the capacity to play the role of the municipal reform leagues in the West. There are doubtless some local civic forces quietly at work, in a positive sense, of which we have no clear knowledge. Local crises and the most pressing needs do probably generate united efforts among the various authorities which have a hand in running every city. There may be further changes in local government and economic management which would afford a certain leeway to what might be called, in Soviet conditions, ' enlightened localism '. The industrial reorganisation of 1957 and the many local government statutes issued since then contain some partial reforms, but no sweeping shift of responsibility to urban areas themselves. It still appears that the organisational and psychological obstacles of the present will determine the shape of the future. This, sadly, has been the case with all too many cities of the non-communist industrial nations, in totally different political circumstances. The Soviet Government has had the urban dilemma of the West from which to learn, and the power and the means to take action. One might have expected more foresight in a planned society.

26 See Robert C. Tucker, ' Towards a Comparative Politics of Movement Regimes ', *American Political Science Review*, Vol. LV (June, 1961), p. 285.

THE UTOPIAN TRADITION

Thilo Ramm

THE connection between Marxism and early ('utopian') socialism does not appear to require any further analysis. After all, in the *Communist Manifesto* Marx and Engels scoffed at Saint-Simonism, Fourierism and Owenism. In these early versions of socialism 'activity by ingenious individuals' had come to replace mass activity, and a 'cut and dried social order', the gradual organisation of the proletariat. 'The best possible plan for the best possible society', 'a blue-print for a future society'. With these jeers, the plan for the social order to be were discredited and rejected out of hand as 'utopian'. Later on, in *The Civil War in France* (1871), Marx wrote that the working class has no ready-made utopia to be implemented by popular decision. In the light of these words, Marxists might well consider a concern with early socialism as superfluous, if not downright deplorable. Although from the intellectual and humanistic point of view it was the most interesting and attractive period of socialist development, early socialism sank into oblivion, while Marxism went on gathering momentum as a political movement.

*　　*　　*

It is no easy task to summarise the mass of individual suggestions for a new order put forward by the early socialists. To begin with, they appear to be agreed only on the rejection of liberalism, which would confine the scope of state functions to as few fields as possible: maintenance of law and order at home, and warding off aggression from without. State administration was to be kept to a bare minimum, an official social policy was inadmissible, and even care of the poor was to be permitted only in so far as it did not interfere with the 'free play of forces'. Liberalism recognised only the individual. Groups, corporations, and associations of workers or employers, were considered detrimental to free competition, in which only the individual should take part.

This system became the target of early socialist criticism, whose relentless attacks shook the very foundations of liberalism. Is it really the best and most efficient alone that prevail in the competitive struggle? Answering in the negative, they pointed to circumstances which lay beyond human control, as well as to the unscrupulousness of the successful. In his brilliant satire on the *Hierarchy of Bankruptcy*, Fourier made it his main concern to expose and denounce fraudulent dealings. Early socialist critics pointed out that competitors never had one and the same point of departure : not only were they not endowed with the same capacity, but there was also a disparity in training and in the means each one had at his disposal. There was therefore no such thing as equal weapons in that ' fight of all against all ', as free competition used to be called. The workers, who in these early stages of industrialisation lived under a constant threat of unemployment, had to make do with any wages that might be offered them. This exploitation of labour, a direct sequel to the recently acquired freedom of contract, widened even further the gap between haves and have-nots, robbing the worker of any hope of achieving a substantial improvement in his standard of living. This perpetuation of misery came under heavy fire in the writings of Saint-Simon's disciples.

THE discrepancy in liberal society between actual inequality on the one hand and equality before the law on the other, led to the question whether this had really been the aim of the great French revolution. Was not equality before the law only an initial step towards real freedom? Babeuf thought so, as did later Cabet and Weitling. Fourier rejected the idea of equality, but revealed the questionableness of any system which would grant only political freedom while ignoring the need for economic independence of the individual. Long before Anatole France's sarcastic formulation of ' freedom to sleep under the bridges of Paris ', Fourier wrote : ' People are told that they are free, but free to do what? To die from starvation! That they have inalienable rights. What rights? Not even the right to work for bread! ' With his proclamation of the right to a basic subsistence minimum and the right to work, he opposed to the liberal right to freedom a new type of basic ' social ' rights.

The isolation of man in liberal society became the central theme of early socialist criticism. Does not the system of free competition lead each man to look on every fellow man as an adversary? Can it be denied that Thomas Hobbes' ' man is a wolf to man ' describes accurately the individualistic liberal order? Agreeing on this, the early socialists turned their attention to the idea of fraternity, the second magic word of the French revolution. At times, as in the case of Saint-Simonians, they based their conception of a new social order on the tenets of a new ' industrial religion '. The fraternal life takes the form of small communities—numbering 500 to 2,000 persons, according to Fourier and Owen—whose members would know each other personally, so that public opinion could exercise full control over human relations. The village and small town of the middle ages are compared favourably with the modern big city in which the individual lives in anonymous isolation. ' No more capital cities, no more big cities! ' says Buonarroti, Babeuf's comrade in arms and historian of the ' Conspiracy of the equals ', ' Large cities are a symptom of public ill-health '.

The various blue-prints differ markedly from one another in their economic and political proposals. Saint-Simon thought that the liberal system could be improved if it were combined with a large-scale employment programme, such as could be provided, for example, by public utility works like the construction of canals joining the seas and oceans. The moderate claims he voiced under the exhilarating effects of the early stages of the industrial revolution did indeed allow for the increasing extension of public planning at the expense of free competition. His disciples were more radical. Sobered by the crude realities of the competitive struggle, they wanted to nationalise the means of production. The production plans submitted by *entrepreneurs* would be co-ordinated by the central banks and the necessary credits granted accordingly, so that credit policy would become an instrument of state planning. Fourier, too, sought to maintain and even promote competition, directing it, however, along channels that served the needs of society. Once competition is thus approved on principle, inequality has been recognised. The Saint-Simonians placed their new social hierarchy under the banner ' From each according to his capacity, to each according to his performance '. Fourier detached these concepts from their strictly economic context and applied this hierarchical principle to all spheres of life : every one can distinguish himself in some field or other and draw a certain spiritual or material advantage, for every talent and endeavour is of some benefit to society. The great mistake in all previous social orders was—to his mind—that human faculties were curbed, suppressed and diverted into false channels. Fourier also recognised and accepted private property : the difference between ownership of the means of production and other forms of property had little significance for him, for he ignored technical progress and was concerned in his proposals only with agriculture and the artisan. But while recognising the desire for profit as legitimate, he proposed to prevent property from becoming the dominant factor by applying the principle of co-operative enterprise, the proceeds of which were to be distributed among the labourers strictly according to their performance and their share in investment. His proposed reform of the right of succession was another means to the same end. Thus he hoped to achieve an approximation to equality among all members of society.

This picture of the future closely resembles that sketched by Owen, though the latter recognises only collective ownership and, furthermore, takes into consideration technical progress. In his blue-print for the New Lanark model factory, industry and agriculture were to be combined. From the political point of view, his equalitarian seniority scale occupies an intermediary position between the hierarchical society of the Saint-Simonians and the direct democracy proposed by Babeuf.

IN all early socialist theories, new emphasis is placed on education It was to be without exception one of the responsibilities of the community, in some cases (Fourier and Owen) exclusively and absolutely so, while in others (Babeuf, Cabet, Weitling), the parents were to be allowed some say up to a certain age limit. The function of education is envisaged differently, according to the different general attitude of the writer. In Babeuf's writings we find the characteristic order of precedence : physical training, fostering of ' kindness and vigour of heart ', and intellectual development, and the deliberate exclusion of all speculative sciences. Strongly influenced by Rousseau, his brand of education has one single purpose, to form good citizens. In sharp opposition to this, Fourier disavows such conditioning. According to him, the only purpose of education is to develop human individuality, to foster the particular talents with which a person is endowed by nature, and not to cripple them. Owen and the Saint-Simonians adopted an intermediary position. Owen saw in the shaping of man's environment— he is the first environmentalist—the proper means for counteracting negative impulses ; all-round practical training for all jobs required by the community enables all members of a society to be fully integrated into it. The Saint-Simonians, on the other hand, denied such a possibility in view of the continuous advance of specialisation and division of labour and were content with providing the young with moral education, a suitable professional training, and a general theoretical education, to counteract the crippling effects on the personality of specialisation. The relationship between the sexes was also deemed due for reform. Apart from the bold theses advanced by Fourier on group marriage, free love appears to be, among early socialists, the most popular substitute for the usual indissoluble or barely dissoluble marriage.

This picture of the future social order should be completed by a glance at the criminal law. The early socialists were conscious of the fact that criminal law and penal practices are the real yardstick of freedom under any social order. The Saint-Simonians believed that in the future the court itself would show a high degree of sympathy for those found guilty, so that punishment would become a means of healing, a paternal educational measure, rather than an act of retribution. Fourier, Owen, and Weitling wanted no criminal law at all, although the last two were prepared to substitute ' hospitals for the physically, mentally, and morally ill '. Weitling makes it quite clear, however, that this would mean a formal change only, and that criminal law would continue to exist under a different name. Anyway, we should not take too seriously the far-reaching rejection of criminal law by the early socialists. Every revolutionary theory tends to perfectionism; its advocates want more than a gradual improvement in human relations ; they want a radical one. Therefore they often overestimate the importance of new institutions until experience shows their weaknesses and flaws.

Even this short survey of the different proposals for a new social order shows that the early socialists took seriously the problem of individual freedom. The experience of the French revolution and an examination of his own political tactics convinced Babeuf that freedom threatened the new social order. Therefore, he had to devise preventive measures for the revolutionary period. Among these are to be found concentration camps for political opponents and the sealing of the national frontiers. Furthermore, the resulting social order itself had to be protected from further revolution. On the other hand, Babeuf was too deeply influenced by the libertarian elements in the French revolution to allow such considerations to lead him on to total rejection of the doctrine of liberty, and he worked out certain compromises. Freedom of speech was to be preserved in some sort of popular assembly, without prejudice to the principle of equality or to the sovereignty of the people. Such freedom of speech would be the more harmless since no decisions could be taken in these assemblies. Apart from this, individual freedom would be limited by the strictest equality. Everything would be organised by the state, there would be no private fields of activity, or, as Buonarroti puts it, ' In the new social order the state takes charge of the individual at birth and abandons him only when he is dead '. The only alternative, though scarcely a practicable one, would be for all young people, upon completion of their education and before enrolment as adult citizens, to be given instruction in the nature of the social contract and the rights and duties it implies. They would then be asked whether they were willing to be part of that society. Whoever answered no would be exiled and sent over the frontier with food provisions.

Contrary to Babeuf, Fourier approves of unrestricted human freedom. No other thinker advocated more energetically than he the free development of the personality and its immense potentialities. He took this for granted because in his extreme theoretical radicalism he considered man to be good, evil being not a human characteristic but an outcome of the shortcomings of previous social systems. It was this impressive and splendid, though dubious conception, which makes Fourier one of those great innovators who soar above traditional judgments and prejudices and open new horizons which must always remain closed to the sceptic. Fourier wanted to solve the problem of freedom with his knowledge of human nature, with his many brilliant but often bizarre projects : even daily work was to be performed with joy—an understanding of the psychology of labour which is far ahead of its time—thus yielding unprecedented increases in productivity ; the primary requisites for this were pleasant and beautiful places of work and frequent changes of occupation. The full expression of individuality would thus be to the advantage of society ; freedom and order were not incompatible. On closer analysis, however, his theory shows that he did not consider all human impulses as equal. He uses an ingenious steering mechanism, operated largely by social respect, to avoid the conflicts which might be created by the unchecked yielding to impulse. This does not give a new answer to the age-old conflict of interests between the individual and society : he has, however, by discarding force, refined it. Between the solutions proposed by Fourier and Babeuf stand those of the other early socialists : Cabet and the Saint-Simonians are rather nearer to Babeuf, Saint-Simon and Weitling are more akin to Fourier. Combining elements of these proposed solutions, Owen suggested that the citizen should be obliged to work till the age of thirty, and thereafter be completely free.

ALL these philosophies, apparently so divergent, have one point in common : the change they make in the concept of freedom : it no longer means that the individual determines his own fate ; but that he has a right to participate in the exercise of a collective decision. This follows logically from the assumption that the decisive factor in the new social order is no longer the individual but the community. This also explains why ' fraternity ' became the dominant idea. The conflict of individual interests characteristic of liberalism is eliminated, for the community takes over the regulation of all the vital tasks ; relations between members of the community therefore become more harmonious. The drawback, admittedly, is that personal responsibility disappears along with the freedom of the individual to choose. The early socialists sought the way out of this difficulty in two directions : for personal responsibility they substituted education in conciousness of responsibility to the community, and just as, in the individualist system, the lack of responsibility brings disadvantages to the individual, so in the new social order the lack of conscious responsibility to the community would be harmful to the individual, in so far as it would lead indirectly to the disintegration of society. It appears, however, to be completely inadequate to place the issue on this subjective factor alone, since the community has the practical possibility of evading such a consequence by the correct disposition of the abilities of all its members ; the way in which this is done is a subsidiary matter. It is of little consequence whether a personal interest in a bigger share in the proceeds of production is created by competition, by free choice or education, or by legal sanctions. But even if the right of participation in collective decisions were to become the primary meaning of freedom, the question still remains whether the individual has freedom as against the community. From this question follows a second one : will not the individual demand the return of his freedom to decide? These two questions would be considered inadmissible in a consistently conceived theory. The second one, because the solution proposed to the eternal problem of how human beings should live together was thought to be, if not perfect, then at least better than those already known. The first question was inadmissible because there is no need for arbitrary individual freedom in a brotherly community. Nevertheless, some attention was paid to this need ; did this mean that the theory in question had not been pushed to its logical development, or that a tactical concession had been made to the individualistic propensities of that time? Neither of these explanations is satisfactory. Since all these thinkers wished to go over directly from the liberal regime to the one which they contemplated, individual freedom would appear to be no more than a temporary solution, until the communal life made the right of being different from others no longer necessary. The idea underlying this conception can be found in Fourier's theory. The free development of the personality, the full play of impulse, destroys the personality. The individual becomes a bundle of faculties and functions, but no longer an independent being. He reacts to external stimuli—and this was precisely the point of departure of the social mechanism, as Fourier sees it—but he no longer settles any conflicts. He does not rise above himself, gives no interest priority over any other, or concentrate on the attainment of an aim. Such men are not dangerous. But if in spite of his education he were again to become independent, this would immediately become obvious, since all social relations are open, and remedies could be found.

IN the *Communist Manifesto*, Marx and Engels dealt at length with their predecessors, although in a manner which clearly reveals due respect for political and tactical considerations. Thus they make no mention of Weitling, whom in 1846 they had turned down as leader of the German communist movement ; and devote only a marginal comment to Cabet, who at the time was preparing to found a communist settlement in the United States. Their attitude towards Babouvism was rather ambivalent. Babeuf's writings were described as part of that literature which ' in all great modern revolutions has voiced the demands of the proletariat ', and given no further consideration. In fact they are included anonymously in the following paragraph, as part of the revolutionary literature of the first proletarian movements, which are by their nature necessarily reactionary, preaching ' universal asceticism and a crude equalitarianism '. The explanation of this peculiar indulgence was that Babeuf's followers, on account of their revolutionary drive, were most important allies. On the other hand, the Saint-Simonians, Fourierists and Owenites, with their affirmation of a peaceful transition to a new social order, were considered political opponents and as such to be bitterly attacked ; this did not mean that those elements in their conception of the new order with which Marx and Engels agreed had to be set out, particularly since in any case they would be of interest only after the triumph of the revolution. Such agreement is to be found primarily in the ten transitional measures proposed in the *Manifesto*, those ' despotic inroads upon the rights of property and . . . bourgeois methods of production ', which apply to the most advanced countries. The abolition of the right of inheritance, the centralisation of credit in the hands of the state by means of a national bank with state capital and an exclusive monopoly, belong to the Saint-Simonian school of thought ; the organisation of industrial armies especially for agriculture to Fourierism ; 'agriculture and industry to work hand in hand ', so by degrees obliterating the distinction between town and country, as well as the combination of education and material production, to Owenism.

It is even more significant that the " positive precepts ' of the early socialists for the new society, for example, elimination of the contradiction between town and country, of the family, of private profit, of wage labour, the proclamation of social harmony, the transformation of the State into a mere managing authority for production, are not in fact described as incorrect : all that is said of them is that, because class contradictions were not yet fully developed at the time they were written, they still had a purely utopian character. From this to Engels' later statement that these thinkers ' brilliantly anticipated countless things ', which he and Marx had now scientifically proved to be correct, was only one step, and in fact we can both build up a very clear picture of the total concept held by Marx and Engels from their numerous particular statements—mainly from their early writings, but also from their later works—put together like a mosaic, and demonstrate their far-reaching agreement with their predecessors. These were influential, too, in their analysis of the events of the French revolution, especially those of the years after 1793. It is not the *contents* of the blue-print for a new social order drafted by Marx and Engels which is new, but rather, and especially in so far as Marx is concerned, its more profound philosophical elaboration and reasoning.

In contrast to their predecessors, Marx and Engels were not greatly concerned to safeguard individual freedom, not only because they were politicians to a greater extent than the utopians. The materialistic conception of history offers the clue to their attitude : Individual freedom is the ideological foundation of a society based on individualistic principles. But in communist society man would no longer need this because he would be part of the collective, and feel himself as such over and above the fulfilment of his normal obligations towards society.

Marx and Engels were, however, concerned to prevent the misuse of political power. This did not lead them towards accepting ' direct democracy ' (like Babeuf, Cabet, and the Fourierists) ; they occupy a position somewhere in the middle between these thinkers and Weitling who wanted institutional safeguards for the pre-eminent position of ' talents and geniuses '. Marx and Engels wanted to achieve their aim by making provision for the recall of the people's delegates at any time, and by similar safeguards in the structure of public administration. While there was still this close link between Marx, Engels, and the utopian socialists, this gradually vanished among their successors.

Only Bebel made a fairly detailed study of Fourier, whereas Wilhelm Liebknecht wrote a rather superficial essay on Owen. Socialism remained a revolutionary movement but, curiously enough, there was less and less thinking about its more far-reaching aims. The epigones were mortally afraid of being branded 'Utopians' and busied themselves with the materialist conception of history and the theory of revolution.

A number of interesting and highly relevant problems pertaining to the impact of ideas first developed by the 'utopian socialists' arose after the Russian revolution. Not so much perhaps during the very first years after the revolution, when it was not yet clear whether it was merely a transitional stage, the first short-lived phase of the world revolution; but after Stalin's 'socialism in one country' had prevailed, some of the ideas of the 'utopians' became again relevant. This trend became even stronger after Stalin's death and with the increase of self-confidence among Soviet leaders following their successes in the technological and economic field.

It would be idle to speculate whether the utopian conceptions discussed here have been directly taken over; in view of the ban on 'utopian socialism', direct and open reference is out of the question. If, however, these ideas have not been simply taken over but, so to speak, resuscitated, this would on no account diminish the signficance of utopian socialism. On the contrary: It would demonstrate that the utopian socialists had succeeded in elaborating solutions that, however fantastic in detail, were basically of universal validity. Be that as it may, we cannot simply regard our preoccupation with utopian socialism as a mere essay in *Geistesgeschichte*—its legacy still seems to be very much alive.

MARX, ENGELS, AND THE FUTURE SOCIETY

Iring Fetscher

ALTHOUGH both the founders of 'scientific socialism' always declined to give a coherent sketch of the conditions in and pattern of a communist society, since neither wished to be Utopians or prophets anticipating the future, there are enough pointers strewn throughout their works to enable us to build up a more or less complete picture of communism. But in using these excerpts one must give due weight to the *development* of their thought, which, at least until 1848, underwent fundamental changes, as well as to the *context* of their utterances.

It is therefore preferable within the bounds of a short essay to attempt a systematic presentation which gives a relatively full and many-sided conception of their picture of the communist future. Although the various features of a communist society make for one whole and are inter-dependent, we must examine them one by one. The order of analysis is not that of its inherent logical structure : it is chosen on purely didactic grounds. We begin with the well-known thesis of the withering away of the political functions of the state ; turn then to the conditions necessary for this—the abolition of classes and of the division of labour—and then, in the last and most important section of the discussion, to the change in man which affects his attitude to work, his fellow men, and even his relationship to nature. Only then, at the end of our exposition, will the whole become clear and comprehensible.

THE WITHERING AWAY OF THE STATE

Among the definitions of the classless communist society of the future the thesis of ' the withering away of the state ' (Engels) is the best known. It arouses the imagination : it is contrary to ' common sense ' as well as to the Christian doctrine of man's irrevocable sinfulness and his consequent need of rulership. The formulas in which Marx and Engels prophesy the decay, or superfluity, or withering of the state remain the same from 1848, in the *Communist Manifesto*, to 1884, in Engels's *Origin of the Family, Private Property and the State*.

In the Manifesto it runs

> When, in the course of development, class distinctions have disappeared, and all production has been concentrated in the hands of a vast association of the whole nation, the public power will lose its political character. Political power, properly so called, is merely the organised power of one class for oppressing another.

And Engels says

[The classes] will fall as inevitably as they once arose. The state inevitably falls with them. The society which organises production only on the basis of free and equal association of the producers will put the whole state machinery where it will then belong—into the museum of antiquities, next the spinning wheel and the bronze axe.

But, in contrast to the anarchists, Marx and Engels constantly stress that this abolition of the state as an instrument of government would become possible only *after* the eradication of class differences and is therefore the consequence and not the beginning of a successful social revolution. Furthermore, even after the revolution there would also be a ' state ', i.e. a political force which, in the *Critique of the Gotha Programme*, is described as the ' dictatorship of the proletariat '. Only after this political ' transitional period ' can the state really die out.

But even that does not mean that the populace can live together, unorganised, like a herd of animals. Regulations must be made for the control of production and for the education of the coming generation, as well as for other less important questions arising from human social relationships for which those elected by the community must be responsible.

In his *Critique of the Gotha Programme*, Marx also writes : —

The question now arises : what change will the form of the state undergo in communist society ? In other words, what social functions will remain then still in existence analogous to the functions now performed by the state ? This question can only be considered scientifically.

Some indications as to how Marx would answer these questions are to be found in *Capital* where we find the growing importance of accountancy repeatedly stressed. He says in so many words that ' the regulation of working hours and the division of social work amongst the various production groups ' together with the ' accounting ' involved will remain necessary even after the abolition of a capitalistic organisation of society. In the analysis of the profits of enterprise under capitalism Marx draws an interesting distinction between the role of the capitalist as owner of capital, and the role of a capitalist or factory manager in his ' organisational work ' of superintendence and management, which—even under socialism —will be necessary . . . ' all labours, in which many individuals cooperate, necessarily require for the connection and unity of the process one commanding will, and this performs a function which does not refer to fragmentary operations, but to the combined labour of the workshop, in the same way as does that of a director of an orchestra. This is a kind of productive labour which must be performed in every mode of production requiring a combination of labours '.

The same division can also be perceived in state functions : in part they are based on the necessity of repression to favour a privileged class, in part they represent the means ' for performing the common operations arising from the nature of all communities '. Surely Engels had the same thing in mind when he said that ' the government of persons is replaced by the administration of things and the conduct of processes of production '. Neither in Marx nor Engels can one find any information as to how the people, whose lot it is to direct this ' administration of things ', are to be chosen. Nor does it seem possible to deduce from their conception of the democratic pattern of political bodies during the transitional period (the dictatorship of the proletariat) any firm conclusion about the form of social life *after* the ' withering of the political functions of the state '.[1]

One can only say with certainty: (1) Since these functions no longer deal with government, the voting for functionaries can no longer be ' democratic '—for it has lost all political significance. (2) Unless *all* members of society are equally qualified for directional functions (a thing which Marx thought within the bounds of possibility once they enjoyed the uninhibited development which was to be expected), then it will be necessary to *seek out* the *right* individual. The authority which must inevitably reside with the directors of production would, however, be based entirely on professional competence.

The basic thought behind the doctrine of the withering of the political functions of the state is, then, that government will become superfluous the moment there is no longer a privileged class which must defend its interests, if necessary by force, or by the constant threat of force. From this hypothesis it follows that most incentives to individual crime will fade away and furthermore, that, in a communist society, the moral predisposition of mankind will be able to develop freely. Since Marx and Engels were still convinced that the proletarian revolution could be successful only as a ' united action of the leading civilised countries at least ' (*Manifesto*), the foreign policy functions of the state would disappear with the revolution ; and, since they understood nationalism to be an expression of bourgeois hegemony, it seemed to them that the end of the rule of the bourgeoisie would also abolish the incentive to an aggressive nationalist foreign policy.

In proportion as the antagonism between classes within the nation vanishes, the hostility of one nation to another will come to an end (*Manifesto*).

[1] This applies particularly to his discussion of the problem of bureaucracy. This —in its relevant political form—was according to Marx and Engels a specific feature of continental social development and a sign of the weakness of the most populous (the French small-holders) or the economically leading (the Prussian bourgeoisie) classes, and of their inability to rule in their own name. Though Marx hailed the Paris Commune of 1871 as the ' at last discovered pattern ' for the transitional phase between the dictatorship of the bourgeoisie and the final classless society, Engels suggested later that parliamentary democracy might be an appropriate transitional form. Nor is the question one of the method of appointment of the organisers in the stateless society of associated producers which was to mark the end of historical development. Cf. my inaugural address ' Marxismus und Bürokratie ' in *International Review of Social History*, Amsterdam, 1960, vol. 5, pp. 378–399.

CLASS DIFFERENCES AND THE DIVISION OF LABOUR

For Marx and Engels the abolition of social classes was a relatively simple matter. Since they saw the possession or non-possession of the means of production as the deciding feature distinguishing one class from another, this was bound to disappear when means of production were no longer private property. The proletarian revolution would put an end to capitalist class-society just as the bourgeois revolution had put an end to feudal society. This revolution must not, however, be content to replace private property by cooperative property owned by more or less large groups, since these would still retain, in relation to the economy as a whole, the characteristics of a capitalist market economy. Instead, all the means of production should be handed over to and be held as the common property of all members of society.

In a posthumous Ms. ' On the nationalisation of land ', Marx declares categorically :

> to give the soil into the hands of associated labourers, would be to surrender all society to one exclusive class of producers. The nationalisation of land will work a complete change in the relations between labour and capital and finally do away altogether with capitalist production, whether industrial or rural (*Kleine ök. Schriften,* East Berlin, 1955, p. 321).

Only under such conditions can, according to Marx, class privilege and also the state disappear.

> There will no longer exist a government nor a state distinct from society itself ! Agriculture, mining, manufacture, in one word all branches of production will gradually be organised in the most effective manner. *National centralisation of the means of production* will become the natural basis of a society composed of associations of free and equal producers consciously acting upon a common and rational plan (ibid.).

With the simple question of abolishing the class structure of society (taking Marx's definition of class as a basis), there is bound up the much more difficult one of overcoming the division of labour : for originally the division into classes springs from the division of labour. Even after its abolition, there remain essential differences, in the quality of work rendered by various members of the community, in their lives and ways of thinking. Differences in quality that—on the still valid principle of equal rights—lead in practice to inequality. It is true that, in a society where no one is entitled in virtue of property to enjoy the fruits of the labour of others, all who can work must work. But since everyone for the same amount of work has the right to the same amount of consumer goods, while the performance and also the circumstances of the individual will vary, inequality will in fact arise. Equality in the first phase of a communist society (socialism)

> consists in the fact that everything is measured by an *equal measure,* labour. But one man will excel another physically or intellectually and so contribute in the same time more labour, or can labour for a

longer time ; and labour, to serve as a measure, must be defined by its duration or intensity, otherwise it ceases to be a standard measure. This *equal* right is an unequal right for unequal work. It recognises no class differences because every worker ranks as a worker like his fellows, but it tacitly recognises unequal individual endowment, and thus capacities for production, as natural privileges. It is therefore a right of inequality in its content, as in general is every right (*Critique of the Gotha Programme*).

This inequality and injustice originate because the legal point of view comprehends mankind only one-sidedly, only from an abstract viewpoint. This viewpoint is in capitalist commodity society the value of commodities produced ; under socialist assumptions, the quantum (and quality) of labour expended.

This critique of the abstract quality of law still reflects Hegel's conception of its abstract character. But, while Hegel wishes to abolish the abstraction of law in favour of the ' concrete morality of the state ' (wherein every citizen is elevated to and recognised as ' a universal being '), Marx expects that the one-sidedness of the bourgeois legal conception will be overcome only by a higher social-economic formation. The abstractness of law would not be overcome or outbid by a subordinate and rational morality of the state, but by the humanism of a communist society in which there are no masters.

Following straight on from the exposition of factual inequality in the ' first phase of communist society ' (socialism) there comes the famous paragraph :

In a higher phase of communist society, after the tyrannical subordination of individuals according to the distribution of labour and thereby also the distinction between manual and intellectual work, have disappeared, after labour has become not merely a means to live but is in itself the first necessity of living, after the powers of production have also increased and all the springs of cooperative wealth are gushing more freely together with the all-round development of the individual, then and then only can the narrow bourgeois horizon of right be left far behind and society will inscribe on its banner ' From each according to his capacity, to each according to his need '.

This excerpt calls for some explanatory words. What is to be abolished is the ' tyrannical subordination ' to division of labour, not division of labour itself, which is a technical necessity of modern production. But within the framework of this modern industrial division of labour everyone will, nevertheless, be in a position to choose various functions that he can fulfil, and not have to spend his whole life bound to a single task which would hinder the development of his potential capacities. That such a goal was absolutely compatible with industrial development seemed clear to Marx.

In *Misère de la philosophie* (1847) he says:

Ce qui caractérise la division du travail dans *l'atelier automatique*, c'est que le travail y a perdu tout caractère de spécialité. Mais du moment que tout développement spécial cesse, le besoin d'universalité, la tendance vers un développement intégral de l'individu commence à se faire sentir. L'atelier automatique efface les espèces et l'idiotisme du métier.

The same thought—that ' idiotisme du métier ' will disappear for technical reasons—is repeated in *Capital,* where it is said to be ' a matter of life or death ' for large-scale industry to replace the monstrosity of an industrial reserve army (the unemployed) by the absolute availability of men for various kinds of labour, i.e. in place of a mere fragment of a man there must be a *fully developed individual.*

It is reserved for the socialist revolution to liberate what had been nurtured as a tendency in the capitalist womb. Concluding this passage from *Capital,* Marx goes on to demand a planned development of polytechnic and agronomic schools, which had been started here and there even under capitalism.

The antithesis of intellectual and manual work is inextricably bound up with the division of labour. Indeed, in *Die Deutsche Ideologie* (1845–46) it is explicitly stated that ' the division of labour really becomes a division from the moment when a division of manual and intellectual work occurs '. The division between physical and mental work is accorded so high an importance because in time it leads to the non-manual worker taking a ' higher ' position and successfully demanding privileges for himself, while the labourer, on the other hand, becomes duller—and this will lead to the brutalisation and alienation of the workers. There is no enjoyment in sheer unintelligent labour, and it must therefore, more and more, be forcibly imposed. On the other side, intellectual work will become abstract, remote from reality, and lead to the formulation of ' ideologies '—by which are here meant theories which attribute an autonomous existence and power of action to ' consciousness '. According to Marx

From this moment onwards consciousness *can* really flatter itself that it is something other than consciousness of existing practice, that it is *really* conceiving something without conceiving something *real* ; from now on consciousness is in a position to emancipate itself from the world and proceed to the formation of ' pure ' theory, theology, philosophy, ethics, etc.

The abolition of the division of labour means here getting rid of the unfair inequality in apportioning tasks. Obviously Marx is of the opinion that, with all the given difference of circumstance no man (or only a very few men) can be so untalented that he cannot be entrusted with some mental work.

We must leave till the next section a more detailed examination of how, once the division of labour is abolished and there is no longer a difference between intellectual and manual work, work becomes a ' necessity of life ' for everyone, and how the all-round development of the individual is achieved.

With the difference between manual and intellectual work abolished, the difference between town and country will also disappear (*Manifesto*).

But the abolition of the division of labour in both these respects certainly does not mean that everyone can pick and choose as he pleases. There is no free choice : it is rather ' Society that regulates overall production '. Yet precisely for that reason, and through the possibility of educating himself in any chosen branch, it will be possible for a single individual to change to various occupations which at different times fulfil his need for activity. As a member of society everyone is indeed bound to work ; but he is able—within the framework of necessity which arises from the needs of the community—to choose freely. A situation in which socially necessary work attracts no or too few volunteers is, for practical purposes, not envisaged in the Marxian anthropology of a communist society. Furthermore, the amount of work demanded of every able-bodied member of society will be so small that the ' need for a normal quantity of work ', which is characteristic of most people ' in a normal state of health, vigour, activity, skill and craftsmanship ' will be sufficient to enable them to fulfil the necessary tasks.

THE TRANSFORMATION OF MAN

The abolition of the division of labour, the withering away of the state, etc., are all, in the end, only the premises and at the same time the consequence of a change in man himself. This is where we come up against the central complex of ideas analysed by Marx. Everything else is preparatory to this.

Marx posed the problem most clearly in his third thesis on Feuerbach which, written to clarify things for himself, gives us a glimpse into the workshop of his mind.

> The materialistic doctrine concerning the changing of circumstances and education forgets that circumstances are changed by men and that the educator himself must be educated. This doctrine has therefore to divide society into two parts, one of which is superior to society. The coincidence of the changing of circumstances and of human activity or self-changing can only be comprehended and rationally understood as *revolutionary practice.*

It is this thesis that can always be brought into the field against a materialistic vulgarisation of Marx's conceptions—and one which even Engels seems not entirely to have understood. It means that the ' revolutionary practice ' of the proletariat is the decisive action for the realisation of the new society and the new man. In *The German Ideology,* which is contemporaneous with the *Theses on Feuerbach,* Marx plainly states :

> Both for the production on a mass scale of this communist consciousness, and for the success of the cause itself, the alteration of men on a mass scale is necessary . . . because the class which overthrows [the ruling class] can only in a revolution succeed in

ridding itself of all the muck of ages and become fitted to found society anew.

The theory of revolution cannot, therefore, be separated from the theory of communist society : the two make up an indivisible unity.

This being understood, the changing of circumstances coincides with the self-transformation of the revolutionary proletariat, since the one is identical with the other. Their activity consists in their joining together, and in doing so they destroy the power of the minority who oppose them, the property owners. Inasmuch as they become changed people, so changed circumstances arise ; and inasmuch as they create new circumstances so do they become new people.

In communist society, as it gradually emerges from socialism after the revolution has created the necessary conditions (public ownership of all means of production), the next change will be in the relationship of man to work.

Work will become the ' first of life's necessities '. In order to understand this statement by Marx we must take a rapid glance at his anthropology, more especially as it is expounded in the Paris manuscripts of 1844, and as it quite obviously underlies the whole of his work. Work, which must be distinguished in principle from the instinctive production by animals, is the characteristic attribute of the species man. But to work means to transform the surrounding natural world by human intervention.

If work is the characteristic of the human species, then man humanises himself to the degree in which he humanises nature and recognises himself as undertaking such a task. But, according to Marx, as a direful consequence of the division of labour and the divorce between work and ownership, society produces a blind and fateful relationship which rules inexorably over the destiny of everyone. Human relationships are transformed into ' things ' and ' connections between things ' : as ' Capital ' or ' Money ' they are turned into fetishes.

Stark necessity now forces the proletarians to form themselves into a revolutionary fighting union and this fighting union represents, as we have seen, the ' identical subject-object ' of History. In it and through it both man and society are freed from the fetters of alienation and from dependence on the blind forces of destiny. Only after this has happened can work again be acclaimed as the activity peculiar to the human species and felt as a need.

In the *Grundrisse* it is explicitly stated that at present work is indeed ' repulsive, forced labour ', but under communism objective and subjective conditions must be created to make labour *attractive,* the self-realisation of the individual—which nevertheless does not mean ' that it is just a joke, just amusement, as Fourier so naïvely conceives it '. As an example of such ' serious ' work which is nevertheless ' attractive ', Marx cites the task of composing which calls for the ' damndest seriousness and the most intense application '. Against this and similar remarks by Marx, from which one can conclude that he believes in a total transformation in the character of work and the attitude of men to work, it is expressly stated in the third volume of *Capital* that ' the realm of freedom does not commence until the point is passed where labour under the compulsion of necessity and of external utility is required '. In connection with this Marx emphasises that ' freedom in this field [in the production of necessary consumer goods and the means of this production] cannot consist of anything else but of the fact that socialised man, the associated producers, regulate their interchange with nature rationally, bringing it under their common control instead of being ruled by it as by some blind power '.

Freedom, therefore, comes to the associated producers only in their capacity as associated producers, directing the economic process in planned fashion and no longer at the mercy of its characteristic laws.

' But it always remains a realm of necessity ', Marx adds, obviously because here there is a ' must ', since the work required to cover all needs simply cannot be avoided. ' Beyond it begins that development of human power which is its own end, the true realm of freedom which, however, can flourish only upon that realm of necessity as its basis. The shortening of the working day is its fundamental premiss.'

From this declaration in *Capital* one might infer that the later Marx had renounced his daring speculations and was content with the lesser task of creating more leisure for the workers. But it would be misleading to draw this contrast, for it does not conform to Marx's dialectic thought. Here again a passage from the *Grundrisse,* which in date comes between his main economic work and his youthful philosophical writings, can be of help. Here Marx writes, on a piece of paper dated March 1858, ' The saving of working time is the same as the expansion of free time, i.e. time for the full development of the individual, which itself in turn as the greatest productive power reacts on the productive power of labour. . . . It goes without saying that direct working time in itself does not remain the abstract antithesis of free time. . . . Free time—which is time for leisure as well as time for higher activities—has transformed its owner into a different subject, and as a different subject he then steps into the direct production process '.

But that means, with a shortening of working hours, man will be given the opportunity to transform himself into an evermore scientific person ; i.e. one who works with full consciousness of the meaning of his activity. Through this transformation of the subject, the ' abstract antithesis ' of working time and free time will increasingly disappear until at last work—necessary work of course—will be acclaimed as the free employment of a man's highest potentialities.

Looked at thus, the statement in *Capital* is no renunciation in principle of the earlier conception, but purely a pointer to the first objective on the way to the realisation of the final phase of communist society. Marx should not therefore be understood as finding voluntary and pleasurable activity only in ' free ' time, that is, time taken up with ' the development of human powers as an end in itself ', or work as an evil to be reduced to a minimum and, so far as possible, shared out equally.

Hand in hand with the change in attitude to work, man's behaviour to his fellow men changes. In a capitalist society, to produce is for everyone only a matter of self interest—the labourer to get a living wage, the manufacturer to use his capital. Therefore for every man other men are merely a means to his own ends. At the same time everyone finds it in his interest to pretend to other people that he is working only for their good. Manufacturers and workers therefore produce neither for the sake of their fellow creatures nor for society. But things should be quite different in a 'human society', the communist society as Marx conceives it.

This altered attitude to one's fellow men means also another attitude to mankind as a whole. This no longer appears as an antithesis—rather the whole duality of individual-species falls to the ground. In *National Economy and Philosophy* Marx emphasised that we must avoid regarding society in the abstract as in opposition to the individual. The individual is a social being and in that sense is society. In order to express this unity of the individual and the community within a communist society, Marx liked to call into play the ambiguity of the word ' *Gemeinwesen* '. ' Communal being ' may denote both a single being or the community which he creates in association with others.

The most radical philosophical formulation of the meaning of communism is to be found in the Paris manuscripts of 1844. There Marx distinguishes first an ' early crude communism ', which maintains a purely negative attitude to established society, and then declares that communism, as the positive abolition of private property, means the resurrection of man as a social, i.e. human being. As perfect naturalism-humanism, it offers the true resolution of the conflict between man and nature, between man and man, freedom and necessity, the individual and the species. It is the conscious solution of the riddle of history.

Present-day Soviet Marxists do not care to be reminded of this metaphysical passage in Marx, and seek to belittle it as a bit of left-over Hegelianism. In fact it shows, as hardly any other utterance of Marx does, what philosophic claim lay behind his theory of history and what epochal importance was to be given to the final phase of communism. Even if nowadays the formula is denied, the claim remains.

A few pages further on Marx adds, ' Society [i.e. human or communist] is the perfected essential unity of Man and Nature, the true resurrection of Nature, the realised naturalisation of man, and the realised humanisation of nature '.

According to this thesis of Marx, in human society nature becomes humanised at the same time as man becomes naturalised. This means that his humanity has become for him the whole of nature ; nature is no longer alien to him but has become, through human activity and investigation, something intimate and close. Whether one should read into this formula that Nature only finds her realisation in and through a human (communist) society must remain a moot point. We should have, in that case, to deal in fact with a sort of naturalistic transposition of the

Hegelian system. While, for Hegel, the divine *logos* which in nature is alienated is liberated by nature's human thought to become its true self and is ' resurrected ', Marx's nature experiences its resurrection through the transformation of nature into a human society that has, by its conscious activity, transformed itself.

It can scarcely be denied that Marx's critique of the alienated capitalist world makes a good starting point to evaluate his image of what man and society should be. But this normative picture of man was never consciously drawn by Marx, though he assumed it as a positive starting point. Instead, he expected the liberation and ' resurrection ' of man not through a moral effort but through a political one—the revolution. In the perfect post-revolutionary society moral efforts would no longer be required, since the existence and behaviour of every individual would coincide with the expectations and desires of all. It is therefore wrong to praise Marx for the lofty ethos of his communist humanity or to criticise him for the exaggerated moral demands he makes on it.

So long as there is still need of ' morality ' to enable men to live together there will be tension between the natural instincts and impulses of the individual and the conditions of a secure existence for all. Once this tension ceases, once it disappears as man and nature become one, these men will again become, in an extra-moral or post-moral sense, ' good '—as once, according to Rousseau, they were innocent in a pre-moral state.

Friedrich Engels, who had less understanding for the higher flights of philosophical speculation, later described the development towards communism as the victory of the eternal components of human morality. Out of the varying historical and distinctive class moralities there would remain what was common to every class and age. Along this trail opened by Engels there have been further theoretical advances. Since Marx only a few thinkers have given further thought to his humanistic hopes of a good society and a society of good men, though that is what the orthodox Soviet Marxists invoke when claiming to have gone farthest along the way towards the final phase of communist society.

THE PARTY AND THE STATE

Leonard Schapiro

THE relationship between the party, or more accurately the professional apparatus of the party, and the administrative institutions of the state has never ceased to be one of the most complicated problems of Soviet political life. It is all quite simple in theory, and the theory has been re-stated again and again over the past forty years, but unfortunately, in Soviet society perhaps even more than in most other political systems, theory and practice tend widely to diverge. The theory is that the party should be the leader and inspirer of effort, the carrier of the national policy, the nerve system of the whole body politic, but yet at the same time it should not actually attempt to replace the activity of the corresponding administrative organ of the Soviet pyramid. Put in simple terms, it should always be ready to tell other people how to do the job, but should not attempt to do the job itself. In practice, this division of functions has proved quite impossible to maintain over more than forty years. Indeed it is probably, with the best will in the world, quite unworkable to maintain in being an administration which is liable to be held responsible for all its actions but which at the same time has no influence over the policy which governs that administration. It is incidentally because of this unworkability that the British system strictly requires the political head alone of an administrative department to take the responsibility for the errors of his permanent subordinates. In the Soviet Union the party and the government continuously find themselves in this conflict : if the party official who is in charge of the local party nucleus—primary organisation or district committee, for example—contents himself with organising a few compulsory meetings on Marxism-Leninism for a bored audience to attend, then he will very soon find himself blamed for any shortcomings in plan fulfilment, housing or the like, of which the local Soviet or industrial unit is supposed to have been guilty ; if, on the other hand, he takes over the running of the job with zeal, and interferes at every step, the life of the factory director or local Soviet executive committee chairman becomes impossible and efficiency suffers. Of course in practice the situation is not always as critical as this, and some kind of symbiosis is worked out in many cases—with that genius for accommodating themselves to government inefficiency which has characterised the Russians for centuries. However the problem persists, and there has been no period in Soviet history when it has not been the subject of discussion. Looking almost at random through the general periodical literature which I read in the course of my work, I can find without any difficulty reflections of this problem. Here, for example, is a secretary of a district party committee writing in his diary :

> Looking at it from the outside you would never make out what I am—the secretary of the party committee or the chairman of the Ispolkom [Soviet executive committee] or an employee of the Sovnarkhoz? Really, I am a kind of multiple tool! Of course one has to take part in economic affairs, but surely there ought to be a difference in the approach, in the style of work of a district committee and a district soviet, of a district committee and a factory, of a district committee and a sovnarkhoz? But somehow or other the boundary lines have disappeared.[1]

The rest of the diary is a complaint that the author is required to do everyone's job. One can easily imagine the factory director's or the Ispolkom chairman's version of the situation!

Of course it is natural enough that as educational standards rise, technical ability develops and confidence increases, the great majority of men and women who, whether members of the party or not, actually keep Soviet production going should increasingly resent interference by the party professional. This is reflected for example in a recently published pamphlet which takes the form of an attack on the views of Veblen and Stuart Chase for (so it is said) urging the liberation of the American technicians from the control of the American business man. Since the Soviet reader is not presumably very interested in the views of American sociologists on the management of American business, it is not unreasonable to suppose that the purpose of this pamphlet is to reprove those who have been urging that the technicians should be allowed to take over control from the Soviet ' business men '—the party apparatus. Indeed, the pamphlet ends with an assertion that ' the salvation of mankind does not lie in establishing the supremacy of the " managers " or organisers as the ideologists of the bourgeoisie assert, but in the victory of communism, the road to which is illuminated by Marxist-Leninist theory '.[2]

The trouble is precisely that Marxist-Leninist theory fails to provide any illumination on the solution of this particular problem. It is, I think, fair to say that the present party leader, Khrushchev, has been making steady efforts to keep the boundaries between party and state more distinct than at any time before in Soviet history. He has tried to diminish rivalry between the two administrations by insisting on technical training for the party officials. Or, to take another example, his recent economic reorganisation, which gives more power of decision, at any rate in the administrative sphere, to the regional economic councils, also had the result of creating something of a more logical

---

[1] M. Ivashechkin, ' Thinking Aloud. The Diary of a District Party Committee Secretary ', *Nash Sovremmenik*, No. 3, 1961, p. 5.
[2] G. V. Osipov, *What is ' Technocracy '?*, Moscow, 1960.

division of function between the local party secretary and the council of national economy because the party secretary retains the function of safeguarding national or All-Union policy from encroachments by local interests. Although it is customary to deride his theoretical abilities, he has at any rate evolved a theory on the ' withering away of the state ' which is a good deal more logical, on paper, than Stalin's. This theory makes a clear distinction for the purposes of ' withering away ' between ' party ' and ' state '. As communism approaches so the state machinery will progressively wither away in the sense that ' public organisations ' will gradually take upon themselves. functions hitherto performed by state organisations. The state apparatus, including government departments and the courts, will gradually diminish in size as more and more of its functions are handed over. Indeed, in the past year or two there has been an actual reduction in the number of state organs, in the sense that central ministries have been abolished and their functions taken over by republican ministries, while some of the functions of the regular courts and police have been taken over by communal organisations. In this process, as Khrushchev was careful to point out, the role of the party, so far from diminishing, must increase. It is quite clear that the party is intended to be the guiding element in this increased public activity, since to allow the emergence of communal or public activity which was not controlled by the party would be to allow the emergence of rival institutions. But this in turn would lead to the beginning of the end of communist monopoly of control, which is after all the linchpin of the Soviet system. Khrushchev's explanation, however, was rather more sententious :

> The party has a stronger foundation than government organs. It owes its origin and existence to something other than some kind of obligations of a legislative nature. Its development was called forth by circumstances which flow from people's political views, that is to say, from circumstances of a moral nature. And mankind will always need some moral factors.[3]

NOW all this really makes very little sense in terms of practical politics. Indeed, the withering away of the state to which Marx and Engels subscribed must be regarded as one of those wildly Utopian flights of fancy from which neither of these thinkers was ever immune. Engels' famous phrase that the administration of things replaces the government of men is on analysis quite without meaning—and especially so in a large modern state. Experience of English local government, for example, would amply confirm the fact that even the humble parish meeting could scarcely run without some ' government of men ', that is to say, by relying solely on the harmonious agreement of all its members without any compulsion or vote—which is what is implied in ' administration of things '. The experience of the Soviet

[3] Interview with the foreign editor of *The Times*, *Pravda*, 16 February 1958.

Union does not suggest that even the tentative experiment in withering away of the last few years has been a success. Already the problem of dealing with crime has led the Soviet authorities to return to the old-fashioned method of shooting in place of the new method of communal persuasion. In other respects, too, the government machine, which was reduced in size after 1957, has once again begun to grow. The All-Union Council of Ministers has substantially increased in power, while at the level of the economic regions created in 1957 it has been found necessary to interpose centralised co-ordinating government councils. The new draft programme of the party stresses the need for constant *state* as well as public control.

Indeed, if one contrasts the new programme as published in draft on 30 July with some of the theoretical discussions on the relations of party and state which have preceded it, it looks very much as if there may have been second thoughts on the subject of withering away. In May of this year the official organ of the Central Committee published an article on the subject of the state under communism by P. Romashkin.[4] Since Romashkin is chairman of the Legal Institute of the Academy of Sciences and has for some time past been the spokesman of the official view on legal matters, whose function seems to have been to keep the more liberal-minded lawyers from going off the rails, his views can be taken as an expression of official opinion, or at any rate of Khrushchev's opinion at the time. Indeed, Romashkin is very careful to base his views squarely on Khrushchev's new theory of the withering away of the state. He stresses first the fact that as communism approaches, so the functions of state organisations will gradually pass to public organisations. At the same time Romashkin emphasises that the role of the party during this transition period will increase in importance. He goes rather further than Khrushchev in one respect, suggesting that as communism approaches, so the various forms of organisation, namely soviets, trade unions, and the party, will fuse into one organisation. Since it may be presumed that in any such new composite organisation the party would retain its predominant role, this novel gloss on Khrushchev's theory may be regarded as an improved method of transition to a state of affairs when the country will be run frankly and openly by the party apparatus alone. Romashkin is obviously also concerned to deal with the question, which no doubt has arisen in some minds, as to why the party itself should not eventually wither away. He firmly pours cold water on any such illusions. This is what he says:

> The question is fully relevant : what will be the fate of our party after the construction of communism? The second congress of the Comintern in its resolution on the role of the communist party in the proletarian revolution noted the fact that after communism had ceased to be the object of struggle, the communist party will dissolve fully in the working class and the entire working class will

4 P. Romashkin, ' Sotsialisticheskoe gosudarstvo i kommunisticheskoe samoupravlenie ', *Partiinaya Zhizn*, No. 9, May 1961.

become communist. This is a logical development. The party is striving for such a growth of the communist consciousness of members of society as will raise all to the level of the vanguard. However, when talking about the fate of the party we cannot ignore the fact that to raise the level of consciousness of all members of society to the level of the vanguard is a task which is not less difficult, but more difficult than the task of creating the technical and material basis of communism. In order that the consciousness of the whole people should become communist a considerable period of time will be required. Therefore the party will continue for long to exist and to work, to direct and to co-ordinate the activity of the disjointed system of organisations of communist self-government, and the party must be strengthened in every way. Moreover, until the historic task of constructing communism has been accomplished, it must be said of the Soviet state as well that it must not be weakened. Every weakening of the socialist state in contemporary conditions entails serious dangers for communism and for the task of peace.

Romashkin does not explain how the state should both wither away as communism approaches, and not be allowed to weaken. I fear, moreover, that Marx and Engels might raise an eyebrow at the suggestion that for the working class to attain communist consciousness will require longer than for the material bases of communism to be constructed. However, what is involved is not so much theory as the hard problem of keeping a party ensconced in its monopoly of power long after society has attained a technical competence and a standard of living which are inconsistent with this form of tutelage. The draft of the party programme seems to suggest that the withering-away theory in its original form is now considered too dangerous—perhaps because it gave rise to the kind of hopes that Romashkin was concerned to dash, i.e., that the party would wither away ; or because it encouraged the kind of critics inside the Soviet Union that Osipov was intending to answer when polemicising with the seemingly irrelevant theories of Veblen and Stuart Chase.

The draft programme is very cautious on the subject of withering away. While paying lip-service to the enhanced importance of public organisations, it stresses that the functions of the soviets, the trade unions, and the courts, so far from being reduced are to be increased, and that state control as well as public control is to be increased. It is true that at the same time the draft stresses the need for improving and enlarging democratic principles in the government of the soviets and in the organisation of the trade unions. Since resolutions of this nature have been repeated throughout Soviet history since 1920, it can only be hoped that the intention this time is to carry them out. The historian, however, cannot help but recall the re-iterated claims in the past, from Lenin's time onwards, that the Soviet system was already then the most democratic in the world. Like Romashkin, the draft programme envisages an eventual fusion under communism of all organisations such as soviets, trade unions, co-operatives, etc., into one united form of communist self-government. But it adds the following warning, which is strangely reminiscent of the way in which Stalin in his time postponed the withering away of the state to the final victory of communism on a world scale :

> Historical development inevitably leads to the withering away of the state. For the complete withering away of the state it will be necessary to create not only internal conditions—the construction of a developed communist society—but also external conditions—the definitive resolution of the contradictions between communism and capitalism in the international arena in favour of communism.

Meanwhile the programme stresses that during the period of constructing communism, the role of the party in guiding state and public organisations will continue to increase.

WE are thus back in the more sober world of party-state relations. The wilder flights of theoretical fancy are conveniently postponed, and the practical problem of the relationship between party and state remains, as hitherto, unresolved. To attempt a forecast of the future course of development of this relationship is to come back to the realm of politics and to leave the realm of nineteenth-century Utopianism, and perhaps one should add twentieth-century cynicism. That the party, always in the sense of the party apparatus, will strive to preserve its monopoly of power for as long as it can need hardly be doubted. This means that it will use every endeavour, as it has done hitherto, to ensure that no institution or organisation of any kind is allowed to emerge which is not ultimately under the control of the party apparatus through the normal channel of central secretariat—local network of secretaries—local party committee or primary organisation. Whether the party will succeed in preserving this monopoly is not a question of communist or other theory, but a question of the relationship of social forces. With every improvement in the Soviet Union in the standard of living, technical achievement and education, the pressure for independence must inevitably grow. The party is fully aware of this. It has used the most ingenious methods to counter this pressure and to try to keep it under its own control. The built-in apparatus, the experience, the vested interest of thousands of officials, the lack of any traditions of self-government under Soviet rule—all represent enormous advantages on the side of the party. However, the fact is becoming more and more apparent that to exclude the entire active elements of the country from participation in policy-making is anachronistic and at times patently unworkable (one has only to think of the state of affairs that was disclosed in January 1961 at the Plenum of the Central Committee). I am not a ' Marxist ', but I find very convincing the central argument of Marx, and especially of Engels, that when the form of a government becomes inconsistent with the social realities of the country governed, it must go. In other words, it must adapt or collapse.

FOREIGN POLICY AND THE TRANSITION TO COMMUNISM

George Brinkley

THE newly topical question of the transition to communism is most frequently dealt with in terms of Soviet internal affairs and the withering away of the state. Yet the international implications are equally significant, and indeed success in achieving foreign policy goals appears to be a prerequisite to the completion of the transition. There is, of course, an inevitable link between internal developments and foreign policies for all countries, but this is especially notable in the case of the Soviet Union. It has always been so, and the discussion of the building of full communism once again confirms the bond between these two aspects of policy.

In his theory of imperialism Lenin indicated that the class struggle had taken on a more definitely international character because of the development of interlocking capitalist controls and the expansion of European domination to much of the rest of the world. In this context two things were assigned particular significance : the special role of Russia in shaping the destiny of the world, and the emergence of a world-wide mass of discontented and exploited peoples in the colonial and semi-colonial areas who would constitute an enormous 'external' ally of the proletariat. As the weak link in the capitalist chain binding the world, Russia had both a more revolutionary proletariat, which had not been bribed by the higher wages made possible in the West by imperialist super-profits, and a greater kinship in its own present character with the underdeveloped colonial lands.

The grave which capitalism was digging for itself through imperialism, however, would not serve its purpose unless the capitalists could be pushed into it. With cartels and colonies the capitalists could, at least for a time, stave off the revolution and corrupt their own proletariats with slightly higher standards of living. The instrument necessary to arouse the proletariat, to take advantage of the discontent throughout the world, and to organise the actual seizure of power was, of course, the Communist Party, which in Lenin's strategy became a primary prerequisite of success. The combination of these ideas provided the ideological foundations of the Bolshevik march to power in Russia in 1917, but the subsequent failure of the revolution to spread as predicted then created a certain anomaly. This circumstance, which was a major factor in shaping later Bolshevik policies, did not, however, change the basis of the communist outlook.

As Lenin subsequently argued, the preservation of the Soviet state now had higher priority than other considerations.[1] This was necessary because only by retaining power in Russia and then building up that power as the citadel of the world revolution could the party achieve its ultimate goal and maintain the legitimacy of the revolution. Thus, while Lenin idealised the concept of the withering away of the state and the replacement of the army and bureaucracy by the people in arms and at work, he nevertheless gave warning that this ideal could be fully realised only after ' full communism ' had been attained.[2] The latter, he noted, would be possible only when exploitation ' no longer exists in the world ', and until that time the ' special apparatus ' of the state would have to be used as a ' bludgeon ' against all enemies of the revolution.[3]

In accordance with his convictions, Lenin held that a socialist Russia could not co-exist peacefully on any long-term basis with the capitalist world ; war, he said, was inevitable.[4] But the basis for these conclusions did not lie simply in any belligerency on the part of the Soviet state as such, but rather in the nature of capitalism. It was the capitalists, he held, who could not and would not keep the peace and who could be expected to try to destroy the Soviet republic simply because of the threat posed by its very existence. Thus, within this concept, Lenin could then advocate the adoption of policies designed to prolong co-existence as much as possible. Russia, he insisted, had to offer concessions, make peace, trade with the capitalists, and even time its internal developments to accord with external conditions if need be. Meanwhile, however, in the knowledge that peace would be temporary, the Soviet government would play upon differences between capitalist countries, encourage anti-imperialist movements, and whenever a suitable opportunity arose support revolution anywhere in the world to weaken the capitalist camp and undermine its position both at home and abroad.[5] The ' closest union ' between colonial liberation movements and Soviet Russia was to be fostered, while Communist Party units around the world (organised in the Communist International) did everything possible to support the Soviet government and render it ' every possible assistance '.[6]

In this strategy the ultimate aim did not change, but tactics were adapted to the realities of a weak revolutionary centre surrounded by its capitalist enemies. Stalin's basic task and his real contribution was to put into practice the programme laid down by the master. It was Stalin who made the USSR the ' base of the world movement ', the ' centre of international revolution ', and the ' most important factor ' in the ' international emancipation ' of the proletariat everywhere. Stalin, in short,

[1] V. I. Lenin, *Sochineniia*, 3rd ed. (Moscow, 1935), XXII, 199.
[2] Ibid., XXI, 431-32.
[4] Ibid., XXVI, 12.   [3] Ibid., XXIV, 377.
[5] Ibid., pp. 14-23.
[6] Ibid., XXV, 287; see also No. 14 of conditions of admission to the International approved at the 2nd Congress in August 1920.

created the powerful, monolithic vanguard state, the military and political instrument of the party, which not only saved the revolution but gave it a base for further advances.   With this in mind, he could declare that the old idea that bourgeois nationalism alone could liberate oppressed nations was obsolete ; the Soviet state provided ' a powerful and open base for the world revolutionary movement never possessed before and on which it now can rely for support '.[7]   Stalin made this boast long before the Soviet Union was a great power, however, and further advancement could not proceed on a world-wide scale until the base had really been consolidated and made adequate to the task.   Most of Stalin's era, 1928–53, was thus devoted to accomplishing this goal within a relatively weak country isolated by ' capitalist encirclement '.   His was essentially the time of preparation and build-up, although of course he also took advantage of the opportunities for expansion which appeared during and after World War II.

With specific reference to the question of the withering away of the state, Stalin stated flatly that, unless one simply ignored international conditions, no weakening of the state's power would be possible until ' socialism is already victorious in all countries, or in the majority of countries . . . a socialist encirclement exists instead of a capitalist encirclement, . . . there is no more danger of foreign attack, and . . . there is no more need to strengthen the army and the state '.[8]   By way of dialectical logic, Stalin therefore concluded that ' the state will wither away, not as a result of a relaxation of the state power, but as a result of its utmost consolidation '.[9]   Indeed, he based the achievement of full communism so decisively upon a world victory through Soviet power that he even suggested the possibility that the state might have to continue to exist even after the foundations of communism had been laid if there were still enemies threatening Soviet ambitions.[10]

In his later years Stalin himself initiated discussion of a possible modification of certain aspects of policy in view of Soviet successes and new world conditions.   In the year before his death he spoke of ' moving ahead towards communism ' and declared that the combination of the growing strength of the Soviet Union and the mounting crisis within the capitalist camp made the ' inevitable ' war more likely among capitalist powers than between the USSR and a united capitalist bloc.[11]   This reference to the shifting balance of power was significant, for Stalin had demonstrated before that Soviet foreign policy was determined by three basic factors and the relationship among them at any given time.   Drawn from both ideology and power analysis, these factors were : (1) the strength of the Soviet Union, (2) the strength of the world revolutionary

[7] J. Stalin, *Problems of Leninism* (Moscow, 1953), p. 242.
[8] Ibid., p. 793.
[9] Ibid., p. 538.
[10] Ibid., p. 797.
[11] *Pravda*, 3 and 4 October 1952.

movement in general, and (3) the strength of the capitalist countries.[12] A change in any one of these elements in some significant degree would modify the conclusions drawn for policy. In 1953 such a shift was already being indicated.

IT is Khrushchev, of course, who has elaborated upon this change in line, since it was not until after the struggle for power internally had been settled with the rise of a new dictator that such a revaluation could be undertaken on a thorough-going scale. Like his predecessors, Khrushchev illustrates the unity of theory and practice, the correlation of internal and external policies. It is, of course, true that he took advantage of Stalin's unpopularity to introduce his innovations initially within the framework of 'de-Stalinisation', but his contribution maintains the pattern of adapting the heritage to changes. Khrushchev thus carries forward Lenin's concept of communist power as the initiator and source of world victory, and Stalin's justification of internal power on the basis of foreign policy considerations. The continuity suggested here has indeed been repeatedly stressed in Khrushchev's own remarks and in the 1960 Manifesto of the 81 parties, both of which date the beginning of the 'triumph of socialism and communism on a worldwide scale' from the Bolshevik revolution in 1917.[13] It has been emphatically reaffirmed in the new CPSU programme.

However, this is not to say that there are no differences in Khrushchev's policies. On every suitable occasion, Khrushchev declares that Leninism is the 'source of all successes', but at the same time rejects certain assumptions made by Lenin, such as the theory of the inevitability of war and the necessity of violent revolution. He takes over all the advantages and accomplishments of Stalinism and yet denounces certain attributes and ideas of Stalin as no longer suitable, such as 'capitalist encirclement' and the accompanying rigidities in Soviet policy.[14] At the present stage the basic fact behind these modifications is the alleged decisive 'change in the balance of forces in favour of socialism' emphasised by the Moscow conference of 81 Communist Parties in November–December 1960. It is this claim and its implications which more than anything else shape Soviet policy today.

As Khrushchev explained at the 21st Party Congress in 1959, the 'capitalist encirclement no longer exists', and for the first time the USSR can assert definitely that it is 'able to repel any attack by an enemy'.[15] Moreover, it is of decisive significance in the current view that the world is now witnessing numerous 'national liberation revolutions' and 'the breakdown of imperialism' as predicted by Lenin. It is precisely this

[12] J. Stalin, Report to the 15th Party Congress, 1927, cited by Theodore H. von Laue in G. A. Craig and F. Gilbert, eds., *The Diplomats, 1919-1939* (Princeton, 1953), p. 245.

[13] *Pravda*, 6 December 1960.

[14] See Khrushchev's speech to the 20th Party Congress, translated in *New Times*, No. 8, 16 February 1956.

[15] *Pravda*, 28 January 1959.

simultaneous weakening of the capitalist camp, the growth of Soviet power through the development of nuclear weapons and rockets, and the increasing strength of the anti-imperialist world revolution which is said to have profound significance for Soviet foreign policy. These considerations were valid for Lenin and Stalin, too, but it is Khrushchev who must assert and explain the implications. This he has done, notably in his statements on the meaning of peaceful co-existence and in his formulation of the relationship between the transition to communism now announced in the Soviet Union and Soviet foreign policy.

Khrushchev has made it quite clear that the ' new stage in communist construction ' which will involve the withering away of some of the state's functions will ' not at all mean weakening ' the state's power. Most particularly, there will be no lessening of the power of the armed forces and the state security agencies, a point included in the new Party Programme to be adopted at the 22nd Congress, for ' as long as imperialism exists, the economic base giving rise to wars will also remain ', and internal subversion will continue to be a threat. Until there is a complete guarantee ' against the possibility of aggression by the imperialist states ' there can be no relaxation of the struggle, and the police must continue to exercise vigilance against the ' provocational actions and intrigues ' of agents sent into the country by the enemy. These aspects of state power can never wither away until the ' complete triumph of communism ' Khrushchev asserts, or until the capitalist threat to any socialist country has been wholly eliminated.[16]

The basis of peaceful co-existence and of the possibility of a peaceful victory of socialism in other countries is thus not world cooperation today, any more than it was in the past ; it is still power and struggle. In the first place, peaceful co-existence ' does not at all demand that one or another state abandon the system and ideology adopted by it '.[17] Moreover, since Khrushchev himself has cited the seizure of power in the East European satellites to illustrate the point that it is only when the choice is between peaceful surrender and suicidal war that the conversion to ' socialism ' may occur without violence, it goes without saying that ' the greater or lesser degree of intensity which the struggle may assume, the use or the non-use of violence in the transition to socialism, depends upon the resistance of the exploiters '.[18] It is still maintained that ' the exploiting classes will not relinquish power voluntarily '.[19] The confidence that all-out nuclear war can be avoided rests upon the conviction that Soviet military power is capable of deterring Western states from the use of such weapons in their own defence. War is no longer ' fatally inevitable ' because there is a balance of terror, and for a capitalist country to risk it would be suicidal.

16 N. S. Khrushchev, Report to the 21st Party Congress, loc. cit.
17 N. S. Khrushchev, ' On Peaceful Co-existence ', *Foreign Affairs*, Vol. 38, No. 1 (October 1959), p. 4.
18 Report to the 21st Party Congress, loc. cit.
19 Draft of the new Party Programme, *Pravda*, 30 July 1961 (*New York Times*, 1 August 1961).

PREVENTING nuclear war, however, is only one side of the picture. In his significant and revealing speech after the meeting of the Party representatives from 81 countries, Khrushchev added to his discussion of war and co-existence the notable observation that the power of the Soviet Union now enables it to intervene in both local wars and national liberation wars to see that their outcome coincides with the preconceived course of history. As he put it, ' Once it was customary to say that history was working for socialism. . . . Today it is possible to assert that socialism is working for history. . . .' [20] The progress of the USSR in its effort to overtake the United States in economic competition may indeed point to ' the biggest turning point in history ', but Khrushchev does not by any means limit his methods to economics or even to political struggle. He fully intends to support the ' just wars ' which benefit Soviet strategy, and encourages communists everywhere to take the initiative in ' waging liberation struggles '. Such ' revolutionary ' and ' sacred ' wars are ' not only admissible but inevitable ', and in fact he goes so far as to claim that without the growth of Soviet power ' there could have been no question of the abolition of colonialism '. Imperialism and capitalism mean a continuing danger of war, for there will be limited wars even if total war is avoided ; a struggle against an imperialist or capitalist country so-called (especially the major Western powers) is therefore a ' struggle for peace ' ; and, to complete the syllogism, the struggle for peace is thus a ' struggle for communism '.

Thus under the umbrella of Soviet military might, and with the tactical assistance of the foreign aid programme developed since 1954, Khrushchev has served notice that he will use all methods short of all-out nuclear war to win control of the world. In this effort, moreover, he will with notable flexibility seek out and use every possible ally ' no matter if inconsistent, shaky, and unstable ', for every advantage won and every step forward helps ' clear the way for the ultimate movement towards socialism ' on a global scale. If it is a case of communist support for a national independence movement, the Communist Party (with Soviet assistance) will do all in its power to ' influence the prospects of the further development ' of the movement in the direction of socialism, as in the Congo and Cuba. If it is a case of a parliamentary majority won peacefully, the aim will be ' the overthrow of the military bureaucratic machine of the bourgeoisie and creation of a new proletarian state system in parliamentary form '.

This ' general strategic line ' is furthermore one which will employ the apparatus of the international Communist Party more openly and vigorously than at any time since Lenin's day and the establishment of the International. Although no ' International ' as such exists today, the conferences of the Party representatives from an increasingly large number of countries in 1957 and 1960 resolved to act as an organised

[20] Speech delivered 6 January 1961, *Kommunist*, Vol. 37, No. 1 (January 1961), pp. 3-37. All following quotations of Khrushchev are from this speech.

vanguard in support of Soviet foreign policy. The tasks set forth demand greater cohesion and control than ever, despite the fact that there may be different roads to socialism. The ' common aim of the struggle of all communists of the world ' requires a relentless offensive against the twin evils of revisionism and dogmatism, as Khrushchev has reminded both Tito and Mao Tse-tung. ' Solidarity, solidarity, and again solidarity '. Khrushchev intoned, ' such is the law of the international communist movement '. The Party is a great force precisely ' because it is organised ', he declared. Communists the world over ' must synchronise their watches ' and as a ' powerful army ' keep in step with the ' universally acknowledged vanguard ' of international communism in Moscow. When decisions are made, Khrushchev concluded, ' every party will adhere to these decisions in a strict and sacred manner, throughout its activities '. Thus the two instruments of Soviet foreign policy—diplomacy and subversion—will continue to work together.

This is the line of Soviet policy and communist strategy in the era of the transition to communism. Since communism can be fully achieved only when capitalism is destroyed and all major countries are in communist hands, the Leninist elite throughout the world must devote itself to the mastery of ' all forms of struggle—peaceful and non-peaceful, parliamentary and non-parliamentary '. It is in this context that peaceful co-existence ' strengthens the position of the world Socialist system, promotes the growth of its economic might, international prestige and influence among the popular masses . . . facilitates the activities of Communist Parties and other progressive organisations . . . the struggle the people wage against aggressive military blocs . . . (and) helps the national liberation movement to gain success '. Peaceful co-existence is the ' intense economic, political, and ideological struggle ', which, with the aid of military force when expedient, will constitute the ' only way to bring imperialism to heel '. The campaign for disarmament, as a part of this effort, ' is an active struggle against imperialism, for restricting its military potentialities '.

WHILE the goal of full communism thus points a sword at the heart of the non-communist world, it may also turn out to be a two-edged blade. The economic and political foundations of communism will continue to be built internally, as the twenty-year plan in the new Party Programme indicates, and these foundations of strength will certainly have major implications for Soviet foreign policy. Yet it has become a notable feature of Soviet history that each transitional stage leads to another. Stalin completed ' socialism in one country ' by redefining the terms ; it is therefore not entirely impossible that a variety of ' communism in one country ' may emerge in the future.

This certainly would not be the ' fullest ' communism, but it would facilitate a future declaration of the completion of the communist ' foundations ' in the USSR. Moreover, communism in one country, as a face-saving device in case Khrushchev's predictions fail to materialise, would enable the Soviet Union to remain ahead of the other ' socialist ' countries while they were being prepared for closer integration into the Soviet federation. Such a development might have been implied in Khrushchev's interesting comment on the ability of the Central Asian and Caucasian peoples of the USSR to take ' their place in the ranks of the industrially developed regions of the country ' because of the great assistance rendered ' by the more advanced Socialist nations, notably by the Russian nation. . . .' It is even more directly implied in the draft of the new Party Programme, where to Khrushchev's earlier statement that all the socialist countries would enter communism ' more or less simultaneously ' has been added the explanatory phrase : ' within one and the same historical epoch '. During this ' epoch ', it is stated, ' the first country to advance to communism facilitates and accelerates the advance of the entire world socialist system to communism '. This may speed the others' entry into communism, but it certainly leaves the door open for the USSR to get there first. And the Party is solemnly promising that ' the present generation of Soviet people shall live under communism '.

There would, of course, be ample precedent for the ultimate incorporation of the East European satellites into the Soviet federation, which has always been described as potentially a world federation and which absorbed several formerly independent states as recently as 1940. Moreover references (such as those just noted) to the construction of communism under Soviet guidance imply that the building of the pathway into the Union is included. Solidarity and closer ties within the ' Socialist commonwealth ', a theme stressed in the new Programme, have long been emphasised by Khrushchev, who has asserted that with their ' coming closer and closer together ' and establishing a ' common economic base ' they are indeed creating ' the prototype of a new society for all mankind '. At the same time, however, it is also true that actual steps toward the incorporation of new republics would depend to a considerable degree upon international circumstances, quite apart from the theoretical possibility of a phased introduction of communism followed by political amalgamation. Moreover, it remains an article of faith that ' socialism will inevitably take over from capitalism everywhere ', and thus whatever degree of integration the bloc may attain on any basis of timing it would still be only a step along the way. Indeed, even if the entire world were won, there would still have to be another phase during which the various parts of the world socialist federation were prepared under Russian guidance for full communism.

Stubborn barriers remain, but at the same time Soviet policy is apparently geared to the determination not to tolerate such obstacles any longer than necessary, and possibly even to put the claim of decisive power to the test. This does not have to mean a willingness to go to war, especially all-out war, but it does mean a willingness to risk war with greater confidence that it will be the other side which will be reluctant to carry brinkmanship as far as he does.

It remains unlikely that Khrushchev will deliberately bring about a violent shown-down directly with the West, and not only because he says so. He may be very power conscious, but he must also know the odds. His exaggerated claims for the power of the Soviet camp do not conceal the fact that the building of communism still has a long, long way to go in the Soviet Union, much more than the twenty years now being suggested ; that the bloc itself will require considerably more time to consolidate its position before undertaking any aggressive action, especially in view of certain tensions generated by the different approach (to the common end) contemplated in Peking ; that there is no warrant for the assumption of an easy victory ; and that the national liberation movements are not all conforming to Moscow's preconceived image and plans for their use, but rather are demonstrating a will of their own. The profession of confidence in the ability to win without taking the mutually destructive path of nuclear war implies the necessary degree of discretion to maintain the thin line between limited and total engagement. That Khrushchev is willing to make this distinction is indicated by the position taken in the new Programme and by his statement that ' to win time ' is now ' the main thing ' ; but of course whether or not he is capable of the necessary restraint remains to be seen.

EDUCATING THE NEW MAN

S. V. Utechin

THE Soviet educational system is now undergoing a thorough reorganisation in accordance with the law of 24 December 1958.[1] The reform, decreed by the party authorities on Khrushchev's personal initiative, has as its declared aim to eliminate what Khrushchev called ' the divorce of school from life '. This, according to him, had manifested itself in the lack of any preparation at school for future work in industry or agriculture, particularly for manual work. The chief means of remedying this defect were to be ' polytechnical education ' and the combination of schooling with practical productive work. The concept of polytechnical education derives from traditional Marxist ideology. Marx thought that proper education should acquaint young people with the principles of all production processes, and give them practical skills in a number of trades. The educational policy of the communist government in Russia was based on this idea in the 1920s and early thirties, but it was abandoned in the mid-thirties and not revived until 1952. From then on it steadily gained ground in official circles until it was incorporated in the new reform.

According to the 1958 law, the reform of the school system is to be completed by 1964, so that by now the halfway point has been reached. It is thus a suitable moment to survey the situation : the changes so far introduced in the forms and content of education, the difficulties encountered, new problems that have arisen as by-products of the reform itself, and the shift of emphasis that has gradually taken place in the process of implementing the reform—a shift that involves a quite different interpretation of the past defects and present-day tasks of the schools from that originally given by Khrushchev. The draft of the new party programme envisages a reversal of some of the policies so far pursued by Khrushchev in the educational field and it obviously must be taken into account in assessing the prospects of education in Russia.

Compulsory education, according to the reform law, will extend over eight years, from the age of 7 to 15. There is to be a single type of school for this stage throughout the country, the eight-year school of general education comprising four years of primary education and

---

[1] A description of the state of Soviet education on the eve of the reform may be found in N. Dewitt, *Soviet Professional Manpower*; G. S. Counts, *The Challenge of Soviet Education*; A. G. Korol, *Soviet Education for Science and Technology*; S. V. Utechin, ' Education in the USSR ', *Political Quarterly*, Oct.-Dec. 1958; and articles in *Survey*, Nos. 12 and 28; G. Z. F. Bereday et al. (eds.), *The Changing Soviet School*.

four of what is traditionally considered in Russia as the first stage of secondary education ; the eight-year school is thus regarded as an incomplete secondary school. The first four classes may exist as separate primary schools where this is warranted by local conditions —in practice, that is, in small villages (in 1959–60 there were 111,500 such primary schools, with 4·5 million pupils, and 56,600 seven- or eight-year schools with 10·1 million pupils). The present eight-year schools have in most cases been created during the last two years out of the former seven-year incomplete secondary schools, though some of them (exact figures are not available) are former ten-year secondary schools. The tempo of conversion of the seven-year schools is not the same in all Union Republics. In the RSFSR it lags behind the schedule; there are now 8,300 eight-year schools in that republic and over 21,300 seven-year schools are to be converted during the next two years, many of which lack the necessary equipment and personnel for an eight-year course.[2] Compulsory eight-year education will be formally introduced in the RSFSR from the 1962–63 school year. The situation is different in the Ukraine, where it was officially introduced, and all seven-year schools converted, in 1960. This is said to have been an over-hasty decision, as many schools were not ready for conversion.[3]

Although at present at least seven-year education is in theory compulsory, it has not in fact become universal ; considerable numbers of children, especially in the countryside, either start school late or leave early. The chief reasons are poverty and the inadequacy of school transport. It is true that local Soviets have the power to assist needy families by the provision of shoes, warm clothing, etc., *kolkhozes* are enjoined to make similar efforts, and since 1959 there has been, at least in theory, a ' universal education fund ' at the disposal of every school. There are nearly 1·5 million pupils in the RSFSR alone whose homes are two miles or more away from school. About 40 per cent of them are accommodated in school hostels, while the rest have to rely on school transport which is often non-existent. No wonder that none of the *oblasts*, *krais*, or Autonomous Republics of the RSFSR achieved universal seven-year education in the 1959–60 school year, and only 360 rural districts (*raions*) and towns out of nearly 3,000 succeeded in doing so.[4] A further difficulty in ensuring universal education is the rapid increase in the number of children in the relevant age-groups. The number of pupils in the first four classes fell from 23·7 million in 1948–49 to 12·1 million in 1953–54, due to the low birth-rate during the war. The recovery was slow, since the birth-rate did not start to increase significantly till 1948, but by 1959–60 the number of pupils in the first four classes had reached the figure of 18·4 million. The corresponding figures for the 5th to 7th classes are 14·1 million in 1952–53 (the maximum before it started falling), 7·2

2 E. Afanasenko, in *Narodnoe obrazovanie*, June 1961, p. 8.
3 *Uchitelskaya gazeta*, 23 February 1961.
4 Afanasenko, op. cit., p. 9.

million in 1957–58, and 9·7 in 1959–60. The rising numbers also complicate another problem which has faced the school authorities ever since the thirties, that of over-crowding in the schools. Two-shift work is still very common. A considerable effort is being made to overcome it : 2·2 million new places were provided through the school-building programme in 1956–59 ; in addition, the *kolkhozes* built new schools with a million places during the same period. But the total of 3·2 million new places (the figure includes all primary, incomplete secondary, and full secondary schools) exceeded the increase in the number of pupils only by 300,000, reducing by that figure the number of pupils working on the second shift, which in 1955–56 had stood at 10·3 million.

Most of the boarding schools, the number of which (1,990 in 1961) has greatly increased since 1956 when Khrushchev drew attention to the advantages of boarding-school education, are either primary or eight-year schools. There were over 590,000 pupils in boarding schools in 1961, which falls far short of the original plan of having a million boarding-school pupils by 1960. Another way of achieving some of the advantages of boarding schools is through the so-called prolonged day-classes, where the children remain at school after normal hours under the supervision of teachers until their parents come home from work. This arrangement covered some 300,000 children in the RSFSR in 1961.

THE 1958 reform has affected the content of instruction in the incomplete secondary schools less than in the later part of secondary education. ' Polytechnicalisation ' at this stage has meant chiefly the reintroduction of handicrafts (usually wood or metal work) and an insistence that pupils should themselves clean the school buildings, an occupation regarded as the simplest form of participation in ' productive work '. Another form, work in agriculture, is not new; since the late thirties, *kolkhoz* children over the age of 12 have been obliged to put in a certain amount of agricultural work per year. The main victim of the reform in the curriculum of the eight-year school is history, which now consists of an elementary course in Russian history with a few isolated facts from world history, in place of the former elementary course in Russian history plus (in the 5th to 7th classes) a good course in universal history (ancient and medieval). Another victim, at least in some cases, must be foreign languages, which became optional for those schools in the non-Russian republics where the local language is the medium of instruction.

There are four main paths for those who wish to continue their education after finishing the compulsory eight-year school. Those who want to learn a trade and do not aspire to any kind of academic training can go to vocational technical schools, which provide courses of from one to three years in the towns and one to two years in the countryside and turn out skilled workers. The numbers admitted to all types of vocational technical schools have been fairly stable since 1956, around 700,000 each year, which means that roughly (exact figures are difficult to come by) a quarter of all those finishing the seven-year school went on to this type of training. In recent years the agricultural mechanisation schools have admitted the largest number of pupils going on to vocational technical schools, absorbing between one-third and one-half of all entrants

The effect of the 1958 reform on the vocational technical schools has been to make them more homogeneous : the two extremes which had existed before 1958—the technical schools (*tekhnicheskie uchilishcha*) catering for people with completed ten-year education, and the schools of factory or plant apprenticeship (*shkoly FZU*) which admitted adolescents without complete seven-year schooling—are being assimilated to the main type of trade school requiring the completion of eight-year schooling. Until 1958 pupils were as a rule maintained free at vocational technical schools, but since the reform this has been the case only with orphans and children from large families ; other pupils have to pay for board and tuition but receive ordinary apprentices' wages.

The second type of further education is specialised secondary, received in technicums and other (pedagogical, medical, etc.) specialised secondary schools. There were 3,330 specialised secondary schools in 1959, with 656,000 pupils, of whom 378,000 were admitted as day pupils, 99,000 as evening pupils, and 179,000 as correspondence pupils. The numbers have been rising slightly in recent years, mainly due to the increased admission of evening and correspondence pupils. The normal duration of the specialised secondary course is four years, though this may be varied according to the particular course being followed. Before 1958 the practice was spreading of admitting only people with completed ten-year secondary education and the courses were accordingly shortened to two years, but since 1958 this process has been reversed.

Unlike vocational technical and specialised secondary, the third category of schools for further education—secondary evening, shift or seasonal (the latter for those employed in agriculture)—are not designed to teach a trade or profession, but to provide a general secondary education for employed youths or adults. Before the 1958 reform these were called schools for working youth, schools for rural youth, or adult schools. In his original Memorandum on the school reform, Khrushchev intended to make this the main type of secondary school, but his suggestion encountered strong opposition and these schools were put on an equal footing with other secondary schools. Some schools of this type include classes below the 8th for the benefit of those who for one reason or another have not completed seven-year education. The number of pupils attending evening, shift and seasonal secondary schools remained almost constant at just under 2 million during the second half of the 1950s, but increased to 2·3 million in

1959–60 (one-third of them in classes below the 8th), and to 2·8 million in 1960–61. Schools of this type function for 20 hours a week, of which 6·5 hours are spent on the humanities, 8·5 on mathematics and sciences, 3 hours on individual tuition, and 2 hours on optional subjects related to the pupils' employment. In order to attend these schools an employee who is making good progress at the school is allowed one day a week off on half-pay, and may take off one or two additional days a week without pay.

TRADITIONALLY the principal medium of secondary education, the general secondary school was the main topic of argument in the public discussions which preceded the 1958 reform. In his original Memorandum on school reform Khrushchev vaguely suggested abolishing the general secondary school altogether, but opinion was overwhelmingly opposed and it was finally decided to retain it, though it is here that the biggest changes have been made. The ' secondary polytechnical school of general education with instruction in production ', as it is now called, consists of three forms—the 9th to 11th —which are in most cases not separately housed and administered but combined with eight-year schools. Full figures are not yet available on the number of pupils in the 9th–11th classes ; the available statistics still usually give them together with the pupils of the 8th class. The number of pupils in the 8th and higher classes grew rapidly during the first half of the 1950s, from just over 1 million to 5·3 million in 1955–56, but declined to 2·8 million in 1959–60 and probably further in 1960–61 ; this decline is due both to the low wartime birth-rate and to the educational policy since 1956. Correspondingly, the number of those completing secondary schools (including the evening, shift and seasonal ones) rose from 315,000 in 1950 to 1·6 million in 1958 but fell to 1 million by 1961. According to the 1958 law, the reorganisation of the full secondary schools must be completed in the 1963–64 school year. At first it was estimated that only about a third of the ten-year secondary schools which existed in 1958 would be transformed into new eleven-year schools, while the rest would become evening (or shift, etc.) secondary or would be reduced to eight-year schools. But it now appears that in fact most of them will be converted into eleven-year day schools. There were 15,000 of these in 1960–61—more than the number of remaining ten-year schools.[5] Here again the non-Russian republics seem to have adopted a quicker pace than the RSFSR, where only 38 per cent of ten-year schools had been converted by the beginning of the 1960–61 school year.[6]

The extra year's schooling is entirely taken up with ' polytechnical ' training, to which one-third of the time in the 9th to 11th forms is devoted. In the eleven-year schools it takes the form of apprenticeship in factories, agricultural enterprises, offices, etc.—that is, pupils work

5 *Pravda*, 8 June 1961.   6 Afanasenko, op. cit., p. 10.

two days a week in industry, etc., or one-third of the year in agriculture. The aim is that the pupils should complete their apprenticeship by the time they finish school, if not before. Of 270,000 pupils receiving trade apprenticeship in the RSFSR in 1960-61, over 160,000 were learning industrial trades, 56,500 agricultural, 9,000 building, 3,500 commercial and public catering trades, and the remaining 40,000 mostly clerical or educational (kindergarten) work.[7] By a decision of the central committee of the Party and of the Council of Ministers, the eleven-year schools in rural areas have been given the specific task of training people to be employed in the electrification of agriculture and as combine-harvester operators for the virgin land areas. In the remaining ten-year schools there is another type of polytechnical training, aimed at acquiring not a specific trade, but rather a general idea of modern industrial production, and more closely corresponding to the original concept of polytechnical education. It consists of a general theoretical course in ' fundamentals of production ', engineering, electromechanics, and car maintenance, together with a certain amount of practical work in the school workshops and in factory or field.

Some schools are reported to have had considerable success in carrying out these new requirements, but the general situation is far from satisfactory. Although new draft programmes for most subjects have been issued, there are no suitable textbooks and both teachers and pupils have to make do with what is available. The choice of the trade or trades to be learned presents a difficult problem, since it affects the future careers of the pupils. The available facilities for training, the prospective demand for this or that type of skilled manual work, and to some extent the wishes of the parents and of the pupils themselves—all these have to be taken into account, but are in fact often overlooked. When the choice has been made, new problems arise. Factory managements often object to the idea of young people spending three years acquiring skills which they think can be acquired in three months ; masters who are used to training boys of a comparatively lower intelligence and educational level are often at a loss when faced with the more theoretically-inclined secondary school pupils ; conversely, many school teachers find it difficult to answer questions arising from the pupils' experience of machines and production processes of which they themselves are ignorant. With the stress on acquiring practical skills and the slight prospects of higher education for the majority of pupils, the interest in ordinary school subjects has diminished and many schools show a lower level of achievement in languages, history, mathematics, etc.[8] On the other hand, those pupils who think that they have a reasonable chance of further education resent the necessity to spend so much time and energy on subjects they regard as uninteresting and useless for their future careers.

7 Afanasenko, op. cit., p. 11.
8 Cf. *Sovetskaya pedagogika*, 1960, No. 1, p. 7; No. 5, p. 11; 1961, No. 1, p. 8.

The remaining two-thirds of the time are divided between the humanities, mathematics and science, and physical culture (30 per cent, 31·7 per cent and 5 per cent respectively). Logic, psychology, and Latin (in those few schools where it had been re-introduced in 1946) have been completely eliminated from the curriculum in the process of the reform, while history, literature, and foreign languages have suffered a reduction.

There has been a shift of emphasis in the course of implementing the reform. At first Khrushchev said that the ' divorce of school from life ' consisted in the theoretical orientation of school education and the absence of any training in manual work. But in December 1959 the head of the Department for Science, Schools, and Culture at the central committee of the Communist Party, asserted that the divorce of education from life was expressed in the non-political character of instruction. He declared unequivocally that the main task of the school was ' to bring about through education the conviction of the rightness of Marxist-Leninist ideas '.[9] This may sound surprising, considering that present-day school-children in Russia are the *grand-children* of the generation which witnessed the October revolution in 1917. The charge that the character of teaching was non-political was manifestly untrue. The restoration of traditional school subjects in the 1930s was accompanied by the demand, constantly repeated since then, that the teaching of *all* subjects should be permeated with the ' party spirit '. Certainly nothing was allowed to be taught that contradicted the current party line. But this was apparently insufficient. The central committee, in a number of special decisions during the last eighteen months, has laid down the measures to be taken. One of the most important is the introduction of a completely new history curriculum, which in the three upper forms consists of the modern history of the world and Russian history (as well as local history in schools of the non-Russian republics). The already existing bias in favour of such themes as class struggle, communist party affairs, and the real or imaginary achievements of the communist regime, is now to be accentuated, so that there will be less correspondence than ever between history as taught in Soviet schools and historical reality. Moreover, a new subject is to be added in the 11th form—Fundamentals of Political Knowledge. The stated aim of this one-year course is ' to acquaint pupils with the most important principles of Marxism-Leninism ' in order that they should ' have a good idea ' of the ' advantages of socialist society compared to capitalist ', that they should ' learn to understand the policy of the Party and fight for its implementation, to withstand the influence of religion and of other survivals of bourgeois ideology '.[10]

9 Ibid., No. 2, 1960, p. 159.
10 Editorial in *Sovetskaya pedagogika*, No. 3, 1960, p. 8.

HIGHER education has been expanding very slowly throughout most of the 1950s. The number of higher educational establishments actually declined from 880 in 1950–51 to 753 in 1959–60, though this is mainly due to the abolition of the so-called Teachers' Institutes, which had only given two-year courses. The number of full-time students has been almost stationary around 1,150,000 ; the number of evening students doubled between 1956–57 and 1959–60, reaching nearly 200,000 ; and the number of correspondence students rose from 723,000 to 925,000 during the same period. Khrushchev is on record as saying that full-time higher education would not be expanded in the near future. The discrepancy between the number completing general secondary education and admissions to higher education remains, though it is now slightly smaller than it was at its peak, about five to one as against more than seven to one in 1958. This numerical relation does not, however, mean that one out of every five young people finishing general secondary school this year will be able to proceed directly to full-time higher education. The majority will have to take up employment for at least two years ; they may then apply for admission to higher education if they can produce satisfactory testimonials both from their place of employment and from their party, Komsomol, or trade union organisation.

The 1958 reform obliged the majority of students to combine employment with their studies during their first two years ; for this category, therefore, the distinction between full-time, evening, and correspondence study scarcely exists. According to some at least of the teachers at higher educational establishments, this measure may achieve its intended aim of eliminating the less serious and determined students without doing much damage to academic standards, provided that enough time off for study is allowed. The authorities seem to be mainly concerned with encouraging study by correspondence, and have set up ' general technical faculties ' with evening courses for the benefit of correspondence students in towns that have no higher educational establishments.

On most aspects of the 1958 educational reform public discussion now seems to have abated, but there are some important points on which it is as vigorous as ever. The over-burdening of school children, a problem which caused anxiety even before 1958, has in many cases been made worse by the addition of ' socially useful ' work. An example was recently given in the Press of a secondary school in Vladimir oblast which had taken over responsibility for a cattle farm and where in consequence the senior pupils started their day's work at 5 a.m. and did not finish until late at night. The introduction of Fundamentals of Political Knowledge as a new subject will add a further burden. The second issue on which discussion continues is the difficulty of maintaining academic standards at school when so much time must be devoted to polytechnical subjects and when the majority of pupils have no prospect of higher education. Most vocal are those such as Academician Lavrentiev (chairman of the Siberian Division of the Academy of Sciences), who urge the need to ensure gifted children an opportunity to make the best use of their talents.

THE draft party programme envisages no changes in the educational system after the completion of the present reform. However, there are two major departures from the policy pursued by Khrushchev hitherto, one concerning general secondary education, the other higher and specialised secondary. The draft gives as the party's aim the realisation during the next ten years of compulsory eleven-year general secondary education for all children of school age, and of education corresponding to the eight-year school for young employees who have not previously completed it. During the following decade the aim is to ensure for all the opportunity of acquiring full secondary education. On higher and specialised secondary education, the programme says that admissions are to be considerably expanded every year, new higher and specialised establishments (especially evening and correspondence) are to be set up in all parts of the country with the help of enterprises, trade unions, and other organisations, and that a shorter working day and the raising of living standards will create conditions where all who desire it can receive higher or specialised secondary education. Only two other specific points are mentioned. The expansion of the network of preschool establishments and boarding schools of various types would make it possible for all parents who so desire to have their children brought up in these institutions rather than in the family. And all schools will receive good buildings and equipment and will be able to function without resorting to the two-shift system.

Here, as elsewhere, two questions naturally arise : are the aims put forward capable of realisation, and if so are they likely to be realised in Russia within the next twenty years?

To deal with the question of buildings, equipment, and shifts first. There is obviously nothing inherently impossible in this aim, but to achieve it a much greater allocation of resources would be needed than has ever been made during the Soviet period or is embodied in the current seven-year plan. At the moment, for example, the RSFSR Ministry of Education is concerned with the problem of how to avoid an increase during the coming years in the number of pupils working on the second shift. Since the claims on the available resources are going to be very great, and no particular priority is earmarked for school building, it is fairly safe to predict that this aim is unlikely to be realised.

The case of the boarding schools is different, since the draft programme itself introduces a third factor besides official intentions and material resources—the wishes of the parents. If one were to assume that a majority of parents would wish their children to be educated in boarding schools, then the material resources likely to be available would clearly be insufficient. The question thus turns on the assessment of the number of parents desiring this type of education for their children. There is at present a considerable run on the comparatively few boarding schools available, mostly by poor families, but it is clear that only a minority of parents are in favour of boarding schools. Factors likely to lessen the desire for boarding school education are the probable improvements in urban standards of living, especially housing (no particular prestige attaches to boarding-school education), and a possible improvement of school transport in the countryside ; on the other hand, if secondary education is expanded, this is likely to work in the opposite direction, particularly in the countryside. But none of these factors, nor any combination of them, seems likely to change radically the present balance of parental attitudes. Thus the plan to provide boarding school education for all who desire it may well be fulfilled.

As for eleven-year general secondary education for all children of school age, this is a complete switch from Khrushchev's preference, stated in his original Memorandum, for all young people to leave school and take up employment at the age of fifteen or sixteen and to continue their general secondary education if they so desire through evening or correspondence courses. Universal eleven-year education would in fact bring the compulsory age up to eighteen years, thus fulfilling the task put forward in the party programme of 1919. Universal secondary education was not in fact seriously considered until the 19th Party Congress in 1952, when the aim was proclaimed of achieving universal ten-year secondary education by 1960. The policy of expanding general secondary education was vigorously pursued until 1956, when it was suddenly stopped, obviously because of Khrushchev's intervention. The return to the idea of universal general secondary education, foreshadowed by Kairov (President of the Academy of Pedagogical Sciences) in a recent report, is bound to re-open the problem of the purpose and content of such education. If secondary education is understood in its traditional sense—that is, as bringing the intellectual development of the pupils up to the level required for entry into universities or other higher educational establishments—then the aim is clearly utopian. Even the few pieces of genuine research into children's abilities which have recently appeared in the Soviet Union (after a break of nearly thirty years) show that, despite the official Soviet pedagogical dogma that there are no children incapable of receiving full secondary education, something like 10 per cent of children are unsuitable for secondary education in its present form because of mental backwardness.[11] But leaving aside these 10 per cent, or whatever the true proportion may be, the question of purpose and content would remain.

11 E.g. *Sovetskaya pedagogika*, No. 6, 1961, p. 86.

Broadly speaking, there are three main trends now discernible both in practice and in the thinking on the subject. One lays the main stress on the acquisition by all pupils of definite, mainly manual, trades at the expense if need be of general education ; if this trend were to become dominant then academic levels would drop below those of genuine secondary education. The second tendency is to emphasise the study, both theoretical and practical, of general technical subjects, such as principles of engineering and electro-mechanics, and mathematics and sciences as a necessary basis ; a victory of this tendency would mean a one-sided development of secondary education, and the humanities would suffer. Finally, there exists, in a slightly camouflaged form, a trend which favours the system of secondary education worked out by the Academy of Pedagogical Sciences but rejected by Khrushchev in 1958. Supporters of this trend suggest that the principle of streaming should be introduced, the different streams concentrating on different groups of subjects, including (which is of primary importance for the adherents of this trend) one stream concentrating on the humanities. They are at a disadvantage at the moment because Khrushchev is clearly against it, but in fact it is the only practicable way of preserving the substance of traditional secondary education. If this approach were adopted, then in fact some of these streams would be genuinely secondary while others would naturally fall short. The present official view that all three elements—general secondary education, general technical instruction, and trade apprenticeship—can satisfactorily be combined in one course is not convincing and does not seem to be justified by results obtained so far. But even apart from pedagogical problems, the limited material resources would make the achievement of universal secondary education within the next ten or twenty years highly unlikely if not impossible.

The same considerations apply a fortiori to the plans for higher education. This is self-evident in relation to intellectual ability and limited material resources. But problems of purpose and content would also arise if higher education were to be considerably expanded. There has been no serious discussion of these problems so far, and the only publicly voiced view is that of Khrushchev, according to whom higher education would be taken up as a kind of hobby by employed people in their spare time.

Summing up, one can say that Khrushchev's educational reform has so far had a limited success, has raised more problems than it has solved, and has failed to satisfy informed opinion in Russia. The new party programme introduces new complications. Conflicting interests— of party authorities, industry, scientists, teachers, doctors, and parents —pull in different directions, and it is still difficult to predict the final outcome of the reform.

RUSSIA AND CHINA

I. Two Roads to Communism

Donald S. Zagoria

THE present Sino-Soviet conflict began, broadly speaking, in the fall of 1957, when the two basic complexes of issues arose around which the controversy has since been waged. The first and most persistent element in the conflict concerns communism's global strategy. Peking rejected the Khrushchev version of 'peaceful coexistence' as unworkable. The second revolved about domestic revolutionary strategy, how to build socialism and communism in a country already ruled by a communist party.

Although the conflict over revolutionary strategy abroad is more acute than the conflict over how to build communism, the two issues cannot really be separated. For its part Peking not only rejects the 'general line' of Soviet policy; in many areas of the world, particularly in the underdeveloped countries, it seeks to impose its own line. It seeks to change the strategy of many of the communist parties in the underdeveloped countries in a left-wing direction, and in those underdeveloped countries ruled by communist parties, it seeks to export some of its own experience in building communism at a headlong pace with limited resources and a rapidly growing population. The Russians, for their part, although aware that they cannot impose their will on the Chinese, will not allow the Chinese to set themselves up as leaders of communism's Eastern empire. The result is competition in many areas, which has already produced profound changes in the relations between Moscow and Peking, in the relations within the communist world, and, not least important, in the relations between the communist bloc and the Western world.

THE PRINCIPAL DIFFERENCES

The differences between Moscow and Peking on the 'transition to communism' turn first of all on the question of timing. The Chinese conception of how to build communism is shaped by the desire to go faster than the Russians believe desirable or feasible. While the Chinese suggest that the Russians, by taking the slow road to communism, are putting into jeopardy the social revolution in the bloc itself, the Russians accuse the Chinese of trying to move faster than 'objective conditions' allow. The newly published Soviet party programme gives warning, as the Russians have done persistently since late 1958, against trying to jump over stages in the advance toward communism.[1]

---

[1] Much of the section on the 'transition to communism' in the new programme must be viewed against the background of Mao's challenge to Soviet doctrine.

Secondly, there is the specific question of the communes. For a variety of reasons, the Russians have been cool towards the Chinese commune experiment, which they believe is premature and potentially disruptive for China's economy; it is, in any case, an ideological challenge to them. This is so because the Chinese claim that the commune, however modified since it was first introduced, and however much it will change in the future, is the final unit of communist society, a unit for which the Russians are still groping. Moreover, the Chinese have introduced in the commune a part-supply system which they claim represents a ' sprout ' of the final communist form of distribution according to need, a form of distribution which the Russians say must await the distant future.[2]

Third, the Chinese conception is characterised by a radicalism or fundamentalism which contrasts sharply with the more pragmatic Soviet attitude. It was symptomatic of this Chinese fundamentalism that in September and October 1958, various Chinese spokesmen went not to contemporary Soviet writing but to the works of Marx, Engels, and Lenin to justify their path to communism.[3] In so doing, they implied that the Russians had abandoned the classical ideological goals and were interested merely in building a modern and powerful economy. This approach has forced the Russians to counter it by putting more emphasis in their propaganda on the spiritual and ideological goals of communist society.

A fourth difference between Soviet and Chinese views is the Chinese insistence on unceasing experimentation with social institutions whenever they seem to hold up revolutionary advance, as opposed to the Soviet stress on continuity and consolidation. The Maoist insistence on ceaseless experimentation is more than a rationale for the erratic commune experiment. It has deep roots in Mao's philosophy, as shown particularly in his writings on contradictions. These indicate that ' contradictions ' can never be fully eliminated from human society, even after the full triumph of communism. The same emphasis on ceaseless struggle and experimentation is manifest in his ' creative development ' of the Marxist-Leninist theory of uninterrupted revolution.[4] First officially noted by Liu Shao-ch'i when he set out the ' general line ' at the 8th Party Congress in May 1958, Mao's theory of uninterrupted

---

[2] For a perceptive comment on the communes as a divisive force in Sino-Soviet relations, see Richard Lowenthal, ' Shifts and Rifts in the Russo-Chinese Alliance ', *Problems of Communism*, Jan.-Feb. 1959. Lowenthal makes the important point that the Chinese ideological challenge to the Russians was deliberate.

[3] In articles about the proper form of distribution in both socialist and communist societies, *People's Daily* throughout October and November 1958 appealed almost exclusively to the authority of Marx and Engels. In seeking to justify the ' emancipation ' of women, writers cited Engels' *Origin of the Family, Private Property and the State*. In articles on education under communism, authority was again sought from Engels. In not one case did the Chinese press refer to recent Soviet experience or doctrine on building communism.

[4] The theory of uninterrupted revolution is of course accepted in its Leninist form in the Soviet Union, but is given greater emphasis in Mao's writings in reference to the post-revolutionary period.

revolution has been the subject of much discussion since. In one of the most revealing of such discussions, the Chinese journal *Study* wrote in October 1958 :

> There are some who ask in alarm : when you advocate uninterrupted revolution in a socialist society, what is the object of the revolution? *Actually, viewed from the standpoint of Marxists, the objects of revolution always are the production relations and the superstructure, which at the time are lagging behind the development of the productive forces and therefore interfering with the development of the productive forces.* . . . Marxists must not conceal contradictions and also must not shun revolution. . . . Whoever understands these general truths will not think it strange that it is still necessary to advocate uninterrupted revolution in a socialist society (my italics, D.Z.).

The theory was both a rejection of Soviet gradualism in the advance toward communism and a complete reversal of the Soviet and Marxist view of the domestic revolutionary process. For what it clearly indicated was that the ' superstructure' may lag behind and interfere with the development of ' productive forces'. The transition to communism— like the world revolution—is marked by continuing struggle, by leaps forward, by periods of rapid advance and periods of consolidation, and, above all, by continuing experimentation.

The Chinese evidently consider that Khrushchev, by making of the ' construction of communism' a rather sluggish process whose primary purpose is to increase the material production base rather than to explore new social forms, puts into jeopardy the achievement of the final revolutionary goal. They apparently fear that Khrushchev, who follows the gradualist Soviet tradition, will make of the ' transition to communism' a meaningless slogan. Thus in 1958, one Chinese writer said, clearly with the Russians in mind :

> According to some, the victory of the proletariat and the advent of a socialist society mean the end of the social revolution, after which there will be all sorts of phenomena of crystallisation, ranging from economic matters to the superstructure and tendencies toward absoluteness, all resulting in interference with the development, by leaps forward of the forces of production.[5]

And in 1960, Lu Ting-i, member of the CCP Politburo, criticised ' the kind of theory' which holds that

> there is no need to develop the socialist system, but only to consolidate it, and even if it is to be developed, to go forward to

[5] Wu Chiang, ' A partisan of the uninterrupted revolution theory must be a consistent dialectic materialist ', *Che-Hsüeh Yen-chiu* (*Philosophical Study*), No. 8, 1959, cited by Stuart R. Schram, ' La " revolution permanente " en Chine ', *Revue francaise de science politique*, September 1960, a good discussion of the evolution of the concept of uninterrupted revolution. Later Wu Chiang wrote that ' there is a theory which maintains that development need not pass through struggle and qualitative leap '. Although ' well-intentioned ', this theory in fact impeded the development of socialism because it would lead to a ' lifeless society '. See *Selections from the China Mainland Magazines*, No. 225, 6 September 1960, pp. 10-11.

communism, still there is no need to undergo a struggle and to pass through a qualitative leap ; and thus the process of the uninterrupted revolution of human society goes up to this point and no farther.[6]

WHOSE MODEL?

The Russians and the Chinese not only differ between themselves on how to make the ' transition to communism ' but—perhaps more important—they differ on the applicability of the Soviet model to other countries. In his draft theses for the 21st Congress, Khrushchev said :

V. I. Lenin foresaw that the Soviet Union would exert chief influence on the entire course of world development by its economic construction. Lenin said : ' If Russia becomes covered with a dense network of electricity stations and powerful technical equipment, our communist economic construction will become a model for the future socialist Europe and Asia.' [7]

In sharp contrast to this, the Chinese contended in effect that Mao has solved the problem of socialist and communist construction for all under-developed areas as well as for China. In one of the first discussions of the Chinese communes ever to appear, as early as July 1958, Ch'en Po-ta, in an article significantly titled ' Under the Banner of Chairman Mao ', contended that Mao had followed Lenin's injunction to the countries of the East to develop Marxist theory creatively ' in the light of special conditions unknown to European countries '.[8]

If Mao had indeed solved the problems of socialist and communist construction for the under-developed countries, did it not also follow that Peking should be accorded leadership of the revolutionary movement in those areas? There is, of course, one omission in this chain of reasoning. In effect, the Chinese communists were claiming in 1958 that Mao had discovered a special path for building communism in backward countries once the communists had taken power. They had not then renewed their earlier claims of 1949–51 that the Chinese road to power was also relevant in those countries. In 1959 they were to fill this gap, and to carry their claims to their logical conclusion. Mao knew best how to make the revolution, how to consolidate it, and how to proceed toward communism. In the countries of the East, the CCP was in effect once again claiming leadership of the revolutionary movement. Having pointed to some of the basic differences between Soviet and Chinese views on the transition to communism, we may now try to find some of the explanations for them.

---

[6] ' Unite Under Lenin's Revolutionary Banner ', in *Long Live Leninism*, Peking Foreign Languages Press, 1960, pp. 94–95.

[7] *Pravda*, 14 November 1958 : cited by John Bradbury in *The China Quarterly*, April–June 1961, p. 20.

[8] ' Under the Banner of Comrade Mao Tse-tung ', *Red Flag*, 16 July 1958; *Extracts From the China Mainland Magazines*, No. 138, 11 August 1958, p. 13.

Differing National Circumstances

The Chinese communists' primitive agriculture barely manages to keep ahead of population growth ; enormous industrial strains are generated by their headlong efforts to outstrip some advanced capitalist countries in the space of a few decades. China is, in the words of Mao, ' poor and blank '. The Russians, on the other hand, have a developed economy long past the point of take-off, an economy which does not produce the tensions and strains inevitable in any country, and particularly a communist one, in the midst of vast social and economic change.

Communist China's ' general line ', introduced in 1958, including the commune programme and the ' leap forward ', represented a direct institutional response to the chronic economic problems that had always plagued the Chinese communists and had, by the summer of 1957, become acute.

It is apparent that some time between the summer and early fall of 1957, there was a struggle between two factions within the Chinese Communist Party, one advocating a radical turn to the ' left ' and the other advocating a massive retreat on the lines of the Soviet NEP.[9] The left wing of the party won the day. It had concluded that China's acute problems could not be solved by continuing to copy Soviet experience, as had been done in China's first Five-Year Plan from 1953 to 1957. A radical solution to these problems was required, and this solution was the distinctive path to communism evolved in 1958—a path whose most notable feature was the communes. The principal aims of the communes were to develop cottage industries, to centralise control over all means of production in the countryside, to increase control over peasant consumption, and to mobilise China's one abundant resource, its manpower, for huge peasant labour armies on a scale unprecedented in modern history. A closely related aim was to substitute ideological for material incentives by holding out the prospect of an early passage to the final communist paradise via communes.

Looked at in this perspective, much of the Chinese communist conception of the process of building communism, with its emphasis on continuing struggle, on the strength of the masses once aroused, on the power of ideology, can be attributed to the desperate need to find a solution to acute economic problems.

This does not of course entirely explain the Chinese insistence on exporting their ideology. Differing ideological perspectives induced by different national circumstances would not have produced so great a strain on Sino-Soviet relations if the Chinese had not suggested, as they

---

9 Reflections of the Right's thinking were to appear in November, after the Left wing of the Party had gained the ascendancy. Thus, on 3 November, the journal *Study* railed against ' certain people ' who wanted to ' learn from all ' (presumably including the West), and believed that there should be ' free competition and fluctuation of prices '. The journal denounced such views as ' preposterous ' and said they would ' obliterate the basic differences between socialist and capitalist economy '. ' Study the Experience of the Soviet Union in its Construction ', Hsüeh Hsi, No. 21, 3 November 1957, in *Extracts*, No. 120, 24 February 1958, pp. 5-6.

did, that their new path to communism was valid for all under-developed countries. If we probe this question of what might be called Chinese evangelism a bit further, it soon becomes evident that deeply-rooted in Chinese communist history and ideology is the conviction that its revolution is the model for Asia and other colonial and semi-colonial areas. As early as the spring of 1946, in an interview of extraordinary importance which has never received adequate attention in the West, Liu Shao Ch'i told Anna Louise Strong that Mao had discovered an Asiatic form of Marxism, that Marx and Lenin were Europeans and therefore, by implication, not very interested in or capable of solving Asian problems, that Mao was the first to have succeeded in adapting Marxism to China, and that Mao's revolutionary theories charted a path to power not only for the Chinese people ' but for the billion folk that live in the colonial countries of South-east Asia '. The passage deserves reproduction in full :

> Mao Tse-tung's great accomplishment has been to change Marxism from a European to an Asiatic form. Marx and Lenin were Europeans ; they wrote in European languages about European histories and problems, seldom discussing Asia or China. The basic principles of Marxism are undoubtedly adaptable to all countries, but to apply their general truth to concrete revolutionary practices in China is a difficult task. Mao Tse-tung is Chinese ; he analyses Chinese problems and guides the Chinese people in their struggle to victory. He uses Marxist-Leninist principles to explain Chinese history and the practical problems of China. He is the first that has succeeded in doing so. Not only has he applied Marxist methods to solve the problems of 450 million people, but he has thus popularised Marxism among the Chinese people as a weapon for them to use. On every kind of problem—the nation, the peasants, strategy, the construction of the party, literature and culture, military affairs, finance and economy, methods of work, philosophy—Mao has not only applied Marxism to new conditions but has given it a new development. He has created a Chinese or Asiatic form of Marxism. . . . There are similar conditions in other lands of South-east Asia. The courses chosen by China will influence them all.[10]

From 1949 to 1951, the two years following the Chinese communist seizure of power, Mao's claims to ideological autonomy and his insistence that he had discovered a model to be followed in other colonial and semi-colonial countries was probably the cause of considerable friction with Stalin. A well-documented survey of the period shows :

(1) Chinese propagandists explicitly claimed that Mao's political theories on revolution were independently arrived at, while the Russians consistently endeavoured to show Mao's complete theoretical dependence on Stalin ;

(2) The Chinese asserted that Mao's writing on the Chinese revolution embodied an ideology—the ' ideology of Mao Tse-tung ' ; there was no recognition of such an ideology in Soviet writings ;

---

[10] Anna Louise Strong, ' The Thought of Mao Tse-tung ', *Amerasia*, June 1947, p. 161.

(3) Between 1949 and 1951 the Chinese viewed their revolution as the model to be followed in other undeveloped countries and they referred to this model revolutionary path as ' Mao's road '. Such themes were absent from Soviet writings, which conceded only that the Chinese revolution had ' inspired ' the people of backward countries in their own revolutionary movements.[11]

The political significance of such claims is difficult to exaggerate. First of all, they suggest that Mao has always put himself on a level not with Stalin, let alone Khrushchev, but with Marx and Lenin, the founding fathers of communism. In the light of this image, Mao's attitude to the hearty peasant who now sits on top of the world communist movement is easy to imagine. Second, the claims imply that Mao has never accepted a position subordinate to Moscow with regard to Chinese domestic or foreign policies. Third, they suggest that Mao has always considered himself to be leader of the revolution in all under-developed areas, including Asia, Africa, and Latin America.

In 1951 the claims for ' Mao's ideology ' ceased to be made, probably because Mao's economic and military dependence on Stalin forced him to greater caution and modesty. But in 1958, as the Chinese communists were becoming more powerful and the balance of forces in the international communist world was changing, similar claims again appeared. Mao was now described as a ' great prophet ' and ' one of the most outstanding Marxist-Leninist revolutionaries, statesmen, and theoreticians of our age '.[12] By the end of 1959, Mao's ideology was being increasingly equated with Marxism-Leninism and sometimes given priority over it. There were also invidious remarks about ' so-called Western Marxists ' who did not understand the problems of the ' East '.

For Sino-Soviet relations, one of the implications of the growing cult of Mao was obvious. Mao was once again, as in the period from 1949–51, being portrayed as an independent source of authority and strategy, who had adapted Marxism to China and whose theories were relevant for all colonial and former colonial peoples.

DIFFERING REVOLUTIONARY HISTORIES

Still another factor behind the differences on the transition is the differing revolutionary histories of the two parties. The Russians had experimented with agrarian communes in the early years of their revolution and had found that such a drastic form of socialisation was not feasible. In Stalin's report to the 17th Party Congress in 1934, his only major pronouncement on the communes, he ascribed their failure to three factors : under-developed technology, a shortage of products, and a premature practising of egalitarianism. The future commune, he wrote, could arise

---

[11] Unpublished manuscript by Arthur Cohen, Phillip Bridgham, and Herb Jaffe, ' Chinese and Soviet Views on Mao as a Marxist Theorist and on the Significance of the Chinese Revolution for the Asian Revolutionary Movement '.
[12] Liu Lan-tao, *People's Daily*, 28 September 1959, in *Ten Glorious Years*, Peking Foreign Languages Press, 1960, p. 296.

only on the basis of abundance of products and a developed technology. It is of course true that the Chinese communes of 1958 were a far cry from the Bolshevik agrarian communes of the 1920s. But the common denominator of both was the attempt to introduce egalitarian distribution, to socialise all means of production, and to introduce a system in which each individual would work selflessly for the good of the state. The Russian failure had been marked enough to convince them that such drastic forms of socialisation required a production base which would allow the sharing of plenty rather than the rationing of scarcity. It left a deeply engrained belief, repeatedly expressed by Stalin and his successors, that the transition to communism would have to be gradual ; the vestiges of capitalism could not be eliminated overnight. It was this firm belief, rooted in Soviet history, that led the Soviet leaders to view with grave reserve the Chinese attempt to introduce communes at a relatively early stage of revolutionary development.

By 1960 the conflict over the communes and the transition to communism had receded into the background, to be replaced by the more acute conflict over global strategy. As a continuing potential source of discord, however, the issue remains. In their vigorous attacks on Soviet policy in April 1960, the Chinese continued to take issue with Soviet views on the transition to communism and continued to reassert the Chinese path and its relevance to under-developed countries. The CCP contended that revolutions in Oriental countries would ' undoubtedly display even greater peculiarities than the Russian revolution ' ; they protested again ' *foreign* and Chinese philistines ' who had ' their heads stuffed with metaphysics ' and did not understand the revolutionary dialectics of the general line, the leap forward, and the communes.[13] The claims implying doctrinal innovation were soft-pedalled when the structure of the communes had to be modified, and some ' leftist ' mistakes were admitted. The Soviet view is made explicit in the new programme, which claims universal validity for the Soviet path to communism and studiously avoids any reference to the Chinese experiments.

IMPLICATIONS FOR WORLD COMMUNISM

An analysis of the issues dividing Moscow and Peking ultimately leads to the most basic of all—the question of authority within the communist world. The Chinese communists are not attempting to supplant Russian leadership of the communist world now ; it is a position which, they are well aware, they are not yet sufficiently strong to occupy. Nor are the Russians, for their part, seeking to enforce unquestioning obedience. which they know to be no longer possible. They are arguing, instead. over the extent to which authority can be divided between two autonomous communist states with divergent interests and needs and differing ideological perspectives.

---

[13] ' Forward Along the Path of the Great Lenin ', *People's Daily* editorial, 22 April 1960, and Lu Ting-yi, ' Unite Under Lenin's Revolutionary Banner ', both in *Long Live Leninism*, pp. 60-63 and 94-96.

If Russia and China offer different models to other communist states, which one should the other communist states follow? The Russians remain convinced that their model is by and large universally valid both for Europe and Asia. The Chinese seem to be equally convinced that the problems of building socialism and communism in under-developed areas, predominantly agricultural, with large peasant populations, relatively little arable land in comparison to total population, are quite different from the problems of building socialism and communism in relatively more advanced countries. A ' division of labour ' on this question between Moscow and Peking thus seems out of the question. For the Russians to concede that the Chinese model is valid in all under-developed areas would be tantamount to surrendering to Peking the hegemony of the revolutionary movement in Asia, Africa, and Latin America. For the Chinese to concede that the Russian model is universally valid would be tantamount to accepting Soviet hegemony in the communist world as it exists today and in the future communist empire that both parties envisage for tomorrow.

If the smaller communist parties throughout the world choose, as seems increasingly likely, not to follow either the Soviet or Chinese model, but to pick and choose from both and to adapt the experience of both to their own peculiar national environments, this in turn threatens in the long run to undermine the ideological and therefore political unity of the communist world.

To the extent that each communist party adapts general Marxist-Leninist principles to its own national setting, ' nationalist deviations ' are bound to occur. What may at first appear as ideological relativism opens the door to ideological erosion. And without ideological sanction the Communist Party loses its very claim to existence.

This is the basic dilemma that has arisen and will continue to plague the communist world. The most likely result is that there will begin to appear other variants of socialism and particular brands of communism. Just as the smaller communist states have already taken advantage of the Sino-Soviet conflict over global strategy to advance their own foreign policy interests as they perceive them, so they will take advantage of the conflict over the ' transition to communism ' to adapt general principles to their own peculiar national environments. While this is by no means an insurmountable problem for the communist bloc, and certainly does not diminish the very real challenge which communism presents to the Western world, it will have important consequences. Ideological ties will become looser and authority in the communist world will become increasingly more diffused. The Russians will have to govern the bloc within the limits of an international communist consensus. As several writers have already pointed out, the spectre of polycentrism is here to stay.

II. A Study in Economic Strategy

Alexander Eckstein

THERE is a frequent tendency to view the economy of China as a carbon copy of the Soviet model. This view ignores the fact that China is an underdeveloped Soviet-type economy with the accent on underdeveloped. There are obviously vast differences in the factor endowments of Russia and China, most dramatically illustrated by the differences in population dynamics. Thus, while the population of the Soviet Union has been growing at an average annual rate of 0·6 per cent since 1913, China's population has expanded during the past decade at about 2 per cent a year. Even if we abstract from war influences and take only so-called normal periods, Soviet population grew only at about a 1 to 1·5 per cent rate. This divergence in population patterns becomes even more significant if we consider the vastly different states of population pressure on arable land resources in the Russia of 1928 and the China of 1952.

In these terms, Chinese conditions are clearly much closer to those encountered in other overpopulated underdeveloped economies than are those of the Soviet Union. However, the same can be said of Chinese development experience only if it can be shown that Chinese communist planners and policy-makers have themselves recognised these differences and have evolved a strategy adapted to their own conditions. This paper, therefore, will attempt to examine, first, what are the general ingredients or requirements of a development strategy; second, to what extent and how are these requirements met in the Soviet model ; third, whether and in what ways the Chinese model departs from the Soviet example; and fourth, what are the implications of this for other underdeveloped areas.

Ideally, a development strategy should be based on a clearly articulated set of objectives—both economic and non-economic—and an arsenal of instruments, means, clearly designed to attain them. The means, in turn, could be classified under three headings : ideology, institutions, and patterns of resource allocation.

This, of course, raises the very difficult problem of whether ideology serves as a guide for the definition of objectives or whether its function is primarily instrumental. Clearly this is not an either-or proposition, but rather a process with a dialectic of its own, with ideology serving simultaneously as a guide to and a tool for action. In this respect, political ideologies seem to have a life-cycle in which the early phases tend to be dominated by programme definition. As the movement becomes stronger, older, more institutionalised, and particularly as it assumes the reins of government, its instrumental functions tend to become paramount.

For the strategy to be fully successful, the objectives must be consistent and complementary, rather than competitive, and the three categories of instruments must be woven into a functionally inter-related and integrated pattern. Thus, a rationally designed plan cannot attempt to maximise a number of objectives simultaneously, such as for instance military prowess and standards of living, or quantity (measured in physical units) and quality of goods produced.

It would probably be possible—though beyond the scope of this essay—to rank ideologies according to their degree of totalism. Societies committed to raising standards of national power or standards of living higher, faster, and with less to work with than the countries they are emulating, will naturally require a more comprehensive and all-embracing ideology of zealotry in the name of which, and for the sake of which, large sacrifices can be demanded or commanded—sacrifices necessary to yield the desired rate of economic growth. From this point of view, the Protestant ethic, nationalism, and then nationalism combined with communism, may be considered as progressively more potent ideologies.

There is obviously an intimate relationship between ideology and institutions. Certain ideologies are compatible with private property relations or decentralised decision-making, as exemplified by the market mechanism, while others clearly are not. Similarly, certain institutions are either consciously designed or at least naturally suited to accomplish maximal objectives, while others may be altogether incompatible with economic development. Systems of land tenure, the character of the banking system or of capital markets, provide good cases in point.

Thus traditional landlord or communal systems of land tenure have tended to block economic development wherever they are found. They have done so in two principal ways : by serving as obstacles to raising agricultural productivity, and by channelling their surplus into consumption credit, speculative land purchase, or conspicuous consumption. It is not surprising, therefore, that one cannot think of a single case of successful industrialisation that was not preceded or accompanied by an agrarian transformation.

Among the most critical institutional means are all those related to mobilising actual or potential savings. In this respect, too, alternative mechanisms could be ranged along a spectrum extending from minimal to maximal, exemplified perhaps by small individual postal savings at one end, on to credit creation through the banking system, and finally by involuntary savings institutionalised through turnover taxation or forced extraction from a highly collectivised agriculture.

Patterns of resource allocation will inevitably be inter-related with institutional mechanisms. Highly decentralised decision-making will necessarily be preponderantly based on consumers' preferences, and will thus yield a rather different resource mix from a highly centralised pattern. It is true that, theoretically, one could conceive of central planning consciously based on consumers' preferences, but in practice this is most unlikely.

To sum up this phase of our analysis, one could say that the function of ideology is to provide the rationale for carrying out the objectives which are actually implemented through the institutional framework, and then translated by the prevailing pattern of resource allocation into the production and distribution of goods and services implicitly or explicitly postulated by the objectives.

APPLYING this framework of analysis to the Soviet model and concentrating first on objectives, it can be clearly shown that at least in this respect the model falls short of the ideal requirements of a development strategy. While it would be difficult to pinpoint precisely what the basic long-term objectives of Soviet policy-makers really are, it is fair to say that the central operational *leitmotiv* of Soviet planning has been to catch up with and overtake the West in industrial and economic power as soon as possible. Concretely, this has meant maximising the rate of economic growth year in, year out.

However, Soviet planning is often based on a multiplicity of mutually inconsistent goals. They would like to maximise several objectives simultaneously, e.g. collectivise while raising agricultural production, overfulfil production targets and improve quality of product, increase production without additional inputs of capital, labour, and raw material. These inconsistencies are then resolved by an implicit or explicit ordering of priorities, with some objectives becoming more maximal than others.

Ideology need not detain us for long in this context, since its implications are fairly obvious. One need only underline the fact that this is a maximal ideology in the sense used above, that is, it is a most potent ideology which harnesses the forces of nationalism and communism into a combined religion ideally suited to command great sacrifices.

The institutional framework is in turn designed to provide maximum control over all the social, political, and economic levers, and thus provide the channels for centralised direction and resource allocation. Public ownership of the means of production, collectivisation of agriculture, the entire banking mechanism, the tax system, the primary reliance on planning through administrative *fiat* rather than through the price mechanism, are all examples of this.

This institutional framework was then used to shape the pattern of resource allocation. In its Stalinist phase, in particular, high rates of saving and investment institutionalised through agricultural collectivisation, preponderant emphasis on the development of industries producing raw materials and investment goods, reliance on large-scale and capital-intensive technology in industry (and to a considerable extent in agriculture as well), relative neglect of yield-increasing rather than labour-displacing investment in agriculture, in consumer goods industries, and in social overheads, may be said to represent the principal features of the resource allocation pattern in the Soviet Union. In effect, it is a pattern of economic development which is bound to lead to rapid rates of industrial expansion at the expense of agriculture, i.e. of both agricultural productivity and rural standards of living.

There is no question that in spite of the many elements of irrationality in Soviet development strategy, they have done remarkably well in attaining their most important and high-priority objectives. However, the extent to which this relative success is a function of the strategy rather than of the country's size and its vast resources is an open question. It is far from certain that the same strategy applied in other settings would yield the same results. But before turning to this question let us examine Chinese communist development strategy.

COMPARING Soviet and Chinese communist development strategies in the context of the elements outlined above, one finds no essential differences in objectives, in ideology, or even in the institutional framework broadly conceived, with the single exception of the communes, about which more will be said later. Of course, there are some differences in degree and in tactics. Thus, the objectives of the Chinese communist leadership are even more ambitious than those of their Soviet counterparts. They would like to go even further, at much greater speed, and with much less to work with. This ambitiousness is, not too surprisingly, coupled with greater ideological militancy, both in its communist and nationalist aspects.

The pattern of development in China has been conditioned not only by ideology on the one hand and the country's economic backwardness on the other, but also by the fact that it enjoys the advantages of being a latecomer among communist states. A host of consequences follow from this fundamental fact. China had a tested model to follow which it could adapt and modify to suit local conditions. It did not have to grope as the Soviets did earlier for even the most elementary guidelines of communist statecraft. The Chinese communists, as a result, did not need to go through the waste motion of debating whether money should be used as a medium of exchange, whether wage or income inequalities should be allowed, etc.

At the same time, the Soviet example provided the Chinese with certain lessons, particularly of mistakes to avoid. Looking from this angle at China's economic development during the first decade of communist rule, one of the most important facts is the extent and pace of agrarian transformation ; a transformation which went further and faster than in the Soviet Union, yet was not accompanied by the same degree of overt violence and disruption. These differences in patterns of collectivisation had far-reaching implications for the whole course of China's economic evolution. They affected the behaviour of a number of economic variables.

One of the central purposes of collectivisation in the Soviet Union, as elsewhere, was to institutionalise a high rate of saving in the economy. However, it led to a considerable decline in crop output and an even more pronounced decrease in livestock numbers. Thus a high rate of saving had to be imposed upon a shrunken farm product and income. This not only reduced rural standards of living but undermined peasant incentives even in the collectives, and thus greatly hampered agricultural recovery. At the same time, capital had to be diverted to replace the animal draft power lost in the process. The more agricultural recovery was hampered, the greater had to be the pressure on agriculture.

In addition to institutionalising a high rate of saving and providing an effective control mechanism for agricultural procurement, collectivisation was designed to provide a readily available supply of labour for a rapidly expanding industry. However, the decline in farm output had a negative effect upon real wages and labour productivity in industry. The decline in productivity was, of course, reinforced by the large influx of unskilled labour from the countryside, and at the same time required an even greater expansion in the industrial labour force if rates of industrial growth were to be maintained.

In China we observe a rather different pattern. Agricultural production and livestock numbers continued to expand slowly right through the collectivisation period, although with fluctuations reflecting variations in harvest conditions. At the same time the evidence, though imperfect, strongly suggests a rising trend in real wages and in labour productivity. As a result, greater reliance could be placed upon increases in labour productivity as a means of obtaining high rates of industrial growth. Conversely, rates of industrial expansion roughly equivalent to those found in the Soviet Union during the first five-year plan period were achieved with relatively slower rates of increase in the size of the industrial labour force. While urban population is expanding very rapidly in China, this process is slower than it was in the Soviet Union during the 1928–32 period. This means that while rural population pressure was declining in Russia it is rising in China. Moreover, it suggests that the Chinese may be able to neglect investment in urban housing and other social overhead facilities with even greater impunity than the Soviets were able to do.

Let us explore briefly what could account for a less violent course of agrarian transformation in China. The roots of this difference may possibly be found in the different relations between the regime and the peasantry in the two countries. In both cases, land redistribution was the first item on the agenda of agrarian reform. But while, in the Soviet Union, the land reform following on the heels of the October revolution came from below, in the Chinese case it came from above, carefully prepared and planned. Moreover, the Chinese communists came to power after a prolonged period of civil war, while in the Russian case the civil war came after the revolution. Thus, while the Chinese were able to carry through their land reform programme undisturbed and in a systematic manner, the Bolsheviks were plagued by very acute food supply problems during the period of ' war communism ', and were thus compelled to resort to forced confiscation of grain and other agricultural produce. This served to alienate the peasantry from the regime, almost from the beginning, and at the same time it turned out to be counter-productive from a procurement standpoint, since it created an atmosphere in which the peasants would hide their grain, feed it to livestock, and consume it themselves, rather than surrender it to the authorities. Furthermore, peasants reduced their plantings to meet only their own consumption needs.

The Soviet regime therefore found it necessary to beat a tactical retreat and to institute the New Economic Policy. One of the essential features of NEP was a considerable reliance upon market incentives as a means of expanding and procuring the marketable share. This brought with it a strengthening of the economic and political power of the kulaks, as Lenin recognised in his statement that ' We must not shut our eyes to the fact that the replacement of requisitioning by the tax in kind means that the kulak element under this system will grow far more than hitherto. It will grow in places where it could not grow before.' The regime committed itself to reliance upon market incentives, but was reluctant to pay the price in terms of reduced savings and investments. Collectivisation was to point the way out of this dilemma. However, this course was bound to meet with strong resistance, so that if the process was to be consummated rapidly it necessitated a resort to violent means.

In contrast, land reform in China went so far that very few ' rich peasants ' were left. At the same time, by launching the collectivisation campaign as soon as the land redistribution programme was completed, the Chinese communists proceeded with the more advanced stages of their agrarian programme before the new and old owner-operators could consolidate their economic position, extend their landholding, and accu-mulate wealth. Thus the potential development of a ' rich peasant ' or kulak class was nipped in the bud, so that both the incentive and the power to resist collectivisation were minimised.

WHILE differences in objectives, in ideology, or in institutional instruments are largely tactical, patterns of resource allocation seem to diverge significantly in the Chinese and Soviet economies. This was much less pronounced during the first five-year plan period (1953–57), when the Chinese policy-makers pursued an essentially Stalinist development strategy. But, given the vastly different factor endowments of China in the fifties as compared to the Soviet Union of the twenties, Chinese planners were forced to modify their original approach and develop a new strategy for the second five-year plan (1958–62), based on intensive utilisation of under-employed labour combined with promotion of technological dualism, as a means of maximising the rate of economic growth.

In spite of five to eight years of rapid industrial growth, the Chinese policy-makers approached the end of their first five-year plan with some serious unresolved problems on their hands. Within this context, they began to grope for a new strategy, one that would provide a way out of the dilemmas facing them. The most intractable issue confronting them was agricultural stagnation. Farm production grew only slowly, possibly just sufficiently to keep pace with population growth. Unless this trend could be reversed, agriculture would increasingly retard the pace of industrialisation in a more or less closed economy. Therefore they sought a strategy which would promote growth in farm production without significant diversion of investment funds from industry to agriculture.

The problem was aggravated by the rising rate of population growth and the increasing pressure of population on arable land resources, and this accelerated the frantic search for an escape from the ' low level equilibrium trap '. All of these problems converged in the course of 1957, when the pressure on domestic saving was also rising because of the approaching exhaustion of Soviet credits to China.

The essence of the problem facing China's planners was most succinctly defined by Eckaus in the following terms :

> Suppose that the respective demands for output are such that a large part of the available capital is drawn into the capital-intensive and fixed coefficient sector. The amount of labor which can be absorbed in these sectors is dependent on the amount of capital available. Since capital is a scarce factor, labor employment opportunities in this sector are limited by its availability rather than by demand for output. The relatively plentiful labor supply is then pushed into the variable-coefficient sector and absorbed there as long as the marginal value productivity of labor is higher than the wages it receives.

It is against this background that a new development strategy began to crystallise in 1958, one better suited to China's factor endowments on the one hand, and to her planners' scale of preferences on the other. At its core, this strategy involved mass mobilisation of under-employed rural labour on a scale not attempted before, even in China.

This additional labour was to be largely used locally for three purposes : (1) labour-intensive investment projects such as irrigation and water reclamation ; (2) more intensive methods of agricultural production based on greater applications of labour designed to increase unit yields through closer planting, more careful weeding, etc. ; and (3) development of small-scale industry. Moreover, all this was to be accomplished while preventing leakages into consumption, thus capturing all of the increase in marginal product at zero marginal cost. The slogan was ' build much from nothing '.

Of course, none of these measures was entirely new. Mass labour projects have an ancient lineage in China and have only been perfected and rationalised by the new regime. However, rural mobilisation before 1958 was much less comprehensive and systematic than since.

ONE of the interesting by-products of this new strategy was a shift in Chinese population policy. Apart from doctrinal incantations against Malthusianism, the Chinese communist leadership apparently paid little attention to the population problem before 1955. However, rising rates of natural increase, primarily due to a reduction in mortality rates, forced a revaluation in population policy. As a result, some birth control measures were instituted between 1955 and 1957. But this new population policy was only half-heartedly pursued, since the leadership could not make up its mind whether to follow its doctrinaire bias and treat population as a productive resource, as a source of labour supply, or whether to stress its role as an actual and potential impediment to greater saving and investment.

With the new emphasis on labour as a productive resource, population policy was reversed and population again was viewed as an asset rather than a liability. This is most clearly illustrated by the following quotation from Liu Shao-ch'i : ' All they see is that men are consumers and that the greater the population, the bigger the consumption. They fail to see that men are first of all producers, and when there is a large population there is also the possibility of greater production and accumulation.'

The development of small-scale industry was one of the uses to which the rural under-employed were to be put. While small-scale industry has been traditionally a subsidiary occupation for the Chinese farm population, it was largely confined to weaving of textile cloth and other handicrafts. Within the context of the new strategy, it was viewed as one of the principal means for increasing the rate of industrial growth. In effect, the planners concentrated on the simultaneous development of two distinct industrial sectors—a modern, large-scale, capital-intensive sector based on fixed factor proportions, and a small-scale, labour-intensive sector based on variable factor proportions. In pursuit of this policy of technological dualism, or ' walking on two legs ' as it is officially termed in Chinese communist writings and pronouncements, the expansion of small-scale industry is being promoted in a number of sectors such as iron and steel, machine shops, fertiliser production, power generation, coal extraction, in addition to the more traditional textile and food-processing industries.

By the end of 1956, practically all Chinese agriculture was encompassed by small collectives (officially termed ' producers co-operatives of the advanced type ') of 35 to 100 households each. The management, supervision, and control of such a vast number of small units placed a considerable strain upon the administrative and party apparatus. Moreover, their proliferation and small size made them ill-suited as units of mass labour mobilisation and utilisation. Therefore, during 1958, a number of such small collectives were merged to form communes. These new units were sufficiently large to harness major labour-intensive projects beyond the resources of the collectives, and to integrate agricultural production with the mass labour projects on the one hand and the development of small-scale industry on the other. At the same time, the communes served not only as an instrument for the better utilisation of the existing labour force, but also for augmenting the force with women released from housework. Last, but not least, the task of managing consumption controls and preventing leakages must have appeared easier with a smaller number of large units.

In its first year (i.e. 1958), the application of the new strategy, coupled with the organisation of communes, was characterised by improvisation, lack of realism, false starts and a great deal of waste. This was perhaps most pronounced in the mass movement to produce iron and steel in the backyard. As is well known by now, the quality of the resulting product was so defective that much of it had to be scrapped. Yet it would be erroneous to base one's judgment of the success or failure of the strategy as a whole on this single example.

In respect to small-scale industry growth, Chinese communist planners seem to have learnt from their failures in 1958. Realising that they had over-reached themselves, they continue to push vigorously for the development of these industries but on a more modest and rational basis. In the course of 1959 and 1960, considerations of technical feasibility received more attention. At the same time, it was recognised that the rural sector could not be left entirely to its own resources ; if it was to grow, it had to receive technical assistance as well as some investment goods from the modern sector. Thus in the course of its adaptation to reality, this model—like all others—lost some of its purity.

In contrast, the attempt to raise farm yields and expand agricultural production through this mass mobilisation of labour seems to have failed, as evidenced by the current food crisis. In effect, China's agricultural difficulties represent an eloquent testimony to the fact that there are no shortcuts to technological progress and technical transformation in farming.

In essence, the ingredients of China's agricultural crisis are very similar to those encountered by the Soviets in the course of their development. Agriculture was kept on a short investment ration and the reward for the peasant's labour was kept to a minimum. From the outset, the Chinese communists were unwilling to devote enough resources to develop domestic fertiliser production and/or import enough fertiliser to raise agricultural yields. At the same time, in order to check increases in peasant consumption, constantly new forms of agricultural organisation were tried out—each involving progressively tighter control by the state. Thus, barely was land distribution completed in 1952 when various forms of producer co-operation were instituted. Then in 1955–56 the drive for collectivisation was on, and just as it was completed, the drive for the organisation of the communes was started. Chinese agriculture was kept in a perpetual state of uncertainty, reorganisation, and disorganisation.

All these factors, low levels of investment, unfavourable farmer incentives, and agricultural organisation, were hardly conducive to agricultural development. In the meantime, the Chinese population has been growing rapidly and steadily, at a rate of about 2 to 2·5 per cent a year, while agricultural production was subject to sharp harvest fluctuations in response to weather. Thus, since the advent of the communist regime, there have been three good harvests in China—in 1952, 1955, and 1958. Each marked the inauguration of some major new move or policy : the first five-year plan in the first case, collectivisation of agriculture and nationalisation of industry in the second, and the introduction of the communes in the last. In turn, each of these good harvests was followed by two or more poor ones. This has given the whole pattern of economic development a zigzag character, with large outpourings of effort and major surges forward at a time of favourable harvest, followed by a slowing down and a pulling back afterwards.

WHAT are the implications of all this for other underdeveloped areas? Are any elements of the Soviet or Chinese communist strategy applicable to underdeveloped countries pursuing different objectives, based on a different ideological orientation?

It could perhaps be said that both communist and non-communist societies are dedicated to the same long-range objectives, namely, raising standards of national power and standards of living more or less simultaneously. But, as was pointed out earlier, these two objectives are, at least in the short or intermediate run, mutually inconsistent. The contradiction tends to be resolved in Soviet-type economies by assigning a high priority to power and downgrading welfare. Other underdeveloped areas, however, tend in varying degrees to follow the opposite course.

There is no question that a Soviet-type strategy, other things being equal, can always attain a much higher rate of savings and capital formation. But will this necessarily guarantee higher rates of economic growth under a wide variety of conditions?

In this context it should perhaps be noted that the Soviet and Chinese strategies are peculiarly well suited to large countries with vast and varied natural and human resources. These strategies are essentially autarkic in character, and, to this extent at least, much less well adapted to small countries, for which the actual or potential advantages of international specialisation are much greater, and for which the penalties of an autarkic policy are much greater, too. This proposition seems to be borne out by the post-war experience of Eastern Europe, where the imposition of the Soviet model has met with much less success than in its own habitat. In effect, a part of savings may have been dissipated through significant diseconomies due to attempts to pursue a domestically based pattern of ' balanced ' growth. Under these conditions, high rates of capital formation were at times accompanied by low rates of economic growth.

What this suggests is that even countries which are prepared to sacrifice present for future consumption, and to disregard social costs and the surrender of individual liberties, may not necessarily reap the high rates of growth which might be expected on the basis of the Soviet experience.

(This article is based on a paper read at the thirteenth annual meeting of the Association for Asian Studies in Chicago, 28 March 1961.)

III. The Roots of Social Policy

H. F. Schurmann

BASIC ORGANISATIONAL APPROACHES

FOR more than a decade now, the Chinese People's Republic has formed the second great communist society in the world. In its development, it has not only been linked tightly to the Soviet Union ; it has followed the path of the Soviet Union in seeking the rapid socio-economic transformation of society through a powerful system of organised totalitarian rule. Yet despite the massive influence of its northern ally, its ' road to socialism ' has in many instances deviated sharply from that of the Soviet Union. Though international communist documents proclaim the unshakeable unity of the ' socialist camp ', the differentiating influences of ' national characteristics ' are now officially admitted.[1] This may not mean much in regard to the small nations held in the Soviet sphere by more than mere ideological solidarity. But it is of much greater significance if a country like China veers from the Soviet model. Differences between the two countries seem already to have produced a certain ideological alienation between them, and this ideological alienation may have been, if not an immediate, an underlying factor in their recent quarrel.

Although the Chinese communists developed their own organisational methods during the Yenan period (1935–45), the changed circumstances facing them after final victory in 1949 brought about a temporary deviation from these methods. The reconstruction phase and that of the slowly evolving first five-year plan witnessed a far-reaching emulation of the Soviet organisational model. As in the Soviet Union, the first five-year plan concentrated on the rapid and select development of heavy industry, notably in a few favoured areas such as Manchuria. Although land reform and a measure of collectivisation were carried through in other parts of the country, agriculture was seen essentially as a source of capital accumulation for industry. Considerable emphasis was put on the development of complex ministerial and technical bureaucracies. Increasingly important structures of economic control, resembling the Soviet Ministry of State Control, began to evolve. In industry, the dominant managerial principle was the ' single director system ', copied straight from the Soviet Union. Though with modifications, the Soviet conception of planning was adopted : detailed, centralised, long-term planning. The organisational accent during this period was on *centralism*, on management from the top down. This emulation of the Soviet model was not entirely a matter of choice, for in Manchuria Soviet

---

[1] Khrushchev in his XX Party Congress speech admitted the existence of national differences between communist parties. References to national differences were repeated in the 1957 and 1960 Moscow Declarations.

influence and the rule of Kao Kang, who had already laid the roots of his power before final victory, had created a miniature ' Soviet ' state. The leadership functions of the party during this period were often dubious, for one saw admonitions to party committees not to interfere in managerial functions.[2]

The effective unification of the state apparatus in 1954, and the downfall of Kao Kang, started a counter-development which was to lead to the formulation of the second five-year plan, and to a second organisational phase at sharp variance with the first. As early as February 1954, the party issued a call for strengthening the functions of party committees in organisational units.[3] The *Su-Fan* movement, which began in the summer of 1955, started a drive against the growing bureaucracy ; the ominous phrase ' bureaucratism ' began to appear again and again.[4] The single director system, which had been praised as an ' advanced experience of the Soviet Union ', began to fall into desuetude. The Ministry of Control, which began to assume Soviet proportions with the development of economic control functions, lost more and more of its power. At the Eighth Party Congress (1958), a new line was proclaimed : ' the mass line '. In its concrete manifestations, it reversed many of the major policies of the preceding period. Centralised, detailed, long-term planning was criticised and abandoned in favour of greater decision-making autonomy at lower levels and periodic plan revision. The single director system was officially abolished. Henceforth, economic development was to take place simultaneously throughout the society rather than in a few favoured regions. Industry and agriculture must develop co-ordinately. Subsequently far-reaching decentralisation measures in industry, commerce, and finance were announced. Above all, the crucial role in the coming period was to devolve on the party, and in particular on mass-level party cadres and activists.[5]

As the second five-year plan (1958–1962) led to the great leap forward and the formation of the communes, the Chinese communists increasingly expressed their conviction that they had discovered a new organisational approach, one by which they could speed up the pace of economic development. The key lay in the maximal activation of basic organisational units : work teams and brigades. If the entire web of organisation throughout China could be so activated, vast new reservoirs of labour energy could be tapped. Labour was, after all, China's one great resource. If the basic unit was the key to the process, that key could be manipulated only by dynamic leadership cadres implemented in their

2 On the first five-year plan, see Choh-ming Li, *Economic Development of Communist China* (University of California Press, 1959), pp. 5-12; T. J. Hughes and D. E. T. Luard, *The Economic Development of Communist China, 1949-1958* (Oxford University Press, 1959), pp. 35-58. On Kao Kang's admonitions against party interference in management, see *Jen-min Jih-pao*, 5 June 1960, section IV 2.
3 *Jen-min Jih-pao*, 18 February 1954.
4 Ho Kan-chih, *Chungkuo hsientai koming-shih* (Hong Kong, 1958), pp. 388-91.
5 Hughes and Luard, op. cit., pp. 59-71.

midst. The massive build-up of the party and organisational decentralisation gave new power to these cadres. They were no bureaucrats, but something in the nature of guerrilla leaders, autonomous in many of their actions, yet totally subordinate to the centre. Military terminology is more and more used to describe the new organisational formations which arose at this time. During the earlier phase, the Chinese communists were often ashamed of their crude rural background, and again and again stressed the need to change perspective in the new urban environment. Many guerrilla cadres could not adjust and were purged during the *San-Fan* movement in the early 1950s. But now the Yenan guerrilla leader became the model for countless commune and factory cadres.[6]

The great leap forward and commune-isation produced phenomena which were alien to the Russians, and even provoked negative reactions. The frenetic mass movements by which the population was aroused to self-sacrificial work-enthusiam were never known in Russia. The communes, which internally were marked by a military kind of discipline, were of a magnitude surpassing anything the Russians had attempted. On the other hand, the extraordinary decentralisation of the national economy, with its deleterious effects on planning, sharply diverged from Soviet ideas of economic centralism. Local cadres were given a scope for decision-making which exceeded greatly that granted by the Russians to lower members of the apparatus. In fact, it has been excessive decentralisation at the national level coupled with oppressive centralisation at the unit level which has been a major organisational factor in the present economic disbalance in China.

The central organisational idea behind the great leap forward was the activation of the basic groups by cadre leaders internally embedded in the group, and living in close personal contact with its members. During this period so-called *hsiafang*—' transfer downward '—movements led to a continuing emptying of managerial staffs as office cadres were sent down again and again to the front lines of production. It was the group cadre who organised ' study ' and ' indoctrination ' through countless small group meetings held after working hours. It was the group cadre, through his exemplary actions, who led the group in its work. It was he, as the committed agent of the party, who supervised the group, checked on its actions and reported to higher echelons. Everywhere, it was the party committee which held decisive authority. The commune committees were dominated by the party, as were managerial staffs in all other organisations.

Despite the formal similarities in Soviet and Chinese communist organisation, particularly that of the party, functionally the differences are very great. The rapid bureaucratisation of Soviet society and the extreme centralisation of power created a mass level organisational leader very different in nature from the Chinese communist cadre. In contrast to communist China, particularly during the great leap period, where party

6 Richard Hughes, *The Chinese Communes* (London, 1960), pp. 34–36.

cadres commanded and led everything directly and personally, lower level decision-making in the Soviet Union has been largely of an administrative character, and hence has been in the hands of bureaucrats. Total subordination to the centre made the kind of autonomous ' spontaneity and creativity ' characteristic of the Chinese cadre impossible in the Soviet Union. Where practical difficulties necessitated adjustments, they tended to be informal and illegal in a technical sense, even though the regime often preferred to ignore this. In the Soviet factory, the dominant figure is the factory director, the ' one-man manager ' ; the party secretary often wields great influence, though usually because of his personal characteristics and access to party channels rather than his formally allocated authority. Although party membership is a sign of elite status, it does not carry with it the expectation of direct personal leadership as in China. As scholars in the field have noted, indoctrination, supervision and recruitment are the three chief functions of the party member. The leadership functions of a party member derive from his particular bureaucratic role, rather than directly from party membership. If the Chinese cadre took on a military character, in Russia he was eminently a civilian, an *apparatchik*. Though the *apparatchik* was formally embedded within an organisation, and though a ' web of mutual involvement ' at times bound him to other bureaucratic figures, his leadership functions tended to be institutional rather than personal. If the ' Stalinist formula ' was one of ' maximum pressure, incentive or coercion ', so the role of the *apparatchik* involved an external acting on those under him—' from the top down '.

THE RUSSIAN AND CHINESE REVOLUTIONS

Obviously there are very great differences between the Russian and Chinese Revolutions. But it is perhaps not always realised to what extent the revolutionary process in each of these countries has influenced its subsequent development. In Russia, Bolshevik power began with the sudden seizure of state power and ended with the effective extension of Soviet authority through most of the old Tsarist Empire. In China, the seizure of state power marked the climax of a revolutionary process, of a gradual build-up of military and political nuclei. These differences have had an important bearing on the subsequent development of the Russian and Chinese communist systems.

The Bolsheviks, almost until the eve of the October Revolution, remained a small, conspiratorial party. Though they undoubtedly enjoyed considerable sympathy throughout Russia's urban working class, severe oppression prevented them from creating a wide organisational network. The ideological split from the Mensheviks, and from West

---

7 Merle Fainsod, *How Russia is Ruled* (Harvard, 1953), p. 154 ff.; Bauer, Inkeles, and Kluckhohn, *How the Soviet System Works* (Harvard, 1957), pp. 44, 51, 161, 164; Joseph S. Berliner, *Factory and Manager in the USSR* (Harvard, 1957), especially p. 264 ff.

European social democracy in general, made the Bolshevik Party a disciplined and powerful organisational weapon, but one ill-suited for the maximal recruitment of revolutionary cadres. The decisive event preceding October was of course the February Revolution, which not only gravely weakened the power of the state, but destroyed its legitimacy. Yet centuries of despotic political centralisation plus the exigencies of war had created an autocephalous state with its exposed pinnacle in Petrograd. Capture of state power was the decisive first step towards total power. In China, as we shall see, the situation was different. But in Russia, the decisive revolutionary act hinged on a sudden seizure of state power. It is significant that France, the one European country with long traditions of political centralisation, offered precedents of similar revolutionary action : Paris was the key to France ! In a sense it was Lenin's organisational ideology which equipped the Bolsheviks for the sudden dramatic event. A gradual policy of encroachment on the *directoire* state would probably have failed ; the exposed head of Russian state power had to be seized at one blow, in a single decisive disciplined action. Among the revolutionary parties, none but the Bolsheviks was equipped and minded for such an all-or-nothing act.

Another important feature of the Russian Revolution was that the disintegration of the monarchy did not lead to the rise of local political formations, with the exception of the separatist movements in the national minority regions. The 1911 Revolution in China was followed by immediate attempts to reconstitute the state apparatus, but the sudden emergence of regional political figures—largely of warlord type—doomed this attempt to failure. Ever since the Taiping Rebellion, Ch'ing policy favoured the creation of embryonic warlords, for to suppress the rebels the Manchus had to allow the organisation of permanent regional armies. But, as had happened earlier in Chinese history, the rise of local armies created the foundations for local political entities, as warlords allied themselves with local power elites. In Russia there were no local political formations, except in the nationality areas. The White enemies of the Bolsheviks, after the October Revolution, aimed at nothing less than total recapture of state power. Their obsession with Petrograd made them oblivious to local conditions, as in the case of Kolchak, who stubbornly refused to compromise with nationality movements. The extension of Bolshevik power after 1917 became a straight military task, in which the Bolsheviks were greatly aided by popular uprisings and support. They pushed their power outward from Petrograd, ' from the top down ', so to speak. Having defeated the Whites, their next task was the destruction of separatist nationality movements, again largely through external conquest.

The sudden and total seizure of autocephalous state power created conditions for the immediate re-institution of a state bureaucracy and the immediate organisation of a regular army. While political and ideological differences still rent the ranks of the revolutionary government, a vast administrative bureaucracy arose once more. The formation of the Workers and Peasants Inspectorate (Rabkrin) in 1919 as a control instrument over the new bureaucracy (significantly dominated by Stalin) indicates the rapidity with which bureaucracy proliferated. Lenin, in his last writings, expressed serious alarm over the rapid and unexpected re-bureaucratisation of the Soviet system. While Stalin busied himself with bureaucracy, Trotsky organised a *regular* Red Army, whose co-ordinated divisions bolstered by Bolshevik organisational discipline carried the revolution to Russia's distant corners.

Despite the gradual elimination of dissidents from the ranks of the party, the general influence of Soviet and revolutionary ideology, plus the sense of freedom prevailing in the early years after the revolution, made it a poor organisational instrument. Much more reliable was the new bureaucracy, and as Stalin consolidated his power, the new bureaucracy began to develop with greater speed. Furthermore, though Soviet ideology had originally allowed for a certain degree of self-determination at local levels, the subsequent period saw a rapid re-centralisation and concentration of power in Moscow's ministries. The proliferation of bureaucracy soon brought with it a concern with problems of ' control ', political and economic. Stalin's growing obsession with problems of control ultimately led to the all-pervasive system of political control through the secret police, and economic control through the powerful Ministry of State Control.

Just as the Russian Revolution was extended ' from the top down ', so also was the emerging Soviet system pressed on to society ' from the top down '. ' Centralism ' became the dominant organisational theme under Stalin. Detailed, long-term planning arose in an organisational context which facilitated rule from the centre. Local ' spontaneity and creativity ', often even by local Stalinists, was brutally destroyed.[8] A secret police system—par excellence a system of ' external ' control ' from the top down '—became the backbone of a despotic and centralised state. Purge after purge soon eliminated ' soviet ' tendencies from the party, and created a hierarchical structure of bureaucratic party *apparatchiki*. The old Russian alienation of state and society once again appeared. Bureaucrat and gendarme were once again the chief figures, with the extremely crucial difference that the state now interfered in everything. The new regime remained thoroughly committed to the Marxist idea that society must be totally transformed through the actions of the polity.[9] The concrete goal of this ideological conviction was the total socio-economic transformation of Russia into a great industrial (if not industrialised) society. To this goal Stalin adhered unwaveringly. If the new instrumentalities echoed alarmingly those of the *ancien régime*, the new ideology was radically different. Soviet Russia was not a simple

---

[8] See, for example, the case of Comrade Rumyantsev; Merle Fainsod, *Smolensk under Soviet Rule* (Harvard, 1958), pp 59–60.

[9] The conceptual distinction between ' polity ' and ' society ' is particularly important in the study of communist systems.

Tsarist restoration, as little as communist China is a new Chinese dynasty. Yet continuities there obviously are, even across the abyss of total revolution.

The process of revolution in China was very different. In China the seizure of state power marked the climax of a long and arduous struggle. During this struggle the Chinese communists suffered two far-reaching defeats and underwent a series of deep internal crises. Yet out of these defeats and crises there emerged a unified party and a powerful army which in 1945 was ready to attempt the supreme push for total power. During the first period (1920–27), the party emerged, more or less on Comintern initiative, from the ranks of China's increasingly Marxist intellectuals. The small ' study groups ' earlier organised by Li Ta-chao were soon transformed into communist cells. The growing trade union movement in China's coastal cities provided fertile ground for creating a mass organisational base for the new party. China was at that time in a state of nationalistic and revolutionary fervour, which reached a climax in the march northward of the Kuomintang. The policy of collaboration with the Kuomintang, ordered by the Comintern, opened up a second avenue towards power : infiltration into the emerging political structure. The example of the Russian Revolution, which lay only a few years back, deeply influenced the thinking of the then leaders of the Chinese Communist Party. If the Wuhan government was indeed to be the *directoire*, then state power could be seized in the same sudden, dramatic way as in Petrograd : by a powerful disciplined party supported by urban and proletarian mass organisations.[10] However, Chiang Kai-shek did not turn out to be a Kornilov, and the feeble structure of the Wuhan government was easily destroyed. China was indeed not Russia, for neither Peking nor Wuhan formed an autocephalous pinnacle of state power, the seizure of which would be decisive for the revolution. The 1911 Revolution had been followed by the rise of regional political entities. The amorphousness of state power was to bedevil Chiang Kai-shek, too, but he felt that the problem could be at least provisionally solved through exchanging formal recognition of his sovereign power in Nanking by the war lords, for a more or less open tolerance of their local power. The first phase in the history of the Chinese Communist Party ended with the bloody purges of April 1927 and the almost total destruction of communist organisations in the urban centres.

If the first phase was marked by the growth of the party apparatus, the second phase started with the formation of the Red Army as the result of defections of units of the Kuomintang armies. The focus of revolutionary action shifted not only from city to countryside, but also from party to army. As long as the Mao Tse-tung and Chu Teh faction did not have complete control of the central committee, they could not

[10] On the complex politics of Chinese communism during this phase, see Benjamin I. Schwartz, *Chinese Communism and the Rise of Mao* (Harvard, 1951), p. 79 ff. For a more or less official communist view in retrospect, see Ho Kan-chih, op. cit., p. 126 ff.

transform the party into a disciplined instrument under their centralised control. Furthermore, the massive recruitment into the party of rural elements, with little training and low consciousness, made it less than ever a usable organisational instrument. But the army was entirely under the control of the Mao-Chu group, and it was the Red Army which provided the power for the organisation of the Chinese soviets. The revolutionary process in the Kiangsi-Hunan region swung sharply from the earlier phase, when the party sought to grasp state power ' from the bottom up ', to one where an army-based revolutionary organisation sought to impose revolution ' from the top down '. Land reform was carried out in a drastic and doctrinaire manner. Peasant soviets were organised wherever the power of the Red Army penetrated. By the time the Mao-Chu group acquired control of the party apparatus, the new revolutionary patterns were already dominant. The second phase reached its climax with the creation of an embryonic state power, the Chinese Soviet Republic. But the Chinese Soviet Republic was short-lived, for under the dual pressure of attacks from Chiang's troops and internal discontent, the party and army, now organisationally unified, embarked in 1934 on their long march into China's remote northern areas.

The third phase (1935–45), the so-called Yenan period, proved to be decisive in the organisational development of Chinese communist power. The popular front policy and the threat from Japan freed the communists from obsession with capture of state power. The popular front policy, followed by all communist parties, also freed them from their doctrinaire approach to organising social revolution. Organisationally speaking, during the Yenan period the communists faced two major problems : (1) building up party and army into tight, disciplined, co-ordinated forces, and (2) constructing mass-level organisations, the building blocks on which their power must rest. It is not coincidental that it is during the Yenan period that one begins bit by bit to detect signs of that ' dialectical ' mode of thinking on organisational problems which has become so characteristic of the Chinese communists in recent years. It was during this period that Mao Tse-tung's theories on guerrilla warfare developed, not as the result of abstract philosophising, but under the impact of the practical problem of organising regular and guerrilla armies in the most effective way. The dialectical opposites of ' commandism ', i.e. too much ' centralism ', and ' mountainism ', i.e. too much ' democracy ', begin to appear in the literature. Guerrilla units and underground party organisations had to be organised, and, given their isolated circumstances, an operational autonomy granted them. Yet though ' spontaneity and creativity ' were expected of them, there also had to be ' submission to the directives of the centre '. On the other hand, despite their widespread reliance on guerrilla warfare, the Chinese communists never lost sight of the basic fact that ultimately the decisive actions against the Kuomintang would be fought with regular armies, though the support of guerrilla units and ' mobilisation of the masses ' would be crucial factors. Organisationally, the Yenan period seemed to combine the ' dialectically ' opposite methods of the first and second periods (revolution from below and from above) into a single system.

It was during the Yenan period that so many of the characteristically Chinese communist organisational practices arose : thought reform, group control, rectification. In fact, the scattered nature of Chinese communist power necessitated control from within units as well as from without. No amount of regular army discipline could effectively control the actions of thousands of scattered guerrilla groups. More and more the function of control devolved upon the politically trained party cadres. Party enrolment during this period rose from 40,000 in 1937 to over one million in 1945. If regular army discipline could not in itself effectively control the guerrilla units, no bureaucratic instrument (non-existent with the non-existence of state power) could control villages and regions once ' liberated ' by Red Army action but again surrendered under hostile pressure. In the face of enemy re-occupation, only organised cadres implanted in the villages and regions could continue to exercise control. It was during this period that the cadre—*kanpu*—emerged as the decisive organisational figure. It was essential for him to have the ability to lead and organise, but it was also crucial for him to be ideologically and politically sound. The constant emphasis on ' study ', to be carried out everywhere and anywhere, was designed to assure not only absolute political commitment, but also the foundations for a communications system on which overall co-ordination depended.[11]

The Yenan period brought into being a powerful party and army, marked by extraordinary organisational perfection. The last chinks in the power of the centre had been closed with the death of Chang Kuo-t'ao and Wang Ming in the later 1930s. Almost a decade of uninterrupted work had built up the system into a sophisticated and effective instrument. The war proved a welcome opportunity for the communists, for while patriotic fervour impelled thousands of young people into the party, where they were trained as cadres, the various battle actions, small and fragmentary rather than large and concentrated, in which the communists participated, provided the ground on which organisational work could rapidly proceed. The final victory over the rotting forces of the Kuomintang probably took place more easily than the communists expected.

State power was seized, but it was still amorphous. Under the influence of the Soviet model and Soviet direction, a new apparatus of state was rapidly reconstructed. Yet the existence of the ' large administrative regions ', notably Manchuria, again posed the danger of localism. Perhaps, paradoxically, it may have been the very ' centralism '

---

[11] Unfortunately the Yenan period has not received sufficient critical study by scholars. See Boyd Compton, *Mao's China—Party Reform Documents 1942–44* (University of Washington Press, 1952), pp. xv–xxxiii. Liu Shao-ch'i's speeches and writings during this period on the subject of leadership reveal the new organisational thinking then developing.

which Kao Kang practised in his ' independent kingdom ' which made it easy to destroy his own autocephalous power sphere. Still, as we pointed out earlier, the very consummation of the process of effective unification of the state apparatus in 1954 was followed by a new organisational policy out of which, ultimately, the great leap forward grew. During this latter phase, the Chinese communists once again made full use of the instruments developed during Yenan days. Cadre leadership of work teams, mass movements, decentralisation with considerable cadre autonomy, and total control and leadership by party organisations became the organisational methods of this period.

RUSSIAN AND CHINESE SOCIETIES

In both great communist societies we see the phenomenon of a complex and powerful political system, a polity, attempting to replace the elements of society with the new institutions of the polity. If the early Marx clearly perceived the distinction between *Staat* and *Gesellschaft*, he felt that in the revolutionary process the new forces of *Gesellschaft* would ultimately destroy the dead institutions of *Staat*. The great communist societies of the 20th century have reversed the process. The ultimate goal is of course the final and irrevocable institutionalisation of the new polity as society. In respect to this drive, there is no difference between the Soviet Union and communist China. But, there are clear and important differences in the specific forms which that process has taken. In Russia, a vast apparatus of state weighs down on the population, by its very power seeking to root out traditional institutions and plant new ones. The new polity has acted on society in an essentially *external* manner. Positive manipulation has taken place bureaucratically, through specificity of role and complex division of tasks. The multiple systems of control have all taken the forms of external pressures : the police, the auditors of the economic control apparatus, and the party *apparatchiki*. Even indoctrination has been external : mass meetings, lectures, massive newspaper propaganda. But in China, despite the formal existence of similar external pressures, the manner of political acting on the society has tended to take more *internal* forms. Instead of reliance on bureaucratic manipulation, the role or organisational leadership has devolved on the cadre, the group leader. Though external control systems are important, more important is internal group control through cadre supervision and group indoctrination. Significant is the relatively minor role played by the secret police. The Chinese communists have always held it crucial to manipulate and control an organised group from within, rather than simply to maintain a firm hold on the group through external coercion.[12]

We have already suggested that these differences can be traced back to the respective revolutionary processes. Are there perhaps factors in

12 See my article, ' Organisation and Response in Communist China ', *The Annals of the American Academy of Political and Social Science*, January 1959, pp. 51-61.

the nature of the two societies which may also account for this difference ? Both Russia and China had long traditions of effective political
centralisation. Ever since the establishment of Muscovite *samoderzhavie*
under Ivan IV, and the final elimination of militarist particularism under
the early Sung, both Russia and China, despite dynastic upheavals and
foreign incursions, have enjoyed a basic internal unity. The creation of
powerful autocratic monarchies did not lead to a merging of polity and
society, but to a juxtaposition of the two. In Western Europe and Japan,
the so-called ' feudal ' period resulted in the development of intermediary
political institutions between the lowest rungs of society and the highest
rungs of the polity. In England, the institutions of local government
proved to be powerful forces, on the one hand supporting unified national
monarchy, and on the other hand exercising a stabilising influence on the
local regions. In Japan, local political formations were strong enough to
resist the centralising tendencies of the Tokugawa. But in Russia and
China such intermediary political formations were absent. The juxtaposition of state and society tended to produce an alienation of one from
the other. In Russia, the *dvorianin* and *chinovnik*, though oppressive
and punitive, were remote figures, living in the capital or other distant
cities. As the wave of European culture flowed into Russia, they even
began to take on foreign mannerisms, and this differentiated them even
more from the great Russian mass. The presence among the Russian
aristocracy of large numbers of nobles of foreign origin, notably Baltic
German, further increased the alienation of polity and society. In China,
the power of the state apparatus rarely reached below the level of the
county township. The magistrate was in theory a man from another
locality. His education and social status established a certain psychic
distance between him and the population. People tried at all costs to
avoid involvement with the magistrate. ' Heaven is high and the emperor
is far away ' was a common saying in traditional China. The state itself
made only few, though heavy, demands on the society : peace and the
payment of taxes.[13]

The nature of these despotic centralised polities gave the state considerable security from internal challenges. All illegitimate political
activity was immediately seen in its maximal implications as a threat to
the state, and was, where possible, suppressed. This meant that political
activity, when it arose on a sizeable scale, had to take on maximal aims.
This was to prove fatal for both the Russian and Chinese monarchies, for
no political activity could be contained at the local level ; it immediately

---

[13] Karl A. Wittfogel, in his monumental *Oriental Despotism* (Yale, 1957), classes both
Russia and China as ' hydraulic societies ', and differentiates them qualitatively from
the ' multicentred societies ' of Western Europe. Since in the hydraulic societies its
power was unchecked, ' state was stronger than society ' (p. 49 ff.). Wittfogel,
however, far overestimates the extent of the ' operational leadership ' of the traditional Russian and Chinese states over society, and therefore fails to appreciate the
crucial change which the Russian and Chinese revolutions brought about. His ' law
of diminishing administrative returns ' (p. 108 ff.) applies much more aptly to phases
of retreat in Soviet and Chinese communist policy, rather than to earlier periods
when as a whole the state did not seek a totalistic transformation of society.

took on national and total implications. Thus the consequence of a concentrated political despotism was a peculiar vulnerability to all-or-nothing challenges.

Yet despite the fact that Russia and China shared these aspects of polity and society, they differed in respect to the kind of relationship existing between the two. Despite the absence of intermediary *political* structures between polity and society, certain intermediary *social* structures did exist in China which were of decisive importance to the state. Though there always was social unrest, a relatively stable social system, particularly in the rural areas, continued down until modern times. Village and clan social ties were perhaps stronger in some areas than in others, but almost everywhere in China the role of traditional social organisations such as village groups, family and clan groups, guilds, native associations, was very strong. This provided a basis of collectivity which was an important factor in maintaining overall social stability. Furthermore, these social formations were dominated by certain traditional leadership groups : men of local power, wealth, and prestige. These were the so-called ' gentry ' families, although there never existed in Chinese a single generic term for this local elite.[14] They consisted of landowners, old families of standing, and families grown influential through present or past political associations. Invariably they persuaded some of their more intelligent members to ' pass the examinations ' and formalise their prestige, and invariably they attempted to get official positions in the bureaucracy for the most promising. Conversely, the closer their associations with the state, the more they expanded their local authority through new prestige, new wealth, and new power. These individuals became the natural leaders of local social organisations (villages, families, guilds, etc.), and it was through them that the local agent of the state, the magistrate, operated to uphold the interests of the state. They tended to be conservative and to support the state, so long as the state did not encroach on their prerogatives. The relationship was a delicate one, and collaboration between state and local elite was not without its breakdowns.

The existence of stable social structures with a leadership elite made it possible for the state to *act through them* rather than simply *on them*. The state was always ready to use external compulsion if more sophisticated methods failed, but centuries of experience had taught the bureaucrat that the disruptive consequences of an act of violence were to be feared and such acts should be taken only in extreme cases. The Chinese

---

[14] The polemic over the ' Chinese gentry ' has occupied Sinologists for some time. The historical term ' gentry ' should be abandoned for a more neutral sociological term to avoid false analogies. The lack of a single comprehensive term in Chinese for this group suggests that it was neither a class nor an estate. On the most general level one can say that they were a local leadership group whose power and status had multiple origins. The relationship between state and society in traditional China was always a tense one, and the position of the local elite over the centuries was always subject to fluctuations. See Eberhard, op. cit.; Chung-li Chang, *The Chinese Gentry* (University of Washington Press, 1955).

communists were very conscious of the existence of this group, and the slogan ' destroy the local gentry ' was a common one throughout the civil war. When the Chinese communists, after final victory, began large-scale land reform, one of their major problems was not the physical annihilation of these local elites, but the destruction of their leadership and authority. Land reform was usually preceded by a ' mass movement ' called ' destroy the bandits and oppose the powerful '. To couple the local elite with the local bandits started the process of discrediting them ; it was completed by the public disgracing of the traditional ' men of prestige '—*wangtsu*—in the villages. They were bound and dragged into public places. Party *kungtsotui*, ' operation squads ', compelled the peasants to denounce them individually. They were forced to ' lower their heads '—*tit'ou*—the final symbolic act of total humiliation. One need not be a Freudian to accept the proposition that the attitude of people towards men of authority is always ambivalent. If centuries of tradition had generated feelings of awe and respect for the local elite, the communists released the suppressed resentments of the people against the elite. Confucian ideology had always stressed effectiveness and success as a sign of legitimate authority. Now total communist victory plus the universal humiliation of the local elite opened the floodgates of hatred. The bloodiness of the land reform period recalls the popular excesses of the French Revolution. The result was the total elimination of the traditional elite ; but their disappearance produced a vacuum, and into this vacuum there stepped the cadre, the agent of party and state. The cadre became the new leader and the new elite, though lacking the security of legitimacy and acceptance. Yet no one saw or could see the cadres as a new ' gentry '. The first step towards the destruction of traditional village social structure had been taken, and no new leadership group could automatically step into the shoes of the old. Furthermore, the cadre came armed with a totally new ideology, one which explicitly rejected the premises of the old. He was a strange figure, even if he was a native of the village and spoke in local accents. But, like the old elite, the cadre was supposed to be an internal and not an external figure. He is the ever-present leader in constant contact with the masses. He is the work team leader, the study leader, the leader of all the new associations into which the peasant masses were pressed. Where in traditional China the state acted through the *wangtsu*, today it acts through the cadres. But whereas the former were non-political, today the cadre is eminently political. The old juxtaposition of state and society is gone. In its drive to transform society, the state has made the cadre its direct instrument. Though equivalent in position to the old elite, functionally the cadre represents a completely different and new figure.

Unlike China, the legal stratification of society into estates in Russia precluded social mobility. Though the lot of the Chinese peasant was as miserable as that of the Russian serf, the former was never bound to the land, and was free to move physically elsewhere or socially upward (if he could). If the old *obshchina* shared with the Chinese village the trait of social integration, little was left of stable village organisation in pre-modern Russia. The *mir*, as Lenin repeatedly pointed out, was created to introduce order into a basically unstable peasant social situation, in the interests of the state.[15] The consolidation of serfdom in the 17th century was a sign of social disorganisation. The destruction of the boyars by Ivan IV in the 16th century eliminated the rural aristocracy and replaced them with a military bureaucracy, and though they gradually evolved into a landlord class, their homes were in the towns. There was cruel exploitation of the serf peasantry, but not that personal contact which elsewhere created a certain community between lord and peasant. The bureaucracy which ruled Russia in the 19th century did not have the same local roots as the Chinese bureaucrat had, roots reinforced by family and religious ties. In Russia, bureaucracy and nobility were segments of the polity without those social links to the society as a whole which were operative in China. State and society were juxtaposed and alien to each other, lacking the intermediate political structures of Western Europe and the intermediary social links of China. The state ruled directly through external pressures : bureaucratic administration and police control. This essentially external approach of the polity to society was to continue in the Soviet period, except that the new system sought to eliminate the gap between state and society by revolutionising the foundations of society. Under the Tsars the state was essentially exploitative and punitive ; under the Soviets a new function was added : organised manipulation to create a modern industrial society.

CONVERGENT OR DIVERGENT PATHS?

No one can answer that question. In many ways, what has been said above may relate to a period now past. Since the death of Stalin, there have been far-reaching changes aimed at reducing the terrible psychic gap between state and society which the Stalin era produced, at drawing people out of their atomistic isolation. There are signs that the Chinese communists, too, have retreated from the extremes of their great leap policies. Since the beginning of 1961 the regime has relaxed its pressure on the society. A piecemeal rectification movement has reduced the despotic powers of the rural cadres, and attempts are even being made to transform them gradually into administrative, i.e. bureaucratic personnel. If the political upheaval following Stalin's death was a major factor in producing liberalisation in the Soviet Union, in China it has been the massive economic crisis. How permanent the changes launched in 1961 will be, no one can say. In both countries the basic systems have remained intact, and the differences we have indicated continue to exist.

15 *Lenin—Collected Works* (Moscow, 1960), Vol. I, pp. 512–3; also, D. S. Mirsky, *Russia, A Social History* (London, 1931), p. 149.

TOWN PLANNING AND HOUSING

Timothy Sosnovy *

THE forcible collectivisation of agriculture and the beginning of the industrialisation programme in the First Five-Year Plan (1928–32) brought the question of the Soviet city into sharp focus because it made necessary relocation of millions of workers who poured into the cities from rural localities. This made the problem of rebuilding the existing cities and building new cities extremely acute. An extensive discussion on the Soviet city was held during the 20s and early 30s.

In this discussion there was unanimity among the various writers in regard to rejecting the old type of 'capitalist' city. They all agreed that 'the Soviet city which is to become the city of a socialist society is bound to be different from the city of the bourgeois society'.[1] Another writer declared that 'our cities must be transformed radically; the modern city is a product of the capitalist era'.[2]

The discussion of the type of Soviet city was to have answered the problem of population distribution under Soviet conditions. One of the participants said : ' Before deciding about the new cities, we must decide in principle : will we have a non-urbanised socialist distribution of population or the old urbanised type? '

In this discussion there were two schools of thought—the ' urbanist ' and the ' disurbanist.' Urbanised distribution, i.e. spontaneous and unlimited growth of cities, was condemned primarily because it was a part of the capitalist system. The basic requirement of the disurbanists was that cities should not be accumulations of large masses of people as in capitalist countries, where they grew up unplanned, spontaneously, and therefore with no limitation as to size.

The decision as to the size of the socialist city was in accord with the conceptions of the disurbanists, who considered that cities should be broken up because ' every large city created undoubted large losses, and designing large cities amounts to the same thing as planning great wastefulness '. Some of the debaters thought that the optimal size of cities should be no more than 100 to 150 thousand.[3] Others considered

* I am pleased to acknowledge my indebtedness to the Russian Research Center at Harvard University for its support of the study on which this article is based.

[1] *Sovetskoe stroitelstvo* (Soviet construction), October 1928, p. 10.
[2] L. M. Sabsovich, *Goroda budushchevo i organizatsiya sotsialisticheskovo byta* (Cities of the future and the organisation of the socialist mode of life), Moscow, 1929, p. 13.
[3] *K probleme stroitelstva sotsialisticheskovo goroda* (On the problem of building the socialist city), Moscow, 1930, pp. 43, 84, 85.

50 to 60 thousand the maximum, and a few went as high as 150 to 200 thousand.[4]

Considerable attention was given to the mode of life in the new type of city. Everyone admitted the need for transforming it. It was emphasised that the main difference between the socialist communities and contemporary cities and villages would be that a number of functions now performed by each individual family would be separated and socialised. Each of these functions would become a separate task that would be performed by a special organisation, as a special public institution.

In the opinion of the participants, the main type of housing was to be huge communal houses (dom-kommuna) equipped with all conveniences. ' Each communal house was to be designed for approximately 2,000 to 2,500 residents, to have three storeys and a norm of seven square meters of living space per person.'[5] Such a communal house would serve primarily as a place to sleep, and that only for adults. The basic element of the communal house would thus be an individual room assigned to each member of the group. The entire area of the communal house could be divided into two parts, private and public ; the first comprising the area of the individual rooms, and the second including all other areas used to serve the various needs of the group. It was pointed out further that public laundries and a large number of other housekeeping and educational institutions for meeting the everyday needs of the populace must be organised in the socialist city.

In June 1931 a special plenary session of the party's Central Committee met to discuss urban renewal and development. The resolution adopted pointed out the need ' to transform existing cities into culturally, technically, and economically developed proletarian centres ' that would satisfy completely the housing and living requirements of the Soviet urban population.[6]

THIRTY years have passed since that discussion. As a result of the policy to force industrialisation, the number of cities and urban-type-settlements has increased from 1,925 in 1926 to 4,713 in 1959, with an increase in their total population from 28·1 million persons in 1926 to 103·7 million at the beginning of 1960. The urbanisation of the population over the same period rose from 18 per cent to 49 per cent.[7] Hundreds of new cities were built, some of which became large

4 B. V. Lunin, *Goroda sotsializma i sotsialisticheskaya rekonstruktsiya byta* (The cities of socialism and socialist reconstruction of the mode of life), Moscow, 1930, p. 28.

5 S. G. Strumilin, *Problemy Planirovaniya v SSSR* (Problems of planning in the USSR), Leningrad, 1932, p. 477.

6 *KPSS v rezoliutsiyakh*, 7th ed., Moscow, 1954, p. 126.

7 *Narodnóe khozyaistvo SSSR v 1958 goda, Statisticheskii ezhegodnik* (National economy of the USSR in 1958, Statistical Annual), Moscow, 1960, p. 19; ibid., 1959, Moscow, 1960, p. 9.

cities,[8] as for example : Karaganda, Magnitogorsk, Komsomolsk on the Amur, Stalingorsk, Angorsk, Norilsk. The population of the old cities had also greatly increased.

The growth of cities and urban-type settlements in the USSR during the last 20 years is shown in Table 1.

TABLE 1

POPULATION OF CITIES AND URBAN-TYPE SETTLEMENTS

IN 1939 AND 1959 [9]

	Years		Population									
	Total		below 20,000		from 20,000 to 50,000		from 50,000 to 100,000		from 100,000 to 500,000		Over 500,000	
	1939	1959	1939	1959	1939	1959	1939	1959	1939	1959	1939	1959
Number of cities and urban-type settlements	2,759	4,713	2,256	3,930	315	474	99	161	78	123	11	25
(In %)	100.0	100.0	81.8	83.4	11.4	10.0	3.6	3.4	2.8	2.6	0.4	0.6
Population in millions	60.4	100.8	15.3	26.2	9.6	14.7	7.1	11.4	15.6	24.4	12.8	24.1
(In %)	100.0	100.0	25.4	26.0	15.9	14.5	11.7	11.3	25.8	24.2	21.2	24.0

From 1939 to 1959 the number of cities with a population above 100,000 increased from 89 to 148, of which those with a population over 500,000 increased from 11 to 25. These days about one half of the urban Soviet population lives in the big cities.

To what extent do these cities meet the requirements as compared with the requirements of thirty years ago? How is their territory organised? How far are the housing, communal, and social-cultural needs of the urban population being satisfied?

The organisation of a city's territory is very closely associated with city planning, i.e. in the final analysis it has to do with the manner in which the people are distributed throughout the area occupied by the city.

As commonly used, the term city planning refers either to the reconstruction of already developed large urban centres with an established physical design and relatively permanent construction in the central districts, or to the building of new cities in connection with the establishment of large industrial enterprises at previously uninhabited or sparsely populated places.

Soviet authors stress that ' Soviet city construction is developing in the favourable conditions of a planned economy, thanks to the absence of private ownership of land and means of production. This creates unlimited possibilities to improve planning and building in populated

---

8 Large cities are those with a population of more than 100,000.

9 Compiled from *Vestnik Statistiki*, 1960, 8, pp. 88, 90.

areas in order to transform Soviet cities into the best cities in the world.' [10]

What do we have in reality? Has the planned reconstruction of the Soviet cities passed the test of time?

In the years 1935 to 1937, following the elaboration and approval of plans for the reconstruction of Moscow, projects were worked out for the reconstruction of Baku, Yaroslavl, Gorky, Stalingrad, Rostov-on-Don, Novosibirsk, Cheliabinsk, Leningrad. Since then 25 years have passed. Evaluating these works, it was noted at a meeting of the Soviet Academy of Construction and Architecture that the planning and building of Baku in the 30s had considerable shortcomings. The failure to draw up workable and reasonable plans was reflected in the large number of changes that had to be made in the course of putting them into execution, particularly in the planning and building of Yaroslavl, Gorky, Cheliabinsk and Leningrad.[11]

Projects drawn up for the development of Soviet cities often have to be amended to take in the construction of new, previously unforeseen, industrial undertakings. This introduces serious changes into the initial factors of city growth, as well as changes in the number of inhabitants, as is evident from Table 2.

TABLE 2

PLANNED CITY POPULATION IN 1975 AND REAL POPULATION IN
1959, IN THOUSANDS

Cities	Planned population in 1975	Real population in 1959
Gorky	840	942
Tashkent	800	911
Novosibirsk	850	877
Kuibyshev	700	806
Minsk	450	509

Source: *Ekonomika stroitelstva* (Economics of construction), No. 3, 1960, p. 30.

THE same miscalculations have occurred in the construction of new cities. In 1949 work was begun on the construction of the city of Angorsk, calculated for 80,000 inhabitants, but later it was decided that the size of the city population would be more than double that figure. The construction of Novaya Kakhovka, for 25,000 inhabitants, was completed in 1960. It was then thought expedient to instal a number of additional industrial enterprises, to utilise the power of the

10 V. I. Svetlichny, *Zhilishchnoe stroitelstvo v SSSR* (Housing in the USSR), Moscow, 1960, p. 28.
11 *Stroitelstvo v SSSR, 1917-1957*, Moscow, 1958, pp. 210, 211.

Kakhovka hydro-electric power station, thus increasing the number of inhabitants to 100,000. The town of Volgodonsk was planned as a workers' settlement for 3,250 people, but the population already exceeds that figure several times.[12]

As a result of these miscalculations and changes, substantial corrections have to be made in the size of cities, their street networks, the numerical capacity of cultural establishments, and all engineering utilities (waterworks, sewerage, gasworks, etc.).

It is interesting to note that notwithstanding the number of decrees passed since 1931 on limiting industrial construction in big cities, this sort of construction has continued. The result is that, according to the 1959 census results (p. 15), between 1939 and 1959 the population of Gorky increased by 298,000, Sverdlovsk by 354,000, Cheliabinsk by 415,000, Kuibyshev by 416,000, Novosibirsk by 483,000 inhabitants.

This rapid growth is characteristic only of large cities : many small cities do not develop at all. The population of the 148 large cities with more than 100,000 inhabitants averages 330,000 people, whereas the average in the 3,930 smaller cities and settlements with a population below 20,000 is approximately 7,000.

An irrational utilisation of urban territories is characteristic of many cities which are being reconstructed in the USSR. For instance, sites inadequately used or classified as unfit represent, in relation to the entire city territory 73 per cent for the city of Stalingrad, 61 per cent for Kuibyshev, 63 per cent for Krivoi Rog, 64 per cent for Tula, and 71 per cent for Kemerovo. Frequently, large urban areas are occupied by agricultural enterprises.[13]

In the reconstruction of old cities and the building of new ones, regional planning is of great importance because of the possibility of locating cities, workers' settlements, industrial enterprises, sovkhozes, kolkhozes on large territories according to a unified plan. In the USSR regional planning is supposed to be carried out in 80 regions. In fact, it is being carried out only in 37, and has been completed only in a few regions.[14]

At the present time more than a thousand Soviet cities are being reconstructed or built according to a general plan. However, a number of these plans are already obsolete and require serious modification.[15] About 600 cities do not have approved general plans, among them are such large cities as Leningrad, Gorky, Sverdlovsk, Novosibirsk, Omsk, Kuibyshev, Kharkov, Dnepropetrovsk, Cheliabinsk, Odessa.[16]

[12] *Stroitelstvo v SSSR, 1917–1957*, pp. 212, 213; *Ekonomika stroitelstva* (Economics of Construction), No. 3, 1960, p. 30.
[13] *Stroitelnaya gazeta* (Construction gazette), 8 June 1960.
[14] *Pravda*, 25 October 1959, *Arkhitektura SSSR*, No. 6, 1960, p. 12.
[15] Ibid., p. 2.
[16] *Zhilishchnoe stroitelstvo*, No. 3, 1960, p. 1; *Pravda*, 1 June 1960; *Arkhitektura SSSR*, No. 6, 1960, p. 2.

Every city must have a general plan, and this plan must be duly approved. Without such approval, as the Soviet writers point out, the plan is ignored, which is equivalent to its non-existence, and construction in the cities is carried out in a great number of cases without any planning at all.[17]

There is a similar lag in planning the siting of housing, and of cultural and communal buildings. Thus in the RSFSR such plans have been worked out only for 30 cities, in the Ukranian SSR for 20 cities, in the Latvian SSR for four cities, in the Lithuanian SSR for five cities. Particularly great is the absence of projects for detailed planning and building of areas of mass housing ; most cities have none, and this is bound to affect the quality of new housing regions.[18]

SINCE the state, through its central and local agencies, is the sole owner of all forms of property in the cities and the sole organiser and director of all municipal activities, its policies largely determine the condition of life of the urban population ; a sharp worsening in both the housing and the conditions of life of the Soviet city population was one consequence of the policy of rapid industrialisation. Between 1926 and 1940 the living space per capita decreased from 6·45 sq. meters to 4·09 sq. meters.[19]

In the USSR there has always been a housing crisis, but it became especially acute after World War II. Intolerable housing conditions, particularly for the workers, resulted in a large labour turnover in industry, transport, and other sectors of the national economy, and endangered the fulfilment of the economic plans. Not to speak of the dissatisfaction of the urban population. It became essential for the Soviet government to increase appropriations for housing construction, and as a result, the per capita housing space ceased to decline at the end of the 40s. But the improvement in housing conditions is progressing very slowly ; from the end of 1950 to the beginning of 1960, the per capita living space increased from 4·67 to 5·26 sq. meters.[20]

Academician S. Strumilin is correct when he writes that in the USSR ' every toiler craves a separate small room, and a family craves at least a small apartment '.[21] But, under prevailing conditions in the USSR, this is still an unattainable dream for a great number of people, as can be seen in Table 3 (this author's calculations) :

17 *Stroitelraya gazeta*, 8 June 1960.
18 *Voprosy ekonomiki*, No. 7, 1960, p. 59.
19 Timothy Sosnovy, *The housing problem in the Soviet Union*, New York, 1954, p. 106.
20 Timothy Sosnovy, *Soviet Studies*, ' The Soviet Housing Situation Today ', July 1959, p. 4; *Narodnoe khozyaistvo SSSR v 1958 godu*, Moscow, 1959, p 641; *ibid.*, 1959, Moscow, 1960, pp. 9, 566.
21 *Novy mir*, No. 7, 1960, p. 213.

TABLE 3

DENSITY OF OCCUPANCY PER ROOM IN URBAN CENTRES IN THE
SOVIET UNION

Year	Persons per room
1923	2·60
1926	2·71
1940	3·91
1950	3·43
1960	3·04

Today, the predominant type of dwelling in Soviet cities is one room in an apartment shared with others, with a kitchen for common use. One third of the housing fund of cities and urban-type settlements belongs to individuals, and their housing conditions are somewhat better.

The living conditions of the urban population are determined also by the standard of cultural establishments (schools, hospitals, clubs, shops, kindergartens, restaurants, etc.) as well as communal services (waterworks, sewerage, gasworks, public baths, laundries, paving, tree planting, etc.).

A recent survey of construction in 20 cities, carried out by the Building Committee of the Council of Ministers of the USSR, has shown a great lag in the building of cultural and communal utilities. For example, the expenditure on cultural constructions should amount to 15–20 per cent, and for engineering equipment and external improvements, to approximately 25 per cent of the total expenditure for city construction. Actually, the rate of such expenditure is considerably lower in most cities. In Stalingrad, for example, in 1959 only 9 per cent was allotted for cultural purposes, and only 6·7 per cent of the total city expenditure for engineering equipment and external improvements. As a result of this disproportionate distribution of capital investment, schools operate in two and sometimes three shifts, and there is a shortage of children's homes ; the number of shops and enterprises providing the population with foodstuffs is one-half the average.[22]

At the beginning of 1960, of 4,713 cities and urban-type settlements, only 74 per cent were provided with a central water supply system, and of these only 53 per cent also had a sewer system.[23] In fact, even in the cities with a central water system, not all the inhabitants have any plumbing in their apartments. In Moscow itself ' only in the next four or five years are all living quarters expected to be connected with the water supply system '.[24]

[22] *Voprosy ekonomiki*, No. 7, 1960, p. 56.
[23] *Partiinaya zhizn*, No. 7, 1959, p. 18; *Stroitelnaya gazeta*, 8 June 1960.
[24] *Gorodskoe Khozyaistvo Moskvy* (The municipal economy), No. 8, 1960, p. 27.

The conditions of water supply in Ulan-Ude (with a population of 174,000 in 1959) is described in *Pravda* (14 September 1960) : ' Early morning. Pink dawn smiles amiably at the people standing by the water pump with pails and cans. But people with pails in their hands are not interested in pleasant smiles. For two solid hours they sadly contemplate the backs of their neighbours. After waiting for another hour or so they disperse. There won't be any water today '.

At the present time, 235 cities have gasworks ; at the end of 1958 only 18 million people, that is 18 per cent of the urban population, used gas. According to the seven-year plan, gas will be supplied to all residential housing only in Moscow, Kiev, and Leningrad by the end of 1965.[25]

A number of commonplace requirements, such as repairs for clothing and household equipment, dry cleaning, laundry, etc., are provided for only in the largest cities and then most inadequately, *Pravda* recently reported (16 December 1959) as a gratifying achievement, that in Moscow ' several laundries, when requested by the customer, now pick up the laundry at the customer's home and deliver it after washing '.

These conditions hit hardest at women workers and employees with small children who, according to a survey in 1958–1959, spend four to five hours on their home chores during week days and even more on their days off. The same survey shows that in numerous cities in Siberia, many workers spend $1\frac{1}{2}$ to 2 hours just to get to their jobs, and at that quite frequently half of this time is spent waiting for transportation. Shopping also takes a great deal of time in Soviet cities.[26] On the whole, the level of satisfaction obtained from municipal utilities in Soviet cities is very low as compared with that in the United States and Western Europe. Even in Moscow, only 39 per cent of apartments have a bathroom, and only 10 per cent have running hot water.[27]

The big cities in the USSR are badly paved ; most other cities have insufficient pavement or none at all. Soviet cities have few hotels, are poorly lighted and inadequately cleaned.

SOVIET writers see as the basic reason for faulty practice in city construction the inadequate elaboration of a number of theoretical principles, as a result of which ' in a great number of instances the science of city construction has, until now, lagged behind the practical side '.[28]

It would not be right to blame all the shortcomings of Soviet city building on this. Actually, the Soviet government never considered satisfying even the minimum requirements for decent living conditions.

[25] *Arkhitektura SSSR*, No. 8, 1960, p. 5; *Plannovoe khozyaistvo*, No. 11, 1958, p. 63, A. Kucherenko, *Plan velikikh rabot*, Moscow, 1959, p. 49.
[26] *Kommunist*, No. 15, 1960, pp. 43, 45.
[27] *Moskva, Razvitiye khozyaistva i kultury goroda* (Moscow, the development of city economy and culture), Moscow, 1958, p. 75; *Stroitelnaya gazeta*, 8 June 1960.
[28] *Stroitelstvo v SSSR, 1917-1957*, p. 213.

Present interests were neglected in favour of 'the creation of a communist society'. This has been characteristic of the Soviet system throughout the plan era. The refusal to consider the interests of the population on the one hand and the defects of planning on the other explain many peculiar urban phenomena. For example, the State Planning Commission of the USSR and the State Planning Commissions of the Union Republics do not participate in decisions concerning projects for the economic development of the cities. In most instances, the work of the city planning agencies, which do not possess the necessary data, is done at their own risk and responsibility. Of 875 cities in the RSFSR, only 212 have really qualified architects.[29] The Soviet Union today has 8,692 architects all told, although requirements have been estimated at 25,000. Schools of architecture turn out on the average 540 trained personnel annually (*Pravda*, 19 May 1961).

It is axiomatic that the general plan for large cities must be worked out in conjunction with projects for the entire suburban area within a radius of about 100 kilometres. In other words, the planning of the suburban zone must be included in the main city plan and be considered as an integral part of it. Up to now only a few large cities— Moscow, Leningrad, Riga and some others—have projects for planning and building in suburban zones.[30]

The planlessness of plans for city reconstruction can be illustrated by the case of Tomsk, for which, in 1959, 48 organisations were working out projects, of which only eight were local organisations. During one year Commissions arrived from Moscow, Leningrad, Irkutsk, Kiev, and Orel. The city of Yakutsk is supplied with drafts from about fifty central planning organisations.[31]

It is obvious that the Soviet cities of today are not what, thirty years ago, it was thought they would be. Notwithstanding the assertions of Soviet writers 'that the embryo of cities of the communist future is already in existence', and that 'one can already name several such cities', the objective has not been attained.[32] In total industrial output, the USSR occupies second place in the world after the USA. In degree of urbanisation it is catching up with the leading countries of Western Europe and the USA, but in housing, municipal services and urban living conditions generally, it is 50 to 75 years behind.

It is against this background that one has to look at the solemn undertaking of the new programme to solve 'the most acute problem in the well-being of the Soviet people—the housing problem'. And it should be remembered that the 1919 programme also proclaimed this as 'the most immediate task'.

29 *Voprosy ekonomiki*, No. 7, 1960, p. 52: *Stroitelnaya gazeta*, 8 June 1960.
30 *Voprosy ekonomiki*, No. 7, 1960, p. 52.
31 *Arkhitektura SSSR*, No. 5, 1960, p. 4; *Pravda*, 10 June 1960.
32 *Voprosy stroitelstva kommunizma v SSSR*, Materialy nauchnoy sessii otdeleniya obshchestvennykh nauk Akademii Nauk SSSR (Problems of the construction of the communism in the USSR, Materials of the scientific session of the social sciences section of the USSR Academy of Sciences), Moscow, 1959, p. 378.

CITIES OF THE FUTURE

Ernst May

IN 1929 I was invited by the Soviet Government to take part in the planning of new towns. This task seemed so important and at the same time so challenging that I had no hesitation in accepting, and at once set to work with a group of selected collaborators, many of whom now occupy important positions in the German Federal Republic and elsewhere.

On arrival we found conditions at first entirely strange to us. Flags, slogans, placards, memorials, and loudspeakers spreading political and anti-religious propaganda were everywhere. Here and there churches were being demolished. Station waiting rooms were graced by identical artificial palm trees. Most people were very poorly dressed, and smiling faces rare. They seemed to take life with deadly seriousness. Lipstick and cheap perfume were to be had in the shops, as well as large quantities of gilt busts of the political leaders ; but necessities like clothing, shoes, and above all food were in short supply.

The towns gave a strange and cold physical impression. The buildings were badly maintained and transportation was quite inadequate. The Underground did not exist yet and the trams were hopelessly overcrowded, causing many accidents to those clinging to the running boards. There was little motor traffic except for the luxury cars belonging to the party leaders, and makeshift parts were common. The general poverty was even more in evidence when we travelled. Whole families with all their belongings slept on the ground in railway stations, the air was foul, the floor covered with spittle. The railways could not handle the traffic yet. The train lavatories were usually disgustingly filthy, even in first class. At the stations filthy and half-starving beggars and orphans in rags with sunken faces approached us, eluding the police who tried to keep them away.

Even our own housing arrangements were far from satisfactory. The flats in a new structure which had been allotted to us were not ready, so that to begin with we were scattered around numerous hotels, all equally forbidding. Yet amid all this poverty the population, particularly our Russian colleagues, were still warm-hearted, and our friendship with them made the rough conditions seem less harsh. We began to adopt their own philosophy of life : to distinguish the essential from the inessential, to stop complaining about petty things, to accept these conditions as normal.

Turning to professional matters, we found architecture and town planning in a radically experimental stage. In the planning offices of the big cities, especially Moscow and Leningrad, functional western architecture was widely accepted. In Moscow, Le Corbusier was building the headquarters of the Central Cooperative, and Ginsburg a block of flats for officials of the finance ministry on western principles. A planetarium, with a roof projecting far out over its entrance hall, was of high quality. Milyutin's *Sotsgorod*, a brief compendium of modern housing and town planning with examples of western architecture, had just appeared. But, as this booklet itself showed, conditions in the provinces were different. The ostentatious official buildings, clubs, cinemas, and so on, that were being planned and put up there can only be described as architectural monstrosities. The suburbs of the big cities (probably over 80 per cent of all buildings) and most dwellings in the smaller towns still consisted of one or two-storey log houses. Housing was even scarcer than food, and most flats were overcrowded.

Town planning was dominated at the time by the determination of the party leaders and of their planning agencies to utilise it for the expression of socialist ideology, and to turn their backs on the class stratification of towns that had prevailed before the revolution. They were committed to organically incorporating the new social achievements in the new districts, giving everyone equal access to sanitary housing, schools, kindergartens, nurseries, clinics, restaurants, and shops. Clubs and cultural centres were to facilitate not only social contact but also the infiltration of communist ideology. A principle which is now accepted throughout the civilised world, the division of towns into easily recognisable units, was making headway in the USSR at this early date. They were called ' quarters ' and their optimum size, as well as that of towns as a whole, was under discussion.

From the beginning the new regime had emphasised the systematic development of heavy industry. Thus all the towns that we planned were intended to become industrial centres of various sizes : Magnitogorsk, Nizhni Tagil, Kuznetsk, (now Stalinsk), Karaganda, Leninakan (formerly Alexandropol), to name the principal ones.

Our technical procedure was to go as near as possible to the site of the projected town in a special railway carriage, which was then shunted on to a siding and used as our living quarters. We would inspect the terrain in cars, carriages, or sleighs, according to availability and the time of year. Often we were handicapped by a lack of adequate maps. In some room placed at our disposal—usually the assembly room of the local soviet—we would sketch out a plan showing public transport lines, roads, water supply and sewage, and an outline of the necessary dwellings and other buildings. By means of a magic lantern, which we always had with us, we then projected the plan at a public meeting and adapted it according to the discussion that took place. When we returned to Moscow, our headquarters, the plans would be filled out in detail.

The enthusiasm—I might even say fanaticism—with which our group worked on these tasks was comparable to that which had been responsible for the success of our most recent town planning activity in Frankfurt. Our experiences on these ventures left us with lasting impressions. To give just one example, from Leninakan on the Turkish-Armenian border, the former fortress town of Alexandropol. We had completed our plans after an intensive study of the unique local conditions, including terrain affected by frequent earthquakes. The local soviet gave a farewell party for us, out of doors on the banks of a river. We made our way in some rather rickety cars down the steep banks of the ravine, with the river roaring down below. A sheep was slaughtered and delicious shashlik was cooked over an open fire. Meanwhile wine had been lowered into the ice-cold water in a dried and inflated pig's skin ; there was also excellent fruit. Under the influence of the food and wine we exchanged glowing assurances of friendship. Then the Soviet members of our expedition performed Armenian folk dances of extraordinary speed and vitality. When it began to drizzle we started back wondering how soon the cars would get out of the control of the rather merry drivers on the slippery road and hurtle down the slope. But, since God protects children and drunks particularly, we reached the uplands safely, where a dramatic spectacle confronted us. Among the ruins of a village destroyed by earthquake an early Christian church of great structural purity reached out towards the thundery sky crowned by a splendid rainbow. In the dimly lit interior a priest with a great white beard, in a silken robe was immersed in a Bible bound in pigskin. He stood as still as a statute in the rays of the light coming down through the round cupola and took not the slightest notice of what was going on around him. The intoxicated Russians at first jeered, but then, impressed by the old man's demeanour, left him alone and returned to the cars.

THE most important task assigned to us was a general plan for Moscow, on the assumption of a maximum population of four million (greater Moscow now has eight million inhabitants). We applied to a city of millions the concept of a satellite town, which I had first invented in 1925 in a competition for a plan for the expansion of Breslau, a medium-sized city. We inspected the environs of Moscow from this point of view, considering the topography and the prospects for the circulation of traffic. We submitted a project, christened ' Gorod Kollektiv ', which grouped 24 satellites round a central administrative district. Every employed person in the area was to be able to reach his place of work within half an hour by means of a system of fast electric trains.

The reception of our labours was disappointing. The authorities concerned were out of sympathy with it, and it was a generation before the significance of the satellite principle was recognised and put into practice in Moscow and Leningrad. It was once again plain that, even in town planning, stages in development cannot be skipped, that every people must arrive at the frontiers of knowledge by its own experiences. At that time the principle of ' monumental ' axes was still unquestioned, leading to planning on the basis of geometric figures calculated to impress the people with the added weight of pillars and columns and, above all, structural masses.

But a further disappointment followed this rejection of the Moscow plan. The first assignment given to me in Russia had been to prepare an opinion of a plan for the town of Magnitogorsk in the southern Urals, containing iron ore deposits of unusually high purity (up to 80 per cent) which were to be exploited by blast furnaces to be built by Americans. The residential town was to be planned for a quarter of a million inhabitants to begin with. I explained to the head of the Tsekombank that my opinion would consist of a counter-project, since I did not think much of carping at the work of others. He agreed, and in the course of the next few years, with the help of a local branch office, we produced a plan and then began to execute it on the left bank of the Ural. From the very beginning there had been lively discussion whether the town should be built on the right or the left bank. But since I had deadlines to meet for the construction of the town, and since no decision was forthcoming, I had no choice but to proceed according to our plans. Nevertheless, as time went on this state of affairs struck me as extremely unsatisfactory, and I decided on a tactic which I have frequently found effective.

To this end I had our draughtsman make a cardboard clock, with one hand and labelled ' Magnitogorsk '. The hand could be turned to the left, pointing to the words ' *na levom beregu* ', or to the right, to the words ' *na pravom beregu* '. The commissar for heavy industry, Orjonikidze, who was responsible for Magnitogorsk, received me in audience. I handed him the clock and asked him to indicate with the hand the direction which I might then take as the final decision of the Central Soviet. Without batting an eyelid and with a deadly serious face he turned the clock over and engaged me in a rather lengthy discussion of the advantages and disadvantages of each bank of the river, promising me a decision shortly. I never received it, but found out later that they had built Magnitogorsk on both banks.

After many disappointments I decided, after three years, to leave the country, and most of my collaborators came with me. During the subsequent twenty-six years I had no contact with the Soviet Union. But in the spring of 1959 I was invited by the *Bewobau* in Hamburg to join a group of German housing experts and bankers on a fortnight's tour of inspection of the USSR. At the same time the architects' association in Moscow and Leningrad asked me to lecture on town planning and housing in the Federal Republic. I was glad to accept this opportunity to get first-hand impressions of the changes and progress that had taken place since my first visit, almost a generation earlier.

WE crossed the Soviet border from Finland at Viborg, and fundamental changes were obvious at once. The frontier formalities
were completed most helpfully and politely. The station was spotlessly
clean ; the artificial palms and slogans were gone. A single statue of
Lenin dominated the lobby. An equal surprise awaited us that night
in Leningrad whose central area, contrary to the impression given by
wartime and post-war newspaper reports, was exactly as I had left it
in 1933, with not a trace of bombing. I even stayed at the same hotel,
the Astoria, which was also still unchanged, including its plush furniture. All the famous old monuments of the city were still standing,
including the rococo structures of Peter the Great (although I understand his palace at Tsarskoe Selo—now Pushkin—suffered considerable
damage). When I expressed my surprise at the unchanged face of
Leningrad, my Soviet colleagues explained that there had indeed been
extensive war damage in the centre of the city but that all important
buildings had been skilfully restored (which I could corroborate).

Numerous new residential structures, however, had been put up in
the last decades. Large blocks have replaced many of the primitive
wooden buildings. Expansion has been in the direction of the Gulf
of Finland instead of, as formerly, inland. Valuable building areas
are being reclaimed from the sea. Parks and sports areas are being
created. Hard by the Gulf of Finland reclamation has made possible
a stadium holding 100,000 people; of impressively simple construction,
it forms the concluding part of a monumental axis consisting of many
parks, and constructed in a markedly formalist style. By contrast,
the Victory Park is characterised by freer landscaping.

In Minsk we were given figures which may have general validity
as to the distribution of the various sizes of flats in the total programme. According to these, 10 per cent consist of one room, 75
per cent of two rooms, and 15 per cent of four or five rooms. Heavy
industry now has priority over residential building. In all the cities
we visited, ambitious programmes, however, testified to a determination
to remedy the continuing housing shortage without delay.

The central town planning offices employ large staffs. The chief
planning officer in Moscow has 3,300 people working under him.
Residential construction follows a few basic patterns which are
occasionally submitted to committees of administrators, architects, and
tenants for their opinions and then adapted or retained accordingly.

Most flats are very simply equipped, but we did see a number of
blocks of flats with fitted kitchens not very different from our own. I
was struck, however, by the extent to which furniture still falls short
of western standards. None that we saw was anywhere near high
quality or free of aesthetic shortcomings. But since the kitchens are
beginning to approach western standards it is doubtless only a question
of time before due attention is given to furniture too.

Since Khrushchev's speech at the 20th Party Congress in 1956 the general conception of town planning in the Soviet Union has come perceptibly nearer to western principles. The division of towns into quarters, systematically aimed at thirty years ago, remains the basic principle. These quarters are nowadays called micro-rayons, and vary in size like our 'neighbourhoods'. But more attention is paid than in the West to the social amenities of residential districts. In the satellites now being built in Leningrad, Moscow, and Minsk the town planning is far superior to ours. It has been recognised that the growth of big cities is usually attributable to industrial expansion, and accordingly new industrial development has already been banned in Leningrad and Moscow. Conversely, new towns have sprung up all over the country at a rate fantastic by our standards. Between 1926 and 1956, 564 new towns have been built, and the number of big cities has increased from 31 to 135 in the same period.

On the other hand the micro-rayons are becoming less dense. In place of the buildings of up to ten storeys all around the micro-rayon, typical of past decades—one gigantic skyscraper in Moscow is topped by a tower—structures of four or five storeys are now preferred, and there are plans for and even a few examples of low one and two-family houses. In Leningrad we were told that these concrete buildings are mass-produced, with a choice of five different types. The state offers loans. The desire for one-family houses seems to be endemic to town dwellers. It is still customary for large numbers of the urban population to go to their 'dachas' in the summer. They rent one and two-storey log houses (or sometimes only rooms in them) in villages near the cities, often picturesquely located in woods, and go to work daily in electric rail-cars. In this way they avoid the oppressive atmosphere of the city during the hot weather. During my short stay I could not ascertain the extent to which the standardised concrete structures described above are intended as substitutes for these dachas, or the extent to which they are being put up as suburban settlements on the immediate periphery of the cities.

In Moscow as well as in Leningrad whole districts of flat wooden buildings have been replaced by massive modern structures. One of the main development areas is the southwestern district of Moscow, which contains the Lomonossov University, a project costing many millions. This is a structure of 2,200 rooms, including quarters for 600 students. In a large area surrounding this imposing edifice a large residential programme is being carried out which can be taken as representative of the historical evolution of town planning in the Soviet Union. Each micro-rayon is an improvement on its predecessor in terms of density and green spaces as well as architecturally. Plans for the newest residential quarters in this district are not much different from those in the west.

In one respect, indeed, the Soviet Union is ahead of us. In all the larger towns that we visited the heating of individual houses had been replaced by remote supply heating with natural gas, brought in from hundreds of miles away and collected in great multiple gasometers. Likewise the planning of Kriukovo, the first Moscow satellite town, with its perceptive exploitation of the topography, is thoroughly modern in conception.

Radical measures have been called for to realise these gigantic building programmes, particularly in view of the shortage of skilled labour and of the traditional building materials. It has been found necessary to extend the short building season and to reduce costs by the mass production of standardised materials. We were told that in some towns up to 70 per cent of residential construction was already mechanised. Even if this estimate should be optimistic we saw with our own eyes that in all the towns we visited primitive manual labour had been replaced by modern equipment and machinery. Large numbers of factories were being erected to produce all kinds of prefabricated building materials.

On the other hand, the great danger in any mechanisation of residential construction is particularly apparent to any visitor to the Soviet Union, namely, the unrelieved monotony of entire districts. This is especially true where the buildings have not been erected in accordance with modern ideas of proportioning and landscaping. No attempt had been made to use colour to liven up the appearance of a town. In my lectures I referred to this lack in terms of the Soviet tradition itself, in which so important an architect as Rastrelli always included colour as an essential element in his building projects.

The recent achievements of our Soviet colleagues are usually contemptuously dismissed in expert discussions. I have no intention here to minimise the tastelessness or the pointless fussiness of the façades of many residential as well as official buildings. Buildings like the Hotel Ukraine in Moscow, the similarly cast headquarters of the ministry of the interior, the Lomonossov University, all more or less indistinguishable from a residential skyscraper, testify to the way in which the planners have succumbed to the temptation to impress the masses by misplaced ostentation and have lost sight of function. But it is wrong to apply this criticism indiscriminately without regard to the large volume of building in the Soviet Union. In Leningrad as well as in Moscow and Minsk I saw numerous planning and architectural groupings which, although they do not accord in their external form with our current ideals, are nevertheless objectively superior to many modernistic post-war complexes. Moreover, I gathered from my discussions that my Soviet colleagues regard the period of ' socialist realism ' as over and are striving to replace it with a modern and objective style.

TWENTY YEARS ON

Alfred G. Meyer

INTEREST in the potentialities inherent in the Soviet social system has been more lively in recent years than for a long time. In the USSR itself, a flood of publications has been coming out (culminating in the new party programme) dealing with the impending transition from socialism to communism, ever since Mr Khrushchev announced a few years ago that this transformation was now on the agenda. Western observers have already begun a lively game of speculating about the reasons behind this new preoccupation of Soviet ideologists. Some relate it to an alleged conflict between party leaders and economic managers, others to the disputes between Khrushchev and Mao. There are those who see in these writings about the coming of communism an effort to maintain control over Soviet society even after the dismantling of the terror system, while yet others interpret them as an attempt to stave off the revolt of rising expectations within the Soviet population. It is indeed interesting to observe that the Soviet writers dealing with the transition to communism seem to be, if anything, more interested in outlining what communism will not, than what it will, be like. True, they point out that living standards will be higher, life will be easier, and the basic needs of all will be met free of charge ; they foretell that ' public organisations ' will increasingly take over the functions of ' the state ', and sketch out a life in which much of the daily routines as well as leisure activities will be carried out in communal associations.

While much of this remains vague, it is very clear that, in their view, communism will bring neither equality nor freedom from a great many social controls ; that it will mean neither the right to privacy nor the encouragement of pluralism or heterogeneity ; and that hedonism in any of its manifestations will be frowned upon. Basic assumptions underlying all these musings seem to include the belief that the tasks of industrialisation will not yet have been solved, and that the USSR will still be co-existing with capitalist countries, hence that major proportions of the nation's output will still have to be spent on investment and military materials, and that the solution of these problems will continue to have priority over the material desires of the consumer. The mixture of paternal kindness and moral severity expressed in this new literature brings to mind boy scout leaders, Victorian deacons, and Prussian professors.

In the West, speculation about trends of development in Soviet society has been popular ever since the October revolution, but has been intensified in recent years on account of the spectacular gains made since the war by the Soviet economy and foreign policy, and received an even stronger impetus from the death of Stalin and the ensuing changes in Soviet society. The views range from the assertion that totalitarianism (whatever that is) can never change, except from outside, to the assumption that the achievement of modern industrialism, having been brought about by Stalinist methods, has now made Stalinism superfluous and will bring about the development of democracy. Between these extremes, we can find a great variety of views concerning probable changes in the Soviet social system.

The lack of agreement, the inability even to define terms so that they become acceptable to all, and, particularly, to agree upon a systematic approach to the problem of describing trends of social development— these failures are bound to impress upon the responsible scholar the limitations of social science. Spengler said that only poetry, not social science, should deal with history. And if a Spengler can despair of reaching a scientific understanding of past developments, how much more difficult must it be to make meaningful generalisations about the present, and how reckless to venture any predictions about the state of Soviet society a generation hence. Yet it is an undertaking which can be attempted.

Let us forget, for the sake of argument, the possibility of global suicide. Let us leave out of consideration the dynamic possibilities inherent in the growing diversity shown by the bloc of communist nations, a diversity which is likely to increase. Let us falsely assume an isolated Soviet society. Can we describe it in a generally acceptable thumbnail sketch, then trace the inherent trends, and thus arrive at a projection of the same society twenty years from now?

Ask a group of social scientists to give a brief description of the United States. Some may decline the offer ; others will give widely divergent descriptions. For even those who might agree on facts are likely to disagree sharply in the choice of those features they would consider as salient. But our knowledge of Soviet society is based on far less reliable data. Hence the thumbnail sketch will be far more controversial ; and the writer's confidence, already shaken badly, will go down even more when he attempts to discuss trends of development. Generalisations about human behaviour and its more complex forms, the development of human relationships, institutions, and society, are comparable to those mathematical equations in which the unknown variable may have either a positive or a negative sign : a sudden rush of adrenalin produces either fright or anger, either cowardice or courage ; a disaster may serve to integrate or to disintegrate a community, or do both at the same time. We see social systems as dynamic structures composed of an infinite number of variables, all of them dependent on each other. If agreement cannot be reached on which of these are the most significant for an analysis of the system, the difficulties of projection are multiplied by the added difficulty of predicting their future course. The most that can be done by a responsible writer, therefore, is to outline various broad possibilities. And even in thus giving his imagination free rein, he may succeed only in demonstrating how little we know to enable us to assess the relative probability of the various alternatives.

L ET us begin by describing the USSR as a society engaged in a forced programme of rapid industrialisation. For the purpose of describing the society, the motives for this industrialisation are not necessarily of concern. What matters is the fact that the exigencies of economic growth have consistently overshadowed all other aims of the Soviet regime ; and the resolve to achieve it as rapidly as possible has done more than anything else to shape Soviet institutions and behaviour. It explains the regime of strict consumer austerity (to put it mildly) which has been imposed on the Soviet population throughout the last thirty years. It is directly related also to the system of economic management, from the central planning institutions down to the pressures for production imposed on management and workers alike. In fact, the entire mode of life, the educational system and the career ladder, the balance of rewards and sanctions, and indeed the very principle which is said to guide present-day Soviet society—from each according to ability ; to each according to performance—all this is obviously geared to the one overriding aim of production and accumulation.

This statement applies also to the political system. Although the dictatorial regime established by the party cannot be explained entirely by economic considerations, it is obviously functional to a crash programme of industrialisation under the conditions prevailing in Russia at the beginning of the five-year plans. Three basic features of the political regime can be related to this programme. One is the terror which prevailed during most of the last decades, and which must be explained, at least in part, as the principal incentive at the disposal of the regime in an era of economic austerity. A second is the party's attempt to penetrate the entire society and all aspects of life by a centralised system of organisations and associations to act as transmission belts between the party and the masses. While this organisational totalitarianism can be explained simply as a measure of control, it can be seen more specifically as an instrument used by the party to transform society, a tool for implementing the cultural revolution which must accompany the establishment of an industrial empire. Furthermore, the cultural revolution can be seen as one of the underlying purposes of the massive indoctrination effort of the Soviet regime, a method of creating the new type of man fit to live in an industrial and collectivist society. But the propaganda machinery of the Soviet state is related to the programme for industrialisation in still another way : while the programme is being carried out, the hardships it imposes are so great that the party does not dare take its subjects into its confidence, does not wish to confront even its own members with the social cost of industrialisation. Instead, it has fabricated an ideology designed to convince everyone that the Soviet world is the best of all possible worlds ; and the gulf between this myth and the harsh realities has been so wide that the urge to enforce lip service to the ideology has been compulsive.

Instead of looking at the relationship between major economic goals and social practices, we may be interested in the power structure, i.e., in the political system. In that case we might describe the USSR as a nation governed by a self-selected elite governing irresponsibly, i.e., without effective public checks or balances. The ruling elite is heterogeneous, comprising industrial executives, military and security officers, leading scientists, opinion makers, and professional politicians. The latter, who constitute the inner core of the Communist Party, have managed to maintain supremacy within the ruling group, even though relations between the various component elements of the elite have fluctuated, and the position of the party within it is obscured by the interpenetration of the various groups and hierarchies. It outlines and prescribes the policies guiding the entire life of society, and is also the final arbiter in all and any disputes and conflicts arising within the power elite from clashes of interest or divergent attitudes. The existence of such interest groups destroys the image of Soviet society as an unstructured monolith which has long been a favourite among non-Soviet scholars ; but it does not, of course, imply the existence of a democratic order, of spontaneous heterogeneity and a free and open struggle of competing groups. The multiplicity of competing hierarchies is much more the deliberate creation of the party, and may be explained in part as a bureaucratic division of powers, undertaken either to correspond with the growing specialisation of functions or for the purpose of protecting the position of the sovereign ruler.

Even when these conflicts come into the open, it would be a mistake to speak of a democratic system, because the broad masses of the population do not participate in any significant sense in the political process. For them, the entire society, despite is multiplicity of commands, is in effect one vast bureaucratic machine in command of their services and confronting them with many authorities which are all part of the same system. This apparatus encourages and even demands the citizens' participation in many of its functions. But, with the exception of narrowly confined areas such as workshop production meetings, the illusion of participating in important decisions cannot conceal the fact that access to, and work in, the centres of genuine power is restricted to a small minority. In fact, it would be no exaggeration to say that the mass of the population has been the object rather than the subject of Soviet history. The regime has imposed permanent revolution, i.e., continual social change, on its society ; all classes and groups have at one time or another felt the heavy hand of manipulated history. But while the dissatisfaction and hostility thus created among the population have been great, they must be weighed against the benefits and satisfactions engendered by the same social changes. The resulting image of popular attitudes towards the regime is bound to be complex and ambivalent.

This thumbnail sketch of Soviet society, inadequate as it is, does at least show what features most interest the present writer. It must be supplemented by a reference to some of the changes that have occurred since Stalin's death. Of these the most spectacular is the dismantling of the terror apparatus. Furthermore, with the removal of the dictator, the variety of groups within the ruling caste has become more apparent, and this in turn has been one of the factors contributing to the intellectual or ideological ferment of recent years. While this has not brought freedom of speech, it has widened the scope of topics which an increasing number of people from among the elite can freely discuss. At the same time, a growing number of citizens from all walks of life have learned to adjust to the regime, to discern a coincidence of their personal goals with some of the aims of the party, a trend encouraged by the recent rise in the standard of living and by the international and scientific successes of the regime. These changes have brought with them new problems. Thus in renouncing terror as a major method of government, the regime has been forced to provide more positive incentives, and this shift in policy may generate a crisis of rising expectations, as consumers become restive. Because of this, and of the various major reorganisations in the economy and administration, tendencies towards private enterprise and localism have been strengthened. Ideological and cultural heresies have crept in in the wake of doctrinal questionings and complex social changes. Summing up, we might say that Soviet society seems now to be in the process of adjusting its institutions and practices to the successes it has achieved since the end of the war. At the same time, each adjustment creates new problems and raises conflicts ; there are forces pressing for more thorough-going adjustments and countervailing forces opposing all change, and these struggles can be explained in terms of power considerations, group interests, differences in temperament, as well as the conflict of generations.

WITH this background in mind, what can be said about the shape of Soviet society a generation hence? Two broad assumptions are necessary at the outset. One concerns the stability or at least continuity of the present Soviet regime. This implies no more than that, whatever the conflicts within the elite or between rulers and masses, and whatever the changes in the social structure, there will be no revolutionary overthrow of the established system. Stability then means evolution, not absence of change. (Five years ago, it would have been legitimate to defend this assumption on the ground that the prospects of a successful revolution against a totalitarian regime are almost nil, but the events of 1956 have undermined belief in the impregnability of communist regimes.) Secondly, we shall assume the continuation of Soviet economic growth at the rate achieved in the post-war years. Some Western economists would question such an assumption. On the basis of analogies with growth rates under capitalism, they predict a levelling-off for the Soviet economy, a prediction which has been certified in the new CPSU programme. In addition, one might cite the great number of serious deficiencies which the Soviet economy still has to overcome before it rivals that of the United States : the preponderance of coal and steel over oil and chemicals ; the low productivity of labour in all but a few key operations ; the increasing cost of converting rural into industrial labour ;

the housing problem and the primitive state of the retail distribution system. The task of removing these and other deficiencies might well be so formidable as to slow down the rate of growth. On the other hand, there are factors which might speed it up even more, such as the advantages of planning by computers over the market mechanism, and the dynamic possibilities inherent in the most modern technology. It therefore seems reasonable to assume a continuation of present growth rates.

On this assumption, it can be asserted that in two or three decades the Soviet economy will have become a mature economy comparable to that of the present-day United States not only in volume of total output, but also in its general structure. We should, in other words, expect the economy to rely for its major sources of energy on oil and perhaps the sun, on controlled fission and fusion. We should picture it as highly mechanised and automated, and using plastic materials in many instances where metals and natural fibres are in use today.

Agriculture is likely to become not only more intensive, but will probably have been reorganised so as to replace all collective farms by state farms. The proportion of rural labour within the total population may have been halved, while the countryside may have been urbanised and electrified. We may expect these changes to have transformed the rural areas of Central Asia and other regions which today have hardly been touched by the industrial revolution. Finally, we ought to expect the USSR to have made significant progress in the development of its food processing industry and its retail distribution system. All in all, the Soviet economy of 1980 may in some respects be less, and in other respects rather more, advanced than the American economy of 1960.

It is also reasonable to expect the USSR to have become by that time a welfare state, i.e., one which provides all of its citizens with certain publicly defined necessities gratis or at a nominal charge and thus maintains a general floor under the nation's living standard. Such public services might include free education for all according to demonstrated talents and trustworthiness (however that may be determined) ; one or more free meals a day in public dining rooms ; free medical services ; social security provisions ; and more adequate housing. To judge from the evidence available today, there is little ground to suppose that Soviet society two decades from now will be a society of equals, as far as material rewards and style of life are concerned, even though the pressures to spread the wealth and promote equality may have become much stronger by then. In that respect, the USSR of 1980 might have become similar to the Sweden of 1960. Nor would it be reasonable to assume that twenty years hence the problem of how best to use the national wealth would have disappeared. Somebody will have to decide what proportions of the country's output should be devoted to the production of capital goods, military equipment, consumer goods and services, the promotion of scientific research, and other purposes. (The assumption made here is that the shares of the national product spent for these diverse purposes will remain roughly similar to the present ; different possibilities for the development of Soviet society would open up if, for some reason, the need for vast military expenditures or ambitious new capital investments were to decrease significantly. This prospect is apparently not being envisaged in Soviet discussions of the shape of things to come, and it is ignored here.)

While we can assume that planning of production on all levels will be done very largely with the help of computers, and that opinion polling techniques may be used to determine consumer preferences (if the latter are not manufactured by the planners with the help of advertising), still, basic choices concerning the allocation of resources cannot be made by machines. Such choices are political rather than economic. But while the mere extrapolation of past growth rates and trends may give us a reasonably adequate idea of what the Soviet economy will be like in a few decades, it is far more hazardous to predict the shape of Soviet politics and the structure of power. It is easy to guess that in future decades computer engineers will be increasingly involved in decision-making. But will it be they who set the basic policies to be fed into the computers ? Or will the party maintain this prerogative ? The question may in one sense be regarded as meaningless because, obviously, the party will want to continue recruiting the top-ranking mathematicians and engineers into its fold, to subject them to its discipline, and keep itself informed on up-to-date management techniques and other technological developments. The question may perhaps be reformulated : In modern industrial societies, with their complex division of labour, there are tendencies towards the development of latent or open conflicts among and between professional experts in various fields, as well as between other interest groups. These conflicts have to be resolved if society is to go on functioning ; and all such resolutions take the form of public policy. Now, whether or not the public generally is involved, we can assume the existence of a group of people whose special job is to resolve conflicts, and hence to formulate policy. These are the professional politicians, who in the USSR constitute the party *aktiv*. This might seem to imply that the group will retain its central position, but matters are not so simple. For one thing, the professional politician need not be the master of society ; under certain conditions he can perform his services in a dependent position, as servant. The question then would be whether there is any prospect of the party's being stripped of its sovereignty without its functions being lost to society. Can the party be either replaced or made subservient ; and if it can be replaced, by what ; and if made subservient, to whom? One obvious and existing alternative to the party is the system of soviets, which on the basis of the constitution should act as deliberative and legislative bodies, as forums for conflicting interests and devices of integration. Few observers would take the possibility of their assuming the functions given them by the constitution seriously, although it might be rash to dismiss it altogether. Such an assumption of power now only granted on paper would be a major change indeed, and to speculate on how it might come about would be fruitless. More likely would be a transformation of the present system into something approaching a constitutional order, in which the rules of Soviet politics, now informal and, in a way, unconstitutional, might slowly crystallise, be made more formal, and become custom, tradition, an unwritten constitution. This in itself could not be described as making the party subservient to other forces ; but since any establishment of formal rules is in effect a limitation of the sovereign, it would be a first step in the direction of creating responsible, or responsive, government. For the same reason, the party can be expected to resist the formalisation of any such political rules. Its aim will be to preserve its present right to experiment freely with the organisation of Soviet society, to create and eliminate agencies and jurisdictions, and to allow no lasting formation of vested interests.

We can imagine that in any conflict between party and managers one of the two contestants may attempt to draw the masses, or at least the industrial workers, into participation. From time to time the party has indeed used this device, and seems to have tried it also in recent times. This at least is one of the purposes behind the new institutions of comrades' courts and people's militia, but later developments suggest that the results have not come up to the expectations of their authors.

But it would be misleading to draw too sharp a line between the party and the managers, between professional politicians and professionals in other fields. In the first place, professional politics itself covers many specialised functions. Secondly, within every field of expertise, integrators come to the top and attain managerial positions—engineers become plant directors, physicians take charge of hospitals ; professors turn editors or deans ; or scientists are placed at the head of research institutes. These are the people who combine expertise in their special field with the talents or personality traits of the professional politician. They are the machine manipulators, the organisation men.

This means that there may be less validity than is sometimes thought in speaking of conflicts between various professional groups and the politicians. In any event, such conflicts are far more difficult to discern, not only because top personnel frequently shift from one group to another, but also because in training and personality traits they may all be very similar to each other. The Soviet power elite may have the homogeneity which Wright Mills attributes to the power elite of the United States.

IS it possible to speculate about changes in the personality traits of the top decision-makers? Will the type of person in charge of Soviet society twenty years from now be essentially different from the men in power today ? Obviously any description of the present-day rulers must be schematic and impressionistic, but it is not unfair to state that those who have come to the top combine ruthlessness with subservience ; that they are well indoctrinated but pragmatic and opportunistic at the same time. Shrewd, calculating, competitive, they conform to the standards of

free entrepreneurs in the period of accumulation ; conformist and conservative, they behave like Western business executives. They are obviously driven by a love of power, and yet manage to combine this with the
ability to evade responsibility. If these are their traits, do they describe
the type of man who will come to the top in any society, or the successful
careerist only in particular types of society ? If the latter, will Soviet
society a generation hence require different leadership abilities from its
top-ranking decision makers ? Is the so-called organisation man about
whom American sociologists have written so much identical with, or
different from, the above type ? And if he is different, will the future
Soviet society develop a similar organisation man ?

This much perhaps we can predict : Most probably the future Soviet
leader will be more mindful of personnel problems than his predecessor ;
and in this his development will follow that of Western business executives. But whatever personality traits may be required to make the grade,
Soviet society will doubtless recruit its elite much as it does at present,
through a selection process involving the educational ladder (which
imparts general knowledge and special skills), youth organisations, where
qualities of leadership can be brought out, and actual work experience.
If we assume a society of unequal status and rewards, we shall also have
to assume continued keen competition for opportunities, recognition, and
promotion, so that what Americans call the rat race will be as much a
feature of society, at least in its higher levels, as it is today. Industrialism,
with its unceasing technological and organisational changes, is characterised by a high rate of social mobility. Society must strive to put all talent,
ambition, and suitable leadership qualities to use, regardless of the
individual's origins. This is usually counteracted by the attempt of those
at the top to provide career advantages for their children. Moreover,
even in the most open societies, class or status origin helps to narrow
down career expectations and thus actual career patterns, so that very
dramatic moves from very low to very high status, or vice-versa, are
comparatively rare. National origin may also distort the aim of providing equal opportunities to all persons of talent, if only because the
general level of education and status prevailing among some national
minorities is still very low.

This is the pattern of social mobility which, *mutatis mutandis,* prevails
in both the United States and the USSR. It seems safe to predict that
the general level of education in Soviet society twenty years from now will
be higher than it is today, and that the Soviet melting pot will have done
much to obliterate status differences among the various nationalities,
perhaps even the hard edges of national consciousness, although it is
likely that, all efforts at indoctrination notwithstanding, feelings of
antagonism as strong as those now prevalent in the Baltic area may linger
on for several decades.

It is fairly safe to assume also that a good many other antagonisms
still smouldering in the hearts of many Soviet citizens will have died
down. We may regard the bitter feelings of peasants and religious

believers as untypical of an industrial society, whereas the apathy or dis-satisfaction of the workers seems to be mainly a response to the arduous conditions of their work. It seems reasonable to suppose that in another twenty years the importance and intensity of peasant resistance to the regime will have diminished, and the industrial workers become more satisfied with the steady improvement of their lot.

It has been argued that the Soviet regime cannot afford to let the standard of living rise significantly, because it would lose control over the population and the economy and would have to yield to an entirely different system of government. Against this it can be stated that the present order in the USSR is already well on its way toward substituting welfare state politics for terror precisely as a means of maintaining control, while retaining the additional methods of indoctrination and education, together with monopolistic control over all organisations, com-munications, and channels of advancement. In combination with such techniques, welfare state politics serve the regime to prevent political deviation, not by violence, but by giving all citizens a stake in the existing order, by encouraging them to identify their own well-being with the success of the state.

For such a policy to succeed, the regime would not only have to stave off any involvement in major military conflicts ; it would also need to solve a number of political problems at home. The party would face the task of curbing the inevitable struggle for the spoils, and of justifying its unique and monopolistic power. But while the political problems created by welfare state politics should not be underestimated, it might be wise for us to look also at the positive side of the predicted general rise in the standard of living. In the long run, we must assume that the self-confidence of the Soviet regime will steadily increase, and so enhance the smug self-righteousness of the regime's adherents. At the same time, it might also lessen the deeply engrained feeling of inferiority sufficiently to relax their dogmatism, and it is conceivable that the party might come to realise that differences in taste or disagreements in philosophy are not necessarily subversive, and that even some of the taboos now protecting social institutions and the historical past from scrutiny may be lifted with safety. How, in any event, will the next generation re-interpret the Holy Writ of Marxism ? Most probably the rulers will have trans-formed it further into a theory of bureaucratic absolutism. Will the rebels have rediscovered the liberational philosophy of Marx, or will the conditions for its re-emergence be even less propitious than they are today ? Will the humanism of Marx's writings have found spokesmen within the ruling elite ?

These speculations end with questions in order to emphasise their tentative nature. There are many questions that have not even been asked. The guesses we have ventured to make have been based on an image of present-day Soviet society which may itself be faulty and inade-quate, and on certain preconceived notions about the structure and functioning of satiated industrial societies.

Five or six years ago, the present author wrote that the history of Soviet society had, with fair persistency, manifested four divergent trends of development : (1) the urge towards the imposition of total, all-encompassing controls ; (2) the urge towards the perfection of rational management ; (3) the striving for the crystallisation of a traditional, conservative class society ; and (4) the yearning for democratic socialism. At the time he did not commit himself to an assessment of the relative strength of these trends and aspirations, although he tried to point out some of the forces behind each of them. The present article reaffirms the general diagnosis made in 1956, but once again he refuses to predict which of these tendencies will turn out to be stronger.

Our Contributors

GEORGE BRINKLEY is Assistant Professor in the Department of Political Science of the University of Notre Dame, and Secretary of its Program of Soviet and East European Studies.

ALEXANDER ECKSTEIN is Professor of Economics at the University of Michigan, author of *The National Income of Communist China*, to be published later this month, and co-author of *The Moscow-Peking Axis* and *Prospects for Communist China*.

IRING FETSCHER is the Editor of *Marxismusstudien*.

JOHN HAZARD is Professor of Public Law, Columbia University, and Member of the New York Bar. Author of *Settling Disputes in Soviet Society*, and other works on Soviet law.

NAUM JASNY is the author of a number of authoritative works on the Soviet economy, of which the latest is *Soviet Industrialization, 1928–1952*.

GEORGE KLINE is Associate Professor of Philosophy and Russian, Bryn Mawr College, and author of *Spinoza in Soviet Philosophy*.

ERNST MAY is a leading architect in the Federal German Republic and an authority on town planning.

ALFRED G. MEYER is Professor of Political Science at Michigan State University, author of *Marxism: the Unity of Theory and Practice*, *Communism*, and co-author of *The Incompatible Allies*.

ROBERT OSBORN, who now teaches at Swarthmore College, formerly worked with the American Friends Service Committee and the Institute of International Education.

THILO RAMM lectures on Civil Law and the Philosophy of Law at Freiburg University, and has written a number of works on labour legislation.

LEONARD SCHAPIRO, Reader in Russian Government and Politics in the University of London, is the author of *The Origin of the Communist Autocracy* and *The Communist Party of the Soviet Union*.

H. F. SCURMANN is Associate Professor (History and Sociology) in the University of California and is working on a book to be called *Ideology and Organization in Communist China*.

TIMOTHY SOSNOVY, who works in the Library of Congress, has written a number of works (English and Russian) on the Soviet economy.

S. V. UTECHIN, born in Russia and educated at Moscow, Kiel and Oxford Universities, is at present Senior Research Officer in Soviet Studies at the London School of Economics.

PETER WILES is Professor of Economics at Brandeis University.

DONALD ZAGORIA works in the Social Science Division of the Rand Corporation and is preparing a book on Sino-Soviet relations.

ALFRED ZAUBERMAN, who is preparing a book on the Eastern and Central European Economies, is the author of ' The Soviet Debate on the Law of Value and Price ' in *Value and Plan*, edited by G. Grossman.

PRAEGER PAPERBACKS

World Affairs and Politics

History

PRAEGER UNIVERSITY SERIES

*If you cannot obtain these titles at your local bookstore, send check
or money order covering the total cost of the books ordered (plus 10¢
per title for postage and handling) to:* Order Dept., Frederick A.
Praeger, Inc., 64 University Place, New York 3, N. Y. *Only orders
totaling $5 or more can be accepted.*

DATE DUE

DATE DUE			
NOV 1 6 '62			
JA 9 '63 MAY 13 1974			
MY 28 '64			
MY 21 '65			
DE 16 '65			
MY 13'68			
OCT 2 7 1969 RESERVED			
75			
MY 21 70			
GAYLORD			PRINTED IN U.S.A.